Delivering College Composition

Delivering College Composition

The Fifth Canon

Edited by Kathleen Blake Yancey

BOYNTON/COOK
Portsmouth, NH

Boynton/Cook Publishers, Inc.
A subsidiary of Reed Elsevier Inc.
361 Hanover Street
Portsmouth, NH 03801–3912
www.boyntoncook.com

Offices and agents throughout the world

Library of Congress Cataloging-in-Publication Data
Delivering college composition : the fifth canon / edited by Kathleen Blake Yancey.
p. cm.
Includes bibliographical references.
ISBN 0-86709-509-3 (alk. paper)
1. English language—Rhetoric—Study and teaching. 2. English language—Rhetoric—Study and teaching—Data processing. 3. Report writing—Study and teaching (Higher). 4. Report writing—Study and teaching (Higher)—Data processing. I. Yancey, Kathleen Blake, 1950– II. Title.

PE1404.D3885 2006
808′.0420711—dc22 2005031813

Editor: Charles Schuster
Production editor: Sonja S. Chapman
Cover design: Jenny Jensen Greenleaf
Typesetter: TechBooks
Manufacturing: Jamie Carter

Printed in the United States of America on acid-free paper
10 09 08 07 06 VP 1 2 3 4 5

To Chuck,
for his talk at WPA that began this book
and for his friendship throughout

and

to David, Genevieve, and Matthew,
always

Contents

Preface

Many—myself among them—have claimed that college composition *today* is different in kind rather than degree from the college composition that preceded it. Sometimes, those claims are made in the language of postprocess, other times in the terms of alt.discourse, still other times in the vocabulary of critical pedagogy or of cultural studies or of . . . (Too) rarely is the claim explored through multiple classrooms, sites, and programs.

This volume does just that: it takes a look at college composition in diverse institutions and regions of the country, using the lens of *delivery* as a way of thinking together about what it is that we hope to achieve in teaching college comp. For our purposes, delivery is defined as site, as agent (faculty), and not least, as technology. In this exploration, the first of its kind since the 1980 publication of *Eight Approaches to Teaching Composition*, we see that the composition of the twenty-first century will indeed take very different forms than its cousin in the twentieth—because of digital technology, yes, and because of new ways of defining the teacher, and because of new ways of understanding both curricular and physical spaces.

It is our hope that in making these differences known, we can all be more intentional about how to make them matter.

Kathleen Blake Yancey
Tallahassee, Florida

1

Delivering College Composition
A Vocabulary for Discussion

Kathleen Blake Yancey
Florida State University

At first glance, the question of how we ought to teach college composition—and thus how we ought to "deliver" its instruction—seems fairly obvious. If we want college students to write, then we should ask them to write. And if we follow Peter Elbow's sometime advice, we don't even need to have faculty available: students can simply write without them.[1]

At second (and third) glances, however, this question—how do we deliver college composition?—isn't quite so simple. Given the ages of today's college students—from fifteen to seventy—what does it mean to be a *college* writer? Given the multiple, complex, and ever changing, often hybrid sites where students can receive credit for a college writing course—from high school classroom to shopping mall to university seminar room to cybercafé halfway around the world—what difference, if any, does the site of instruction make? And what is the instruction in: what is *college composition*? Not least, what does linking these three terms—*college* and *composition* and *delivery*—help us understand about college composition today, and in the future?

By examining and mapping this vocabulary—college, composition, and delivery—this chapter sets the stage for just such an inquiry.

College

The best container for learning is not a course.[2]

A hundred years ago, as James Berlin, Robert Connors, and Sharon Crowley have amply demonstrated, college was fairly easy to define: set off from the world in a world of its own, it was the place that eighteen-year-olds went to be socialized into American culture. In part, of course, college was defined

or: the site (college), the thing (composition), + the method (delivery) through *difference*. It wasn't like high school—in expectations; in attitudes; perhaps most especially in location. High school was here, and college was *there*. As important, college was likewise defined by its difference from high school in population: while the law typically mandated all Americans to complete some high school, college attendance was voluntary and, consequently perhaps, more restricted. As *The Big Test* (Lemann) argues, the eighteen-year-olds who went off to college were more often than not sons of the white establishment.

Like high school, however, the basic purpose of college, particularly in its attention to literacy, was the *normalization of identity*, as Richard Miller explains:

> Whether the writer is Richard Hoggart or Richard Rodriquez, James Baldwin or the students whose work Bartholomae discusses, the movement from the home to the school and to the world of work almost always involves an untiring labor of ascetic self-suppression and refashioning. While debates about writing pedagogy have tended to turn on trivial subjects such as the merits of "clarity" or the need for instruction in "style," literate practices matter as much as they do because they are essential to the normalization of identity. Quite apart from *what* books and classroom lectures may profess, these books and lectures teach people *how* to think and act, how to represent themselves to themselves and others. (41)

The central role that college and composition play in normalizing that which would otherwise not be normal isn't in dispute. Rather, what's interesting is how such normalization—which regardless of how it's phrased (e.g., inventing the university or liberating the students) is still the goal—might still be possible today, when the population is increasingly diversified and the sites of both composition and college increasingly distributed.

During the twentieth century, the collegiate student body diversified through legislation and deliberate political acts, for instance, through the GI Bill following World War II, and later with open admissions. Or: student bodies have changed along lines of race, class, and ethnicity, although not as much as we like to think. In 2000, at the turn of the century, while more than half of graduating high school classes, 57.6 percent, enrolled in some form of postsecondary education, only 24.4 percent of Americans completed what they had begun. For students of color, the picture is considerably bleaker: only 10 percent of African Americans graduate from college, fewer than that for Latinos, which is not surprising given that in that population, 47 percent of those aged sixteen to nineteen aren't in school of *any* kind (Johnson). And don't even ask about Native Americans. So college: demographically, it's changing, if too slowly.

Even more so, the spaces of composition instruction, particularly in their *distribution of sites*, a phrase unheard of one hundred years ago. Even before the campus variety of postsecondary composition, of course, we had off-campus, informal, unsanctioned varieties, that which we in general call the extracurricular curriculum, a way of delivering college learning without teachers, tuition, credits, or degrees. As documented by Anne Gere, Deborah Brandt, and Cindy Selfe, this site welcomes an informal, self- and communally sponsored learning of writing, at kitchen tables and on park benches, often organized by people of little formal education. Some colleges (DePaul, for instance) have made working with this extracurriculum part of their mission, just as some composition curricula—a service learning curriculum, for instance—likewise link to such projects. And there are compositionists, Richard Miller among them, who argue that these sites of learning offer our best hope for the future. He notes that "the most important social changes of our time" are taking place outside the academy, in what he calls "new and uncoercive forms of interaction organized and developed by couples, families, support groups, 'salons,' and congregations" (44).

Howard Rheingold agrees, though he casts his gaze at an electronic landscape. In *Smart Mobs*, he chronicles the use of multiple, interacting telecommunication devices by teenagers who want to gather immediately, who seek new kinds of social interaction, and for whom multitasking seems not so much desirable as normal. While often these smart mobs gather for social and ephemeral (and some might say frivolous) reasons, Rheingold cites some specific instances of political use—in both the Philippines and Senegal. Closer to home, the Associated Press runs a story on the new digital divide, the gulf between the so-called digital "natives" and their digital "immigrant" parents. Some teachers even include instant messaging in their construct of school literacy (although it's fair to note that if the curriculum is what's tested, we're a long way from including IMing or just-in-time social gatherings as school communication tasks). Still others, adults and children, have taught themselves ways to narrate their daily thoughts on blogs and on wikis. Most of these online forms of composition, from the text messaging of cell phones to the instant messaging of college students to the blogging of political candidates, have not generally been taught in the academy, much less sanctioned by it.[3] Moreover, these sites, because of the freedom allowed by the digital, are no longer sites in the conventional, physical, fixed sense: they are mobile, flexible, just in time. It's person as node—or site.[4]

By contrast, composition instruction seems fairly staid, even if on campus it does occur across a wide variety of sites—in classrooms, still, and augmented and expanded in various other sites: writing and learning centers, writing-across-the-curriculum programs, informal individual tutorials, within first-year experience programs and learning communities. At some institutions, instruction can take place on campus *and* off—at off-campus sites such as satellite campuses and at other temporary sites like shopping malls. Increasingly conventional and sometimes short-lived is the virtual site: sometimes video based, these days more often Web based, and in this latter version it often exists inside a course management system separated from any larger context, which, as Darin Payne argues, tends to remove agency at the same time it may increase opportunity. Soon enough, as Chuck Schuster has suggested, composition instruction may arrive in our mailboxes as an interactive CD, with the CD itself as the sole means of educational delivery: CD as college site.

The last principal site of instruction for collegiate instruction, ironically, is the high school, that place that by its difference from college once defined postsecondary education. In the late 1940s, the Advanced Placement Program allowed students to complete their college composition without setting foot in a college classroom, and without any coursework at all (see Jolliffe and Phelan, this volume). They simply needed to earn a score, typically from 3 to 5 on a 1–5 range, that a college recognized as a sign of competence worth college credit or exemption from the standard campus course. Even more popular today, the test itself is not constructed by any college, nor by any group representing colleges per se, but rather by a testing company that is contracted by the College Board. In a second and increasingly popular version of high school qua college, students can earn college credit for composition in dual-enrollment programs where students double-dip, collecting college credit while completing high school courses for which they also acquire credit (see Bodmer, this volume).

In other words, college—if defined by its students and the places it delivers instruction—is no longer a specific place, if indeed it ever was. Rather, college occurs in multiple sites—physical and virtual, informal and formal, official and just in time—that are defined explicitly or function de facto as collegiate.

What does this proliferation of sites mean for college composition? Given this history, is college composition merely an anachronism?

Composition

The real composition is in the being.[5]

That composition has changed in the last one hundred years will surprise no one. As Berlin and Crowley demonstrate, composition as a universal requirement has a long history in this country, one directly connected to the formation of identity. Its briefer, more recent history during the last sixty years, the time when composition morphed from product to process to situated process to digitized "screen text" (Moran)—and became the discipline we know today—suggests both how central it is to the academy and also how shifting. Which, ironically, means that today it is, perhaps more than ever, in search of a definition.

In her 1982 article "The Winds of Change," Maxine Hairston provided a context for understanding the changes in composition that had taken place in the prior fifteen years. Invoking Thomas Kuhn's notion of paradigmatic change, Hairston argued that the teaching of writing had been revolutionized.

Contrasting what came before, she observed,

> It is important to note that the traditional paradigm [of composition and its teaching] did not grow out of research or experimentation. It derives partly from the classical rhetorical model that organizes the production of discourse into invention, arrangement, and style, but mostly it seems to be based on some idealized and orderly vision of what literature scholars, whose professional focus is on the written product, seem to imagine is an efficient method of writing. (78)

This model, she claimed, was being replaced by one oriented both to students and to process, a theme picked up in an advertisement for the new (1982) volume highlighting the various approaches characteristic of this new paradigm, *Eight Approaches to Teaching Composition*.

> Eight new essays reflect a dramatic "paradigm shift" in the field of composition, and offer exciting course options for all faculty members and graduate assistants called upon to teach composition. The focus has shifted from final product to *process*. . . . Approaches include: pure process, prose models and process, experiential, rhetorical, epistemic, basic, conferencing, and cross-disciplinary.

Put differently and as Paul Matsuda has argued, composition in this shift both has and hasn't changed. On the one hand, we still wanted texts, for instance, that had a thesis and support and that were *correct*. On the other hand, we saw the significance of invention, and we were prepared to take a process approach to helping students create text, based in part on new understandings of composing mapped by Sondra Perl and Janet Emig and on work undertaken on invention by scholars like D. Gordon Rohman, Elizabeth and Gregory Cowan, and Alton Becker, Richard Young, and Kenneth Pike.

Still, if composition itself hadn't changed so much, the model for teaching *was changing*, from an analytical, prose- and product-based pedagogy in which class time was spent in analysis and in which the chief purpose of the class—composing—was to take place *outside* of class, to an in-class process-based workshop model that was decidedly social. It still persists today:

> Because our discipline has embraced a pedagogy of draft and revision and close work with a "coach"/teacher, because our classrooms typically promote collaborative learning, and because we often choose to speak at length with students individually as we work with them on drafts of essays, we often form strong bonds with our students. We become invested in our students' successes and failures in ways that are significantly different from those of our colleagues. (Sullivan 378)

Many of the key scholars who influenced this movement early on, since labeled "expressionists," spoke to a particular set of values: "voice" and "truth" and "individuality." Fairly quickly, others spoke to other values: David

Bartholomae to academic discourse, James Berlin to the epistemic role that composing always plays. With this latter claim in particular, composing became rhetorical in another sense: students' work was identified not only as a means of knowledge for us but also as a means of creating knowledge *for* them, which is itself a different enterprise than merely reproducing knowledge delivered *to* them.

As is well known, for nearly a decade the tension between Bartholomae's position and that of those advocating a more personal writing ensnared the discipline. Finally, in a synopsis that reflected the views of many, *College Composition and Communication* editor Joe Harris remarked,

> Indeed the whole argument over whether we should teach "personal essays" or "academic discourse" strikes me as misleading and debilitating—since the opposition between the two tends quickly to devolve into a stand off between belletrism and pedantry, sensitivity and rigor, and thus turns both into something that most students I have met show little interest in either reading or writing. (2)

At about the same time that Harris was pointing to the enervating effects of this divide, some ten years after Hairston's "Winds," Charles Moran invoked the same metaphor to point to the next revolution already under way. In "The Winds, and the Costs, of Change," Moran argued that with the advent of the PC, we had another option before us, a new composing medium that would change both teaching and composing: "It is clear to me and to others . . . that computers have changed our work in ways as fundamental as the advent of the process paradigm announced in 1982 by Maxine Hairston. The change has occurred; it would be foolish to pretend that it has not" (1).

Moran's claim, like McLuhan's before him, was that the medium did make a difference, that the computer changed not only the process of creation but also the product itself. He also suggested that this shift in medium provided students with a novel and difficult rhetorical problem:

> As computer-writers, they were ahead of much of the rest of the institution. If they chose to work in this new medium, *screen text*, they knew that their readers—the professors for whom they were writing in the courses other than ours—were requiring printed text. Somehow they had to write on the screen, all the while imagining their work being read on paper. It is perhaps for this reason that they printed out their work so often. It may be that negotiating this passage—between screen-author and print-reader—contributes to the difficulty writers report having as they read their own work on-screen. (6)

Interestingly, Moran's observation still holds: one way to understand *this* moment in the profession, as Richard Fulkerson in casting a wider net also argues, is to say that we don't seem to have a disciplinary consensus about where our focus belongs: on the print side; in screen and print contexts both; in the passage between; or in all of the above.

And while the nature of composition—what is it?—is contested, faculty continue to introduce new tasks, to be created in new genres, composed not only *on* the screen, which suggests a kind of planar approach, but also *within* new environments, which suggests a place for composing that in its three-dimensionality is like the classroom that they seek to extend, expand, and complicate. Advocates of digital composition, indeed, argue that by comparison, print literacy is limited literacy, and that the digital environment is introducing new genres of writing more quickly that we have time to study them. The Spooner and Yancey article announcing their "postings" on a genre of email was perhaps the first scholarly article to make this claim, but since that time e-genres have themselves diversified:

> Whereas these specialized genres [i.e., genres of academic writing] for students have served as the measure of freshman writing ability for a hundred years, transformation of writing courses by computer technology is a recent phenomenon. Composition instructors first welcomed word processing because it facilitated production of the standard freshman essay. However, the move into electronic environments rapidly began to revolutionalize classroom practices and genres. Today the expanding possibilities for writing engendered through desktop publishing, email, Web-based bulletin boards, MOO's, Web page and other hypertext authoring and presentation software show up the limitations the freshman essay imposes on thought and writing. (Trupe 1)

Classroom writing in new environments has also led to new definitions of writing, ones that are often heavily influenced by spatial notions of production and circulation. For instance, Johndan Johnson-Eilola remediates the process-based, single-author notion of writing into multiple authorship and communal texts. He sees

> WRITING AS THE RECURSIVE, SHARED, (AND SOMETIMES ABSCONDED WITH) COORDINATION OR BUILDING OF SPACES AND FIELDS. In other words, writers are not individuals (or even groups) who produce texts, but participants within spaces who are recursively, continually, restructuring those (and other spaces). (1)

interesting

The role that these multiple genres, media, and environments will play in defining composition, finally, isn't clear, nor can the current major position statements of the field help. The composers of the Council of Writing Program Administrators (WPA) Outcomes Statement, for instance, decided (after much debate) against addressing these issues of digital technology specifically, other than to say that writers should use the appropriate technology. As the previous discussion suggests, the technology chosen is directly related to the definition of composition provided and thus to the composition taught and valorized in whichever assessment scheme prevails. Given that the WPA document was adopted in 2000, we can see how quickly the digital revolution is changing conventional understandings of composing and textuality, and indeed, as of this writing, the WPA is again taking up the issue of technology and its relationship to first-year composition. A quick review of the 1995 Conference on College Composition and Communication (CCCC) Position Statement on Assessment makes the same case about change more dramatically: not only are the more progressive methods of assessment like portfolios, or still experimental methods like online placement or self-directed placement, barely visible, but no mention is made of digitized text, digitized environment, or assessment of the digitized.

All of which leaves us still asking, on the edge of this new century, what does it mean to write? To compose?

Delivery

Classical rhetorical theory was devised a long time ago
in cultures that were rigidly class bound and
whose economies depended upon slavery.
They were invented for the use of privileged men,
speaking to relatively small audiences.
Those audiences were not literate, and
the only available technology of delivery was the human body.[6]

The role of delivery in shaping college composition has taken some peculiar, some invisible, and some ubiquitous forms, but as a matter of concern for American teachers of writing, it has been with us for a very long time. In fact, a quick history of the twentieth century indicates that for compositionists, delivery of composition has been key to our disciplinary identity, a feature that makes us unique in higher education.[7]

In the 1912 inaugural issue of *English Journal*, Edwin Hopkins opened his lead article with the question "Can composition be taught under the current conditions?" Hopkins immediately replied to his own question, "No," arguing that the teaching of writing was a form of "laboratory" instruction, so that as in the case of a science lab, compositionists should be assigned small classes and fewer of them. As Hopkins pointed out, however, labs are small largely because of the material conditions required for the learning of science: lab equipment, stations for each learner, and space to work. From this materialist perspective, the "labor difficulty" in the teaching of composition was that it—unlike science—required no special conditions at all. Much like Socrates, we could meet anywhere, anytime. The teaching of writing did *require* time, admittedly, which functioned as a double-edged sword: it was what cost compositionists (rather than institutions) so much, but because it (unlike material conditions) wasn't commodified, it bore no relationship to the teacher's working conditions or compensation. For very nearly a hundred years, then, our commitment to a laboratory model of delivery—characterized by many assignments, a single teacher, and small class sizes—has defined the field. And even where it has not be instantiated, it nonetheless continues to capture the imagination of many teachers, as Todd Taylor explains later in this volume.

At the same time, all too often, the typical physical classroom—what Barker and Kemp have since labeled the "proscenium classroom" (quoted in Moran)—stipulated a specific model of teaching in which the instructor delivered and the students received in a space designed perfectly, it seemed, for a product-based model that effaced *composing*. Inside that space, this construction of learning was reiterated by the kind of furniture provided as well as by its placement—fixed (and often uncomfortable) chairs with little desk space on which to write, set in rows facing the front, almost as in imitation of the church, with the teacher at the front, of course, as priest. And later in the century, this space for teaching—in opposition, it seems, to learning—remained the same, even as researchers began articulating models of compos*ing* (as opposed to compo*sition*),[8] and the discipline itself seemed coalescing in new ways, with CCCC flourishing, WPA beginning, and new journals being created. The rooms: they stayed the same boxes, stipulating the age-old relationship of students to teacher to materials. To attempt a new pedagogy, then, compositionists needed to work *against* the physical space: gathering chairs into circles (assuming the chairs moved) and moving them back into rows for the next class; using walls for pinups and gallery spaces rather than the blackboard at the front; finding ways for students to contort their bodies so that they could work in small groups; finding more desk space for students to redraft texts and sort through successive drafts of texts as they reflected on process or prepared portfolios, this last the very kind of activity that has been shown to be crucial for the production of knowledge (Sellen and Harper).

From the 1960s to the 1980s three other sites of curricular space appeared—communications programs; computer teaching classrooms; and writing centers—each of which brought with it a demand that the physical space for delivery be congruent with the activity. From each, there are lessons. Communications programs, which lasted from about the 1940s to the 1960s (and which account for the fourth *C* in *CCCC*; see Trimbur and George), required the very kind of support advocated by Hopkins some fifty years earlier. Unfortunately, their promising start led only to a quick demise, in large part because of those material conditions and the cost of maintaining them. In other words, while these programs may have enhanced the material conditions of those teaching in them, that enhancement was temporary: "Given the intellectual demands that communications skills placed upon teachers, and given the administrative support necessary to fund labs, clinics, support staff, and equipment, it does not surprise that communication skills programs did not last long" (Crowley, 183). Those programs in fact died in the 1960s. One lesson here, then, is that creating the material conditions that enhance both teaching and learning may provide a lever for change, but without other supports, the change will not endure.

On the composition side of CCCC, we have seen a similar impulse at work in computer classrooms, the outcome of which is still to be determined. Typically, these classrooms have called for special equipment—hardware, software, furnishings—and in part because the same dollars don't go as far as they do in a conventional classroom, the rooms have been smaller, thus permitting smaller class sizes and something approximating Hopkinian lab conditions. Interestingly, in the creation of these new spaces, there has been much disciplinary discussion about these rooms as to appropriate configuration of desks and workstations. The task was often (though not always) sufficiently new that there was a sense that the old options would not suffice.[9] In addition, the equipment (computers, printers) brought its own set of needs: blackboards create dust that can clog computers, so whiteboards became standard, for instance, and this shift made computer classrooms less like school spaces, more like workplace spaces. Moreover, as postsecondary education has become corporativized, this resemblance of school to work is often viewed favorably.

At the same time, there are real questions both as to the financial sustainability of these spaces and as to their potential to motivate change for the long term. Some of these spaces are finding their purposes being altered as the cost of maintaining machines becomes prohibitive; one-time classrooms are lost as they become labs. And as the world, even higher ed, goes mobile, laptops and handhelds look more attractive. Institutions can require students to buy and maintain laptops, and when the campus requires them, grants and loans are available to underwrite students' purchases. Moreover, the fact that you have computers doesn't mean that you necessarily go small: some composition programs, like Texas Tech (see Rickly, this volume), are using this technology not only to increase size of classes but also, and more importantly, to change the ways those classes are delivered altogether. Perhaps the most fundamental shift this program makes is to separate completely two teaching functions that historically have been unified in a single teacher—(1) instruction and (2) summative evaluation—by assigning them to different people. The lessons from the experience of integrating technology with teaching, then, are still in process.

In the 1970s, we also saw a resurgence of interest in writing centers (Lerner), which provide another site for delivery of composition instruction. Perhaps because they typically operate outside the FTE (full-time-equivalent student) economic structure, perhaps because they often grew from more general learning centers (with a prototypical space of their own) rather than from classrooms, these sites typically construct a much different model of teaching, one based in collaborative learning. The physical site itself tends to be informal, more domestic than institutional, filled with furniture one might actually want to sit on, couches and overstuffed chairs, with an ambience more like home than school. The site thus constructs a different kind of learning than does the classroom; it's a place where peers tutor peers side by side, with experienced tutors coaching those less experienced, a place where grades are deemed superfluous if not indeed harmful; a place where another curriculum, in Steven North's terms, is offered. At the same time, this place has not become the primary means of delivery for composition across the country; it tends to employ few tenure-line faculty; and since it augments the FTE-dominated curriculum, its curriculum too is still largely shaped by that of the predominant model of delivery. To put it succinctly, it has created a new kind of physical site for its curricular work, but since it has not been written into the "regular" curriculum, it seems, it hasn't moved to the center nor offered a viable, sustainable alternative to the standard model. The lesson here, then, is that it is possible to design a physical site congruent with a curricular site, and to do new kinds of curricular work, but apparently only if it maintains its position outside the mainstream. As a lever for systematic and widespread change, it is limited.

Yet another way to think about delivery is through the human: who is doing the delivering of instruction? Earlier in the century, higher education served fewer students and a fundamentally less diverse student body with a staff composed by full-time faculty. As Crowley explains,

> Composition was not always staffed the way it is now. Until 1940 or so, composition classes were taught by full time teachers, although they generally were the newest members of the permanent faculty. This changed when disciplinary specialization began to affect staffing in the undergraduate curriculum. With the narrowing of faculty interests that accompanied adoption of the research ideal, it became increasingly difficult to find full-time faculty who were willing to teach general or introductory courses, and by 1950, American universities with graduate programs had begun to rely on graduate students to staff the required first-year composition course. They had also begun the practice of hiring part-time help to meet staffing demands imposed by the postwar explosion in college enrollments. (119)

Ironically, then, at about the time that Harvard was helping establish general education through its Red Book, composition and its teaching—one of the keystones of most general education programs—were relegated to a faculty labeled as contingent.

Today, the personnel delivering college composition include graduate assistants; part-time adjuncts; full-time lecturers or instructors; and tenure-line faculty. Both the compensation (including benefits) and the material conditions of teaching vary widely, with senior tenure-line faculty earning as much as six figures for the same labor and outcomes produced by adjuncts on a piecework basis, much as in a Fordist model of factory work. At some private institutions, another recent staffing option is the "post-doc": PhDs teach on a multiyear contract, typically combining the teaching of writing with their academic specialty (e.g., history, philosophy) in a first-year seminar model of delivery (see Harris, this volume). Given the diversity in the human agents of delivery, a shared general assumption seems to be that no special expertise, at least in content, is required. It should also be noted that composition's connection to general education often exacerbates this problem. General education is, of course, a worthy program, but it is also the case that its purposes can be somewhat "amorphous" and very general, suggesting again that specialization is not required:

> General education is, in a sense, the most amorphous part of the humanities curriculum. Its goals are perhaps less easily definable and more ambitious than the aims of a major. But the purposes that general-education courses in the humanities should serve for our students are extraordinarily important. In English courses designed for general education, students should learn to participate intelligently and ethically in the discourses of the communities to which they do and will belong as citizens. (Lloyd-Jones and Lunsford 29)

And when composition is said to perform various other noncomposition tasks as well, from introducing students to the library to helping socialize them onto campus, we reinforce some unwise perceptions—that composition has the capacity to be all things to all students and that it can be bent, folded, and turned to serve any and all educational purposes.

Does it matter that these aims are in sharp contrast to those of specialists, whose talents, methodologies, and expertise are well defined? And what, if any, difference does the site of instruction make?

The View from Here

What Is "College-Level" Writing?[10]

The use of delivery, the fifth canon of rhetoric, to talk about college composition, of course, is metaphorical. In this sense, the study of it in this volume is a remediation of the term, with specific application to how we understand both the teaching and the learning of composing. I'm also evoking Lanham's sense of delivery for our conception of the potential of writing. That's a remediated version of the word *composing*: composing as work with various materials to create diverse kinds of communications for various purposes and audiences, a composing that may move us from print to screen, from poster to person—and back again. What kind of curriculum is this, and how is it best delivered? Another way to think about this metaphorical use is to see it as a verbal mapping that permits us to read across various institutional sites as we ask, What is composing? How should it be delivered? The hope is that this vocabulary, and this verbal map, will enable us to calculate the value of our current paradigm of delivery, with an eye toward being intentional about what college composing is, how it is best learned, and what that might mean for a curricular space that is affected and shaped by—indeed in dialogue with—a corresponding physical space.

As Hairston notes, without a new vocabulary, the tendency is to revert to the old:

> As Kuhn points out, the paradigm that a group of professionals accepts will govern the kinds of problems they decide to work on, and that very paradigm keeps them from recognizing important problems that cannot be discussed in the terminology of their model. Thus teachers who concentrate their efforts on teaching style, organization and correctness are not likely to recognize that the students need work in invention. (1982, 80)

Whether or not we need a new paradigm for the delivery of college composition or something less radical isn't clear; what is clear is that an articulation of this issue in these historical and epistemelogical terms helps us see that we are indeed at a critical moment in time, one that allows—perhaps even requires—that we take up a closer examination of composition and its delivery. As we know, the staffing issues do not seem to be improving. Dual-enrollment and AP are growing, not shrinking, suggesting that the composition we deliver on campus is not particularly valued by our own institutions. The role that we have played as socializers of first-year students is now often provided by other academic and student support units: learning communities and first-year experience programs. (And in using full-time staffers and full-time faculty in many departments, they have been smart in their staffing in ways we have not.) As problematic is that the value of college composition, for some, lies not only in the *exemption* of it but also in the role that exemption plays in attracting students:

> [A]bout 15% of our incoming students don't take composition because of very high SAT and ACT scores or because they took advanced placement courses in high school. These are "recruiting issues" and are not to be tampered with. Although the loss of the CLEP [College Level Examination Program] has occasioned some gnashing of teeth among the various colleges, who would like to get their students onto their own revenue-generating soil as quickly as possible, the general sense is that composition and the university are better serving the students. (Kemp)

And as we have seen, schools themselves are changing. The primary role of the college course as a vehicle for delivery of education is being eroded, and even if we opt to retain it, it is likely to look very different than it has. There is the influence of the online. There is the influence of the local: the Council of Writing Program Administrators hopes to articulate a common set of outcomes while schools with specific cultural agendas—like historically black colleges and universities—talk back and rewrite that common curriculum in interesting, provocative ways, as Theresa Redd here explains. There is the influence of the discipline itself, which seems to say to individual teachers, "Here is your set of outcomes," regardless of your individual philosophies (Soles). At which point, Richard Miller asks, referring to students, "Are we prepared to accept non-specialists in the making of knowledge?"

Given this context, these definitions, and these observations, we ask:

- What does this proliferation of sites mean for this thing we call college composition?
- Do we still conceive of college as a place where relationships—between people as between people and materials and knowledges—are central?
- What are the appropriate places and structures for the learning and the teaching of composition?
- What does it mean to write? To compose?
- What is college composition? (What should it be?)
- How does a particular curricular space position teacher, student, materials, and learning?
- How does a particular physical space position teacher, learner, materials, and composing?
- How does the online curricular space position teacher, learner, materials, and composing?
- And not least, how/does the delivery of college composition matter?

Notes

1. See Peter Elbow's *Writing Without Teachers*.

2. This statement was made at the opening session of the Conference of the National Learning Information Initiative, a division of Educause, in January 2003.

3. Some educators are using blogs: see the September 2003 issue of *English Journal*, and see Teddi Fishman's blog for a technical writing class, at http://people.clemson.edu/~tfishma/314/engl314H.html.

4. And if this analysis is correct—students have a communication need and meet it; the fact that they gather when and where they plan to is a pretty good assessment—it's not entirely clear why we need college.

5. Sirc, *English Composition as a Happening*.

6. Crowley, *Composition in the University*.

7. See, for instance, Joe Harris' review of *Rhetoric and Composition as Intellectual Work* in the September 2003 issue of *CCC*: "I am drawn to composition precisely because it values teaching and service, because it defines intellectual in far more expansive ways than most disciplines. The essays collected by Olson in *Rhetoric and Composition* demonstrate that our field has achieved the status of a conventional academic discipline. It remains to be seen what the impact of this discipline will be on the intellectual work of teaching writing" (174).

8. Sullivan, "What Is 'College-Level' Writing?"

9. It's also so that the old can overdetermine the new, as we see in computer classrooms where workstations are lined up in rows so that students can face the front even if they can't see over the monitor to the front.

10. Sullivan.

Works Cited

Berlin, James. *Rhetoric and Reality: Writing Instruction in American Colleges, 1900–1985*. Carbondale: Southern IL UP, 1987.

Brandt, Deborah. "Accumulating Literacy: Writing and Learning to Write in the Twentieth Century." *College English* 57 (1995): 649–68.

CCCC Position Statement on Writing Assessment. Accessed online at http://www.ncte.org/aboutlower/positions/category/assess/107610.htm.

Connors, Robert. *Composition-Rhetoric: Background, Theory, and Pedagogy*. Pittsburgh: University of Pittsburgh Press, 1997.

Crowley, Sharon. *Composition in the University: Historical and Polemical Essays*. Pittsburgh: U of Pittsburgh P, 1998.

Donovan, Timothy, and Ben McClelland, Eds. *Eight Approaches to Teaching Composition*. Urbana: NCTE, 1980.

Elbow, Peter. *Writing Without Teachers*. Oxford: Oxford UP, 1977.

Fulkerson, Richard. "Summary and Critique: Composition at the Turn of the Twenty-first Century." *CCC* 56 (2005): 654–87.

Gere, Anne. "Kitchen Tables and Rented Rooms: The Extracurriculum of Composition." *CCC* 45 (1994): 75–91.

Hairston, Maxine. "The Winds of Change: Thomas Kuhn and the Revolution in the Teaching of Writing." *CCC* 33.1 (1982): 76–88.

Harris, Joseph. CCC Online Editorial. May 1994.

Horns, Joseph. *Review of Rhetoric and Composition or Intellectual Work*, ed. Gary Olsen. *CCC* 55 (2003): 172–75.

Hopkins, Edwin. "Can Good Composition Teaching Be Done Under Present Conditions?" *English Journal* 1 (1912): 1–7.

Johnson, Michelle. "More in NC Getting High-School Diploma." *Winston Salem Journal*. B1 and 6: Aug. 23, 2003.

Johnson-Eilola, Johndan. "Writing About Writing." *Kairos* 7.3: http://english.Hu.edu/Kairos/7.3/features/johnsoneilola.htm. Last accessed 28 December 2005.

Kemp, Fred. Re: AP Cut Off scores. WPA-L: Aug. 20, 2003.

Lanham, Richard. *The Electronic Word. Democracy, Technology, and the Arts*. University of Chicago Press, 1993.

Lemann, Nicolaus. *The Big Test*. New York: Farrar, Straus and Giroux, 2000.

Lerner, Neal. Personal communication. June 2005.

Lloyd-Jones, Richard, and Andrea Lunsford, eds. *The English Coalition Conference: Democracy Through Language*. Urbana, IL, and New York: NCTE and MLA, 1989.

Matsuda, Paul. "Process and Post-Process: A Discursive History." *Journal of Second Language Writing* 12 (2003): 65–83.

McLuhan, Marshall, and Quentin Fiore. *The Medium is the Massage*. Corte Madena, CA: Gingko Press, 1967.

Miller, Richard. "Inventing the University Student." In *Composition in the 21st Century.* Ed. Edward White, Lynn Bloom, and Donald Daiker. Carbondale: Southern Illinois UP, 2003, 252–55.

Moran, Charles. "The Winds, and the Costs, of Change." *Computers and Composition* 9.2 (April 1993): 35–44. Accessed online at http://corax.cwrl.utexas.edu/cac/archives/v10/10_2_html/10_2_4_Moran.htm.

North, Stephen. "The Idea of a Writing Center." *College English* 46 (1984): 433–46.

Payne, Darin. "English Studies in Levittown: Rhetorics of Space and Technology in Course Management Software." *College English* 67 (2005): 483–507.

Rheingold, Howard. *Smart Mobs: The Next Social Revolution.* Cambridge, MA: Perseus, 2002.

Schuster, Charles. "Confessions of an Associate Dean." *WPA: Writing Program Administration* 24.3 (2001): 83–99.

Selfe, Cynthia L. *Technology and Literacy in the Twenty-first Century.* Carbondale: Southern Illinois UP, 1999.

Sellen, Abigail, and Richard Harper. *The Myth of the Paperless Office.* Cambridge, MA: MIT Press, 2001.

Sirc, Geof. *English Composition as a Happening.* Logan: Utah State UP, 2001.

Soles, Derek. "A Comment on the WPA Outcomes Statement for First-Year Composition." *College English* 64 (2002): 377–78.

Spooner, Michael, and Kathleen Yancey. "Postings on a Genre of Email." *CCC* 47.2 (1996): 247–58.

Sullivan, Patrick. "What Is 'College-Level' Writing?" *TETYC* (2003): 374–90.

Trimbur, John, and Diana George. "The Communication Battle, or Whatever Happened to the Fourth C?" *CCC* 50 (1999): 682–98.

Trupe, Alice. "Academic Literacy in a Wired World: Redefing Genres for College Writing Courses." *Kairos* 7.2: 1–9. Accessed online at http://english.ttu.edu/kairos/7.2/sectionone/trupe/WiredWorld.htm.

WPA (Writing Program Administrators). Outcomes statement for First Year Composition. Accessed online at http://www.wpacouncil.org/positions/outcomes.html.

2

The Canon of Delivery in Rhetorical Theory
Selections, Commentary, and Advice

Martin Jacobi
Clemson University

Most historians of rhetoric would tell us that rhetoric's canonical texts emphasize many topics, among them invention, arrangement, and style; the appeals of *ethos, pathos*, and *logos*; the different topoi; and the nature and use of enthymemes, examples, and maxims. What they don't often mention is delivery, which like memory often becomes an afterthought. If one can collect and organize one's thoughts, and if one can select effective tropes, diction, and grammar, of course one can deliver it with but one or two pointers.

Still, as this chapter explains, rhetoricians haven't completely ignored delivery. It has been defined and illustrated in several ways, beginning with the oral contexts addressed by classicists; carried forward by elocutionists; and further defined in the twentieth century as directly connected to ethics. It is this last point, the ethical nature of delivery, that is so important for this volume, for while delivery may function as a trope for ways that learning is staged, that form of delivery, like the canon, is also an ethical activity.

To make this argument, I provide a brief overview of the canon, emphasizing the classical theorists who first discussed it as a major element of rhetoric and who analyzed it and systematized a set of guidelines for its use. Then I examine the implications of identifying an appropriate ethics as well as the implications of denigrating the other-than-logical appeals as somehow seamy, even unethical, in their application as means of persuasion. In the next section I use some classical and modern theorists to develop an identification of the rhetor with her group and a parallel realignment of her ethical stance. Finally, I offer some thinking about what all this means for the delivery of college composition.

The Elements of Delivery in Classical Rhetoric

Neither Plato nor Aristotle speaks well of delivery. In the *Phaedrus*, Plato has Socrates offer advice that in effect conflates style and delivery, saying that the effective rhetor will know how to adjust the material of a speech to the needs of the "souls" of the audience (62–64; 72).[1] Aristotle mentions that delivery for an orator is necessarily different from its use by the tragic actor, but excepting a few brief comments, he does not take up this point, directing us instead to the *Poetics*. Further, he too conflates delivery and style, noting that what is available in one canon is usually similarly so in the other.

In *On Oratory and Orators*, Cicero discusses this canon more fully. He says that "every emotion of the mind has from nature its own peculiar look, tone, and gesture," and the last six chapters of this treatise offer strategies for the effective use of the eyes and the countenance, of the voice and bodily gestures. He differentiates between the orator and the actor in that, for example, the former should use not gesticulation but emphatic delivery, should have "a strong and manly exertion of the lungs, not imitated from the theatre and the players, but rather from the camp and the palaestra," and should stamp the foot "only in the most vehement efforts, at their commencement or conclusion" (258). Further, "the countenance is the image of the mind, and the eyes are its interpreters," and while people are not moved by eloquence if they do not understand the language, everyone understands facial expressions and gestures. The orator thus must be particularly careful to match gesture and tone to the emotion, lest the audience discern "artifice" (259). Artifice, then, is not bad except that it might be discerned; in other words, while both actor and rhetor are concerned with effective delivery, the actor is obviously and appropriately engaged in artifice while the rhetor subtly employs artifice that serves the intent of a more seamless persuasion.

Delivery is more fully developed in the pseudo-Cicero's *Ad Herennium*, which served in great part to standardize the approach of the Romans to rhetoric generally and delivery specifically. Early in the third book, the author notes how many theorists have contended that good delivery is the faculty most important to the practicing rhetor, and while he does not want to rank the canons, he does affirm that this canon has "an exceptionally great usefulness" (189). Asserting that the canon has received very little systematic analysis and development, the author proceeds to do both, in what is the earliest serious treatment of delivery.

The author divides voice quality and physical movement.[2] Under the first category the author lists three aspects: volume, stability, and flexibility. Volume is primarily a gift of nature, but it can be maintained and to some degree enhanced by practice. Vocal stability is primarily gained through cultivation, augmented to some degree by exercise, but primarily conserved. The author goes to some lengths to discuss various ways of developing and maintaining vocal stability, including using a calm and composed voice in a speech's introduction and using long pauses—since "the voice is refreshed by respiration and the windpipe is rested by silence" (193). Speakers should "relax from continual use of the full voice and pass to the tone of conversation; for, as the result of changes, no one kind of tone is spent, and we are complete in the entire range" (193). We should likewise avoid piercing exclamations lest we harm the windpipe, and we should, at the end of a speech, "deliver long periods in one unbroken breath, for then the throat becomes warm, the windpipe is filled, and the voice, which has been used in a variety of tones, is restored to a kind of uniform and constant tone" (193–95). Happily, the author notes, what conserves and otherwise benefits the voice also proves agreeable to an audience, and he takes about twenty-five lines to repeat the reasons for the agreeably persuasive that were just offered for the physically beneficial.

Vocal flexibility, since it depends entirely on rhetorical rules, deserves the author's and readers' careful attention. Vocal flexibility, we learn, has three aspects—conversational tone, tone of debate, and tone of amplification. The conversational tone itself has four kinds: dignified, explicative, narrative, and facetious; the tone of debate two: sustained and broken; and the tone of amplification another two: hortatory and pathetic. For somewhat more than fifty lines, the author then explains "what delivery is appropriate to each of these eight subdivisions" (199), and we learn what we might have expected. For example, with the dignified conversational tone we should use a full voice, yet not to the degree that "we pass from the practice of the orator to that of the tragedian" (199); the pathetic tone of amplification requires that "we use a restrained voice, deep tone, frequent intermissions, long pauses, and marked changes" (201).

After the discussion of voice quality, the author turns to the second major division, physical movement, which "consists in a certain control of gesture and mien which renders what is delivered more plausible" (201). Again, we have a dry summary of predictable suggestions. For instance, "the facial expression should show modesty and animation, and the gestures should not be conspicuous for either elegance or grossness, lest we give the impression that we are either actors or day laborers" (201–3). Additionally, rules for bodily movement ought to correspond to the divisions of tone regarding vocal quality. Thus, the dignified conversational tone mandates that the speaker "stay in position when he speaks, slightly moving his right hand, his countenance expressing an emotion corresponding to the sentiments of the subject," and the pathetic tone of amplification suggests that the rhetor "ought to slap one's thigh and beat one's head, and sometimes to use a calm and uniform gesticulation and a sad and disturbed expression" (203–5). The author concludes this section of the *Ad Herennium* by observing that before undertaking this task, he was not at all sure that he could "express physical movements in words and portray vocal intonations in writing" (205), and he admits that he has only offered some suggestions that need fleshing out through practice. His last suggestion is to remember that "good delivery ensures that what the orator is saying seems to come from his heart" (205)—implying that artifice is part of good rhetoric.

Quintilian's discussion of delivery, in Book XI of the *Institutes of Oratory*, is similar to that in the *Ad Herennium* in its understanding of and advice concerning this canon. He contends that invention "is not so important as the manner in which we produce it, since the emotions of each member of our audience will depend on the impression made upon his hearing" (243); delivery, then, is the most important element of rhetoric (245). It is concerned with "two different things, namely, voice and gesture, of which the one appeals to the eye and the other to the ear, the two senses by which all emotion reaches the soul" (249–50). In Book XI he develops these observations, in the process covering much the same ground covered in the *Ad Herennium* concerning voice quality, saying that it depends upon tone and volume, of correctness and clarity and ornamentation, and of appropriateness. However, his discussion of gesture goes far beyond the simple parallel to voice offered by the psuedo-Cicero. The head, for instance, should be carried naturally and erect to secure grace; drooping the head is suggestive of humility, while throwing it back suggestive of arrogance; inclining it to one side indicates languor, while holding it stiffly and rigidly indicates a rude and savage temper (281). On the more specific subject of the forehead, Quintilian argues for his position over Cicero's and the pseudo-Cicero's, claiming that slapping the forehead is much too theatrical a gesture. Further, and moving to other parts of the body, he says that only rarely is it becoming to touch the breast with the fingertips of the hollowed hand (although if we do employ this gesture "it will not be unbecoming to pull back the toga at the same time") (309). He goes into some detail on how to use the eyebrows to express emotion and spends more than three pages on how to use one's fingers. He also talks about just when one *should* slap one's thigh or one's head, and why one should not "protrude the chest or stomach, since such an attitude arches the back, and all bending backwards is unsightly" (309).

Questions of both voice and gesture are determined by what is appropriate: After all, "the same characteristics of voice, gesture and gait are not equally becoming in the presence of the emperor, the senate, the people, and magistrates, or in private and public trials, or in making a request to the praetor for the appointment of a judge to hear our case, and in actual pleading" (326–27). This advice echoes that given for the decisions concerning invention, arrangement, and especially style, the kind of advice every first-year composition textbook includes regarding audience analysis. Quintilian proceeds to give some advice on just when one will want to be loud or soft, how one might want to arrange one's toga in what situations, and so forth. Finally, he notes that "different methods will often suit different speakers" (343).

One aspect of delivery not taken up in any detail in the classical texts is physical appearance—in fact, the appearance that we read about in Todd Taylor's chapter here—and while it seems important to explain just how and how often one should touch one's hand to one's breast, it also seems important to explain that the hand ought to be clean and the breast covered by a handsome toga. At the close of Book XI of his *Institutes of Oratory*, Quintilian does address clothing and other adornments; he is fairly specific about appropriate lengths and styles of togas for different occasions, advising against too many rings on the hand and against bandanges: "[a]s regards the short cloak, bandages used to protect the legs, mufflers and coverings for the ear, nothing short of ill-health can excuse their use" (323). However, he does not take up in any detail such considerations as the importance of cleanliness, good grooming, or appropriate perfumes and sandals.

Delivery in the Western Rhetorical Canon[3]

In the texts on rhetoric that have followed the Greeks and the Romans, delivery has been treated similarly—that is, in the main ignored and, when treated, treated superficially. Augustine's very general advice in *On Christian Doctrine*, for instance, talks of its importance but does not offer suggestions, Boethius barely mentions it, and Ramus attacks Quintilian on the topic without giving any helpful alternative. At the end of his *Arte of Rhetorick*, Wilson provides very brief mention, and Blair gives one out of the total forty-three lectures to pronunciation (and none to gesture).

Fast-forwarding two thousand years, excepting references to Lanham, delivery today is often sidebarred in rhetorical theory courses, and perhaps because of the privileging of written over oral rhetoric (that is, because in most postsecondary settings first-year writing receives greater attention than undergraduate speaking), it is not studied or taught in the way that invention, arrangement, and style are. As in Athens and Rome, the postsecondary study of delivery occurs through acting courses in theater departments or through elocution and oral interpretation courses in speech departments. So, another way of thinking about the connections and the overlap between delivery and style is through the conceit that delivery is the province of public speaking and the performing arts whereas style is the province of literature and composition. A historical survey would support this conceit, but more importantly, it supports the evaluation of delivery as a sorely neglected canon, at least among the courses and emphases in postsecondary required and general education courses.[4]

In this dash through the two millennia following the ancients, I do want to pause long enough to mention the elocutionary movement in eighteenth-century England. Thomas Sheridan, for one, does provide detailed analysis of and guidelines for elocution, and his advice served his time as the classical writers' advice served theirs: he emphasizes a natural, conversational tone, moderate and conventional gestures and expressions, and conventional grammar and usage. His *Course of Lectures on Elocution* might be updated for our time, but his general advice is still useful to contemporary politicians talking to constituents and voters; to news anchors on network television reading the world's wars, disasters, and threats; and to CEOs explaining third-quarter balance sheets or merger plans. His observations are as predictable and useful as are the observations by Quintilian and the pseudo-Cicero, which is to say that Sheridan dismisses the more flamboyant deliveries recommended by some because they are no longer appropriate for his readers. On the other hand, Gilbert Austin, another writer identified with the elocutionary movement, is less interested in the natural style important to Sheridan and more interested in the grand style of Cicero, the Asiatic style keyed to a more expressive delivery. Austin even goes so far as to prepare illustrations of facial expressions as well as hand and body gestures, and he labels them according to their utility in delivery. It could be said that he promotes a delivery more in keeping with acting than with oratory, although if one dials the radio to a Southern Baptist preacher, or sees on the television a late-night pitch by the local car dealer or the makers of extraordinarily sharp knives and scissors, this distinction is not so easily drawn.[5] The line, of course, is what is appropriate, and in this way we come again to the ethics implied and implicated in the way delivery is understood and used.

Delivery and Ethos

After reviewing the detailed observations on this canon by the Romans, a reader is left with the general impression that all that's needed to understand delivery is a listing of the obvious elements of delivering effective rhetoric. The discussions, then, do not so much serve as engagement for the intellect as they serve as a repository for what memory needs to hold.

Further, in all these treatises the authors avoid the ethical questions introduced in Plato's critiques of rhetoric and in Aristotle's complaint that audiences should be persuaded by good reason alone. In a lengthy and very thorough discussion of why rhetors need to take care of their windpipes, Quintilian assumes that we understand why it would be disadvantageous for a speaker to sound "strangled" or "muffled" or "rasping" or "subject to spasms" (253–55), and of course we do. Dana Carvey, on NBC's *Saturday Night Live*, would exaggerate George Bush Senior's gestures and the audience would laugh, because they found them not only ineffectual but also so distracting as to absorb the attention that should go to the persuasive goals the rhetor has in mind—suffering the double fault of letting the audience see the artifice even as the artifice itself is at best jerry-rigged.[6] We understand, that is, why Cicero contends that delivery is an essential component of rhetoric, and we even see why Quintilian argues that it is the most important component. These theorists' assumption is not that rhetoric can only present what the author knows to be the truth, or even that it is presented most nobly through logos, but that rhetors should use artifice, ornamentation, sweetness to achieve the goals of the persuasion, and that shortcomings in delivery can harm their rhetoric's effectiveness. By avoiding the ethical and otherwise value-laden discussions of Plato and Aristotle, Cicero, the pseudo-Cicero, and Quintilian implicitly hold for a much more sophistic position, that the available means of persuasion for a given case extend, as regards delivery, to virtually anything that will work. Thus, Quintilian speaks of the importance of being able "to exhibit an emotion that cannot be distinguished from the truth" (277).

This connection between truth, rhetoric, and delivery merits greater consideration, and in particular attention to how the study and practice of rhetoric through the lens of delivery—including the practice of acting one way when one believes another way—might rather make a person *more* ethical. In the debate between Plato and the Sophists, some of the lesser sophists of his time contended that rhetoric will make the student a better person, by which they sometimes implied and sometimes stated that they meant a better person in a moral sense. The greater Sophists, like Protagoras and Gorgias, were much shiftier in the sense in which they meant this improved state, so that even in his *Gorgias*, Plato does not have the titular character admit to a clear and simple moral improvement through rhetoric. It is to Isocrates that I want to turn since, in his *Antidosis*, he says that while he cannot promise to ensure happiness, virtue, and success to those who would learn rhetoric, those who follow the precepts he lays out will be helped more speedily toward honesty of character. This change happens, he contends, because the more one writes about and speaks about what is worthy of praise and honor, the more one is effectively supporting honorable causes, and because the more one contemplates what is worthy of praise and honor, the more one habituates oneself to them and begins to feel their influence. Furthermore, the more one studies what constitutes good character for the community and the more one works to present a good character in one's rhetorical activities, the more one habituates oneself to being a good character (77). So, as one speaks and gestures and dresses and otherwise acts in a natural, trustworthy, reasonable, and cooperative manner, one takes on those traits and becomes thereby a better person.

Isocrates is here talking about what Wayne C. Booth calls "hypocrisy."[7] In an interview with Mary Frances Hopkins, Booth recounts the story of a friend who night after night at the community theater played a wicked character. He complained to Booth that he would come home to his wife and children and have difficulty stepping away from the wicked person he played on stage to engage his family as the loving partner and parent he was "in reality." Booth notes, here and in his 1988 *The Company We Keep: An Ethics of Fiction*, that "the word 'hypocrisy' originally meant simply the playing of a role *on the stage*" (*Company* 252). He continues: "Many of the virtues that we most honor are originally gained by practices that our enemies might call faking, our friends perhaps something like aspiring or emulating" (253), so that we "fake" playing the cello, or juggling, or for that matter performing acts of charity with a caring attitude long before we are really able to do these things well. Booth notes in *Company* that while aspiring to and emulating virtuous behavior can help one become good, it is also the case that "if I am really practicing only deceit, and not in fact developing my potentialities for a given virtue, then of course what I will develop is skill in the practice of deception" (253). Either way, practicing virtues or vices, to live in the character's skin, to take on the character's ethos as one's own, will alter the practitioner.[8]

Kenneth Burke also identifies this self-conditioning strategy, identifying it as a "rhetoric to the self," sometimes a conscious attempt at self-improvement and sometimes not, but what functions as self-improvement either way. In *A Rhetoric of Motives*, Burke says:

> A man can be his own audience, insofar as he, even in his secret thoughts, cultivates certain ideas or images for the effect he hopes they may have upon him; he is here what Mead would call "an 'I' addressing its 'me'"; and in this respect he is being rhetorical quite as though he were using pleasant imagery to influence an outside audience rather than one within. . . . For you become your own audience, in some respects a very lax one, in some respects very exacting, when you become involved in psychologically stylistic subterfuges for presenting your own case in sympathetic terms. (38–39)

Further, Burke notes that this rhetoric to the self oftentimes is designed as a "*moralizing* process," a means by which the individual, "striving to form himself in accordance with the communicative norms that match the cooperative ways of his society" (39), identifies with and is identified by the society as one of its own.

The improvement one realizes in a positive rhetoric to the self Booth calls "hypocrisy upward," and the negative effects his community theater friend underwent, or arguably the effects to the character of a propagandist for fascism or an advertiser for cigarettes, he would call "hypocrisy downward." So why would Isocrates say that the practice of rhetoric leads to improvement and not admit that it might lead also to an impoverishment of the character? One answer is that a rhetor wants to represent herself in her delivery as if she is conventionally virtuous, the better to persuade her audience of her position, so her pattern will be necessarily conducive to an uplift. Even if one is arguing that which one believes to be unethical, the work involved in delivering it with conventionally positive ethos actively works against the particular bad arguments with a consistently good character development.

To stretch this argument a bit more, and stretch it a bit outside the bounds of delivery, Plato does contend (as I noted earlier in this essay) that even if one wishes to misrepresent, still one needs to know the truth, lest one inadvertently harm one's persuasive attempt (*Phaedrus* 47), and Aristotle argues that one needs to know all sides of an argument in order to make one's case more effectively. To stretch the argument just a bit further, the ability to see the different sides of an argument, to get critical distance on them, provides one with what Burke calls "equipment for living," a library of various attitudes and strategies as more or less useful in particular situations. To examine all sides of an issue, particularly when the rhetor filters the examination through a conventionally moral persona, does provide one with the situation and the means to see how (again, to reference Aristotle) the good has the natural advantage and attraction. And, within and around all of these reasons is the effect that repetition plays, something like the means by which behavior modification works in psychology, and something like the means by which athletes acquire from hours of repetitive practice the muscle memory that allows them to groove their golf or tennis swings, and something like the way in which people become better writers by writing and writing and writing: a rhetor "grooves" her ethical "memory" not only by residing within the persona of the virtuous person but by continually thinking about how one might construct one's deliveries to represent oneself as a virtuous person.

Conclusion

Despite the relative lack of attention given to delivery throughout the history of rhetorical theorizing, many theorists argue that it is essential to success. That contemporary pedagogical attention on this canon is lacking certainly continues the historical trend. Some professionals—like newscasters, public relations officials, actors, and advertisers—do pay handsomely for voice and movement lessons, and in some cases the payoff is worth the cost, but by and large people's rhetorical effectiveness is hamstrung because of their weakness in the area of delivery.[9]

What is to be done to improve delivery in particular, rhetoric in general, and virtue in rhetoricians? Well, obviously, more attention to the practice of delivery in the schools would improve performance, but I think that there is even more at stake, and I want to slip outside the constraints of this essay's charge for a moment to explain. Because I am outside my bounds, because I think that others in this collection will touch on some of the following points, and because I am addressing some issues with long and complicated histories and arguments of support as well as rebuttal, I ask for my readers' indulgence as I make a series of assertions to prepare for my answer to the question of what is to be done.

Generally speaking, what should be done is to give more attention to delivery in the education of tomorrow's citizenry; that is—as this volume does—to consider not only *how* we deliver education, but also *what* we deliver in that education, and more specifically, the role that *delivery itself* ought to play in it. In both our society's guiding principles and our day-to-day statements, we claim to believe in pluralism and democracy, and we claim to desire the continuation of the first through the responsible practice of the second. A rhetoric course—first-year writing, for instance—lends itself to the development of skills of critical thinking, organizing, and crafting effective rhetoric, all of which are necessary in a pluralistic society and for a democratic system. So, we should be sure that we give our students a good education in these aspects of rhetoric, which might take place at the postsecondary level in first-year writing and public-speaking courses, in writing-intensive courses, and in communication-across-the-curriculum programs. The delivery of this kind of education, then, would support not only our immediate educational mission but also our society and our political system, helping to create virtuous people disposed toward pluralism and democracy. Indeed, an emphasis on guided instruction in critical thinking, organizing, and crafting for the pen or the computer keyboard or the voice, with the implication that practice makes perfect, could be seen as a noble attempt to help students realize hypocrisy upward.

At this juncture, a cynic might point out that one of the first things that antidemocratic forces do after overthrowing democracy—in classical Athens or Rome, in twentieth-century Europe, or elsewhere—is either to close or attempt to gain control of the engines for rhetoric, in the schools and in the mass media; and that cynic might go further to say that the meager funding of writing and public-speaking programs indicates that our government and society have chosen fiscal starvation as a way to keep rhetoric from empowering citizens to act maturely in their political interests. That is, the cynic might say, we have these programs, but as writers in this volume assert (see Neff, for instance, and Rickly), they are too often staffed by underpaid, underqualified, and overworked adjunct faculty or by graduate students who are at best apprentices and are too often less concerned with teaching writing than in completing their own coursework in literature or some theoretical aspect of communication studies. Further, it would not even take a cynic to point out that universities are unlikely to commit additional resources, when what they have is already stretched quite thin, to an additional general education emphasis area.

But—and I suspect it is clear what I am about to say—since there are insufficient resources and attention paid to this essential element of rhetoric, and since such a rhetoric as I have outlined is an essential element in our polity's health, it does seem inescapable that we should promote increasing the emphasis on rhetoric in general, and delivery in particular.[10] Clearly, such a decision would require that speech programs or perhaps acting programs have a bigger role in general education at the college level than they now have. Such a decision might require freeing up funds that currently go to technology or to undergraduate and graduate programs more favored by an institution, yet students would certainly benefit from this refocusing of academic emphases. Quite specifically and practically, my institution has been working very hard to help undergraduates secure prestigious scholarships, fellowships, and other rewards, such as in the Truman and the Rhodes competitions, and the judges for these awards look for and expect rhetorical skills—including skills in delivery at interviews. More generally, all graduating students would certainly be aided by such an emphasis when they interview for positions in graduate schools or in the business and government worlds, when they are called upon to make speeches or presentations or reports, and when they want to be listened to at town hall meetings or political conventions or other public gatherings. More generally still, all of us who live in a democratic system would benefit when citizens possess skills that allow them to participate effectively in governance and that encourage them to do so virtuously.

All of this is to say, then, that if we want a healthy society, and if we want successful students, we ought to work to increase our delivery of Delivery.

Notes

1. As with Plato's treatment of rhetoric—that it is a bad thing that he uses effectively to make his points (including his point that it is normally a bad thing)—so with his treatment of delivery. That is, he ignores it explicitly but uses it effectively—at least at one remove. For instance, Socrates' coy delivery at the beginning of this dialogue is a very effective means of seducing his young interlocutor. It is also instructive to note (and here I am drawing on Richard Weaver's analysis of this dialogue) how the impossibility of a neuter rhetoric—with Lysias' speech by the nonlover being the example—suggests not only the importance of delivery generally but in fact the necessity of learning it. This importance is comparable to the importance (according to Plato, at least) of knowing the truth: ignorance of the truth leads to the very real possibility that one will deliver falsehood; and ignorance of good techniques of delivery leads to the very real possibility that the audience will not understand the rhetor as she wishes.

2. Schematically, the discussion has these parts:

Voice Quality **Physical Movement**

- Volume
- Stability
- Flexibility

* conversational tone	* tone of debate	* tone of amplification
–dignified	–sustained	–hortatory
–explicative	–broken	–pathetic
–narrative		
–facetious		

3. My use of primary sources in this section is aided by commentary in Bizzell and Herzberg's *Rhetorical Tradition*.

4. Perhaps my earlier discussion of the treatment of delivery by classical rhetoricians might seem somewhat dismissive of the attention they do give to the topic and the seemingly commonsense nature of their advice. However, any teacher who has asked students to give an oral report would admit, I think, that, commonsense or not, the guidelines for effective delivery are not well understood or followed by many students in undergraduate courses.

5. It used to be that political speeches had this Asiatic quality to a substantial degree. One thinks of the Gettysburg Address, of Roosevelt's speech about the only thing we have to fear is fear itself, of Churchill's speech about blood, sweat, and tears, even of Kennedy's request that we ask not what our country can do for us but what we can do for our country. We do not get those sorts of speeches anymore. On a similar note, Richard Weaver says in "The Spaciousness of Old Rhetoric" that the oratorical flourishes of the previous century are no longer acceptable; we need not agree with his argument that this

loss comes from certain of his cultural bête noires to agree that political rhetoric has become a diminished thing.

6. Another example can be drawn from a visit to my institution over a dozen years ago by a candidate for a senior position who began his talk in a voice that sounded "strangled" and "muffled" and "rasping" and "subject to spasms"; with gestures that included shuffling his papers, struggling with a paper clip, and dropping a few of the pages; and with body language that amply underscored his lack of comfort in front of the audience. At least some audience members were so strongly empathetic that they slid down, lower and lower, in their seats, embarrassed as they were for the hapless rhetor. Then like Clark Kent transforming into Superman, the speaker straightened up and spoke with appropriate volume and flexibility, telling his audience that his introduction was meant to show them in graphic details the result of not having been taught effective communication skills. The audience should see that the skills he now exhibited were just those sorts of skills the audience wanted its students to have. But the audience could not see, because they were too low in their seats and were feeling not only residual vicarious embarrassment but also a betrayal by the speaker, who made them suffer exquisite discomfort to make a point. His rhetorical decisions were, at least for some in the audience, detrimental to his candidacy.

7. He also seems to me to be talking about some fairly commonly accepted elements of human conditioning, which might fall under a general category of behavior modification and conditioning and which have a long history of practice not only in professional psychology but in parochial schools, the Girl Scouts, and other similar operations. That is, it seems in a way less remarkable in its theoretical articulation than it does in the way it has been neglected in educational theories of rhetoric.

8. Booth even cites as further support the great eighteenth-century British literary figure Samuel Johnson, who asserted that if we try to act better we do in fact improve ourselves (*Company* 54). Which is to say, support for such a position exists not only in psychology and the theater but in other areas as well.

9. Would the arguments I've outlined—that practice in rhetoric leads to virtue—be able to explain why the rhetorically challenged President George W. Bush seems also to be lacking in the virtue of truth telling? I would say that they could, and both Isocrates and Aristotle would help make that case.

10. In "Rhetoric and Reality; or, My Basics Are More Basic Than Your Basics," Wayne Booth offers a sorites that argues this point—that a good rhetorical education is in fact essential for a healthy democracy. See page 36ff.

Works Cited

Aristotle. *On Rhetoric*. Trans. George A. Kennedy. New York: Oxford UP, 1991.

Austin, Gilbert. "From Chironomia." Excerpted in Bizzell and Herzberg.

Bizzell, Patricia, and Bruce Herzberg. *The Rhetorical Tradition*. 2d ed. Boston: Bedford, 2001.

Booth, Wayne C. *The Company We Keep: An Ethics of Fiction*. Berkeley: U of California P, 1988.

———. "Rhetoric and Reality; or, My Basics Are More Basic Than Your Basics." In *The Vocation of a Teacher: Rhetorical Occasions 1961–1988*. Chicago: U of Chicago P, 1988.

Burke, Kenneth. *A Rhetoric of Motives*. New York: Prentice Hall, 1952.

[Cicero]. *Ad Herennium*. Trans. Harry Caplan. Cambridge, MA: Harvard UP, 1954.

Cicero. *On Oratory and Orators*. Trans. J. S. Watson. Carbondale: Southern Illinois UP, 1970.

Hopkins, Mary Frances. "Interview with Wayne C. Booth." *Literature in Performance: A Journal of Literary and Performing Art* 2.2 (April 1982): 46–63.

Isocrates. *Against the Sophists* and *Antidosis*. Excerpted in Bizzell and Herzberg, *The Rhetorical Tradition* (72–79).

Plato. *Phaedrus*. Trans. W. C. Helmbold and W. G. Rabinowitz. New York: Macmillan, 1956.

Quintilian. *Institutes of Oratory*, vol IV. Trans. H. E. Butler. Cambridge, MA: Harvard UP, 1922.

Sheridan, Thomas. "A course of lecture on Elocution," Lecture IV. Excerpted in Bizzell and Herzberg.

Weaver, Richard. *Language Is Sermonic*. Ed. Richard L. Johannesen, Rennard Strickland, and Ralph T. Eubanks. Baton Rouge: Louisiana State UP, 1970.

Welch, Kathleen. *The Contemporary Reception of Classical Rhetoric: Appropriations of Ancient Discourse*. Hillsdale, NJ: L. Erlbaum, 1990.

3

Faculties, Students, Sites, Technologies

Multiple Deliveries of Composition at a Research University

Irwin Weiser
Purdue University

A number of variables affect how composition is taught and learned—how it is delivered and received. Who teaches it, who takes it, what the curriculum is, where and when it is taught, the technologies used (or not) in its delivery and reception vary widely across postsecondary institutions in the United States. In this chapter, I discuss several of these variables, particularly as they impact composition administration, teaching, and learning at the kind of institution with which I am most familiar: the state-assisted research university.[1] Although the circumstances of composition delivery certainly are influenced by the kind of institution in which it is taught, I want to suggest that there are some common features of composition instruction that allow me to claim that the research university can be seen as something of a macrocosm for the various issues involving the delivery of college composition in the early years of the twenty-first century. While most undergraduate students at research universities are traditional eighteen- to twenty-two-year-old native speakers of English, there are also always older students, returning students, and nonnative speakers of English taking composition. While most sections of composition are offered on campus, some may be offered at satellite locations, including area high schools (via both dual-enrollment and evening or continuing education programs), community centers, and industries. While most sections are delivered in classroom settings via face-to-face classes, many students find that their composition course relies heavily on technologies and that some resemble or quite literally are distance-education courses, with much, most, or all of the interaction among students and between students and instructors taking place via email, MOOs/MUD (Multi-User Object Oriented/Domain), telecourses, and so on. And the instructors who teach at research universities reflect the diversity of instructors teaching composition across the spectrum of two-year and four-year, public and private, large and small institutions: they are full-time tenure-line or tenured faculty, full-time or part-time adjunct instructors, and graduate teaching assistants, some regularly teaching a large number of composition courses, others teaching only one or two.

I will be telling the story of the multiple ways that composition has been delivered at Purdue University, a land-grant university enrolling more than 38,500 students. Part of this story will focus on how we have been delivering the course for the past two decades and on our decisions about alternative means of delivery we[2] have agreed to accept or not accept. But another part of this story will be about the development of an alternative means of on-campus delivery for composition, a major curriculum change, and the issues that surround such a change at an institution with multiple campuses, multiple stakeholders, and multiple interests in how composition is delivered—and received. I will be discussing how economics, working conditions, institutional regulations, and interdisciplinary interests and politics all play a part in efforts to change the means of delivering college composition at universities like Purdue. My claim is not that the delivery of composition has been revolutionized, but rather that it has evolved for reasons that combine our desire to improve instruction and learning and our efforts to address the practical constraints that have faced us—and many other educators in the country.

Delivering Composition at Purdue, Part I: A Brief History

Composition has been delivered at Purdue in ways that do not differ significantly from its delivery at other colleges and universities across the United States, at least during the past twenty-plus years. Students followed one of three paths through composition. We offered a two-course sequence of Introductory Composition, taken by the majority of first-year students during their first two semesters on campus. We also offered an accelerated, one-semester version of the sequence for students who appeared to be especially well prepared for college writing and a one-semester developmental writing course for students who appeared to need additional instruction in writing before taking Introductory Composition. Initial placement into one of these paths was done by academic advisers working with data provided by the Office of Admissions—data that included students' SAT-Verbal scores, high school grade point averages (overall and in English courses) and class rank, and several other factors.[3] We do not conduct a formal placement test on campus—with well over six thousand new first-year students every fall since 1995,[4] such testing would be both daunting and prohibitively expensive—but we do ask students to provide a writing sample during the first week of classes in order to see if any might be better served in a different class. As admission requirements have increased, particularly over the past four years in a deliberate attempt to control enrollment at the main campus in West Lafayette, Indiana, we have seen the number of students who are placed in the advanced course increase and the number who are placed in the developmental course decrease to the point that as of fall 2003, we are not offering the course.

The curriculum in our composition courses, like our structure, has been similar to that in many other institutions. In all of our courses, we emphasize the concept of process, the recursive activity of planning, drafting, revising, and editing work. We emphasize as well the rhetorical nature of writing, a person writing about a particular topic to a particular audience, taking into account the interplay of purpose, audience, and language. We encourage students to see writing as a social act, both through the emphasis on audience and through the use of collaborative work, and we try to help students see writing as a means of personal empowerment and reflection as well as a means of practical communication in personal, academic, and professional settings.

Our courses are taught, as is the case in most institutions with research missions and large graduate programs, primarily by graduate teaching assistants. Our graduate teaching assistants are enrolled in MA, MFA in creative writing, and PhD programs in a variety of English and English-affiliated disciplines, including literature, rhetoric and composition, English language and linguistics, theory and cultural studies, American studies, women's studies, and others. They receive support in their teaching through a long-standing mentoring program, which includes both a weeklong preservice orientation program and a yearlong sequence of courses in teaching college composition, taken concurrently with the first year of teaching and required as part of holding a teaching assistantship.[5] We also employ adjunct instructors, either on semester, by-course, limited-term status or on continuing, salaried status, but the number of these adjuncts fluctuates significantly based on enrollment, and they constitute a comparatively small portion of our teaching staff. Faculty in the rhetoric and composition graduate program occasionally teach composition courses, but most of us have administrative appointments and obligations to the graduate program or professional writing undergraduate major that preclude any of us from teaching first-year composition with any regularity.[6]

Our students come from around the United States and all over the world, though as a land-grant university, the majority of our students come from in state: in fall 2004, 20,509 of the 30,747 undergraduate students were Indiana residents.[7] However, Purdue also has the largest enrollment of international undergraduates of any public university in the United States, with 1,943 international undergraduates enrolled in fall 2001, the largest numbers by far coming from India, the People's Republic of China, and South Korea.[8] Depending on their English language abilities, these students may take the same courses as native speakers of English or may be advised to enroll in special sections of

Introductory Composition for nonnative speakers of English, taught by experienced graduate teaching assistants who have taken additional coursework in teaching English as a Second Language and who receive support through an additional mentoring program.

What I have been describing here is a very large first-year writing program, itself part of a larger group of writing, literature, and linguistics courses offered in our department, a number of which are also taught by graduate teaching assistants and lecturers. The economics and politics of the program will be familiar to many readers. The composition courses we have been delivering are of our own design, but they are required not by us or by the Department of English, or even by a central university committee or group charged with developing a common undergraduate curriculum. There is no university-wide general education curriculum at Purdue; instead, each of the ten schools that make up the university sets its own admission and graduate requirements, including composition requirements. Thus we have been teaching composition to students who may or may not be required to take our full sequence, since some schools require only the first course or exempt students from the second course based on their grades in the first. And the number of students we teach is based not so much on our sense of our capacity to teach them as on the expectations of the university that first-year students will be able to enroll in required introductory courses.[9] This has typically meant both last-minute hiring of adjuncts and/or requests for them to take on additional teaching and class-size creep, as pressure for more space in the courses has meant we have increased class size, generally first from twenty-four to twenty-five, and then as necessary from twenty-five to twenty-six, and occasionally from twenty-six to twenty-seven. While we have continued to argue for class sizes and teaching loads consistent with the guidelines of just about every professional organization that has addressed this matter, we have found ourselves unable to bring about any substantial change in these unsatisfactory working conditions.

However, there have been other ways in which we have retained some control over the delivery of composition. In the case of dual enrollment high school–college composition courses, we have been able to determine first, whether we would accept such credits at all, and second, having agreed that we would not categorically refuse to accept such credits, whether courses being offered for college credit in the high schools were equivalent to the courses we offer on campus. We have reviewed program descriptions, course syllabi, and actual student writing as a way to evaluate a number of dual-enrollment programs, and we agreed to accept credit from many of them for our first-semester course. But we also agreed very early in our discussion that we would not accept credit for courses that might substitute for our second-semester course, since we include in this course instruction in research libraries and scholarly publications that are not typically available in high school settings. We have also been responsible for determining whether or not to accept AP and CLEP scores for credit, what scores are acceptable, and what courses students may earn credit for based on these examinations. Following a careful review of the CLEP Freshman College Composition examination with essay, we recently determined that the writing assignments for that examination do not elicit writing comparable with that required in our courses and have stopped awarding credit based on that examination, though we do continue to accept AP credit.

Another kind of delivery that is becoming increasingly common concerns the inclusion of composition courses in first-year experience or retention initiatives. At Purdue, we participate in a cohort enrollment retention program in which students may choose to enroll in two or three courses, usually with a disciplinary connection, with the same group of classmates. Our participation actually began with a program developed by the School of Science at Purdue, which co-enrolled students in the same sections of composition, math, and a basic science, and carried over into participation in a larger retention program sponsored by the Lilly Foundation. We recognized that these programs could be very helpful to new students, particularly at a large institution like ours, and we were intrigued by the possibilities for cross-disciplinary cooperation with faculty from across the university. And our participation has been a successful one, from the perspective of the administrators of these programs, the students, and the composition instructors who have participated in them. However, our decision to participate and to continue to participate in these programs was based on several important principles, which are listed below.

1. The goals of the writing program and the writing course must be maintained.
2. Composition course content and assignments should be determined by the composition instructor, though in collaboration and through negotiation with other instructors in the program.
3. Composition instructors must be involved as equal participants in the program.
4. Composition instructors should have appropriate support from both the writing program and the cross-disciplinary program.
5. Instructors' participation must be voluntary.
6. Initial participation by the writing program does not constitute a permanent commitment.

Rather than take the space to elaborate fully on each of these principles individually, I will instead explain what underlies them as a set. Essentially, these principles articulate our firm belief that the primary purpose of a composition class is to teach students, through practice, to become better writers and rhetors, and that the goals of the composition class must not be compromised by its serving a variety of other purposes, regardless of how worthy those purposes may be. Composition courses do, in many institutions, play an important role in socializing students at the university, since they are often, particularly at large colleges and universities, the only small class a beginning student may be taking, the only one in which the instructor knows students by name, and the only one in which substantial interaction takes place among students and between students and instructors. This is one reason that composition courses are often seen as attractive sites for curricular initiatives of all kinds—another being that composition may be the only required course for all new students and therefore a convenient way to reach them. John Brereton notes that Harvard dean Le Baron Russell Briggs moved Harvard's writing course from the second year to the first and then made his newly originated freshman orientation part of the composition course. Brereton suggests that "the fact that Briggs could add such orientation on to composition instruction illustrates the dual nature of the writing course: important enough to require of every student, but unstructured enough that a third of it can be taken over by a semiacademic orientation to academic life" (28). The principles listed earlier counter this composition-as-empty-vessel mindset by insisting that composition instruction has a purpose, a content, a pedagogy, none of which can be yielded to the goals, however well intentioned, of others. We believe that the composition program—its administrators and instructors—must maintain control over the curriculum and delivery of the course, that instructors must not be seen (and this is particularly important when the composition instructors are graduate teaching assistants or adjuncts and the other participating instructors are professorial faculty) as assistants to the "real faculty" in other disciplines, carrying out their goals, assigning their readings, and evaluating the writing the faculty do not want to read.[10] We insist that whatever additional funding, development opportunities, or recognition that the program makes available to professorial faculty be available to composition instructors as well, and that only instructors who are interested in participating in this program will be assigned to it.

In practice, I am happy to say, our relationship with these two programs has been positive. In fact, it has turned out that the composition instructors are among the most active participants and frequently recognized by their students as having been particularly influential and helpful to them. But the principles suggested earlier remain important and necessary, reminding both us and the those outside our program with whom we cooperate that composition is an equal player, with an educational purpose of its own.

One additional way that we have been delivering composition instruction in our program incorporates technology, particularly computers, the Internet, and the World Wide Web. While I know that we are neither unique nor among the first adopters of computer technology in composition,[11] we have from the start of our use of computers in writing recognized that new technologies, new teaching environments, and new media mean that composition instruction changes. In particular, we have been aware that the mere availability of technology does not mean that it will be used—or used in ways consistent with the goals of a composition course. Continuing professional development opportunities for instructors who want to teach in computer classrooms have enabled us to deliver technology-enriched composition courses that are compatible with our program goals.

Delivering Composition at Purdue, Part II: Evolution

The previous brief discussion of technology serves as an appropriate transition to what is taking place in our program at present. In August 2003, our approach to delivering composition to the majority of students at Purdue-West Lafayette changed dramatically. The two-semester sequence of three-credit courses I described earlier no longer exists. In its place we are delivering composition via a one-semester, four-credit course. I want to emphasize at the outset that this course is one that has been developed, proposed, and supported by the Introductory Writing Program, since on the face of it, it may seem to be a kind of anticomposition move imposed by others. In this portion of the chapter, I will explain the motivations behind this change, motivations that combine pedagogical, political, and administrative considerations.

Pedagogical Motivations

Several pedagogical concerns led us to this revision in our delivery of first-year composition. One of the most important had to do with a fact mentioned earlier: since each school establishes its own graduation requirements, some schools chose to require only one semester of composition or to allow students who earned high grades in the first-semester course to take an elective instead of the second-semester course. What this meant was that approximately one-third of the first-year students were required to take only the first half of what we designed to be a two-semester sequence. Our two-semester curriculum, like that at many other institutions, did not emphasize argumentation or research-based writing until the second semester, which means that one-third of the beginning students at Purdue did not receive instruction or practice in the kinds of academic writing that many of their instructors across campus assumed they received. The new one-semester course has been conceived of as one that will blend the curricula of the previous two courses, providing all first-year students who take composition with instruction in argument and research-based writing. We could have addressed this concern by reversing the curricula of our two courses, moving this instruction into the first semester and instruction in experience-based, analytical, and persuasive writing into the second course. However, as will become clear later, such a move would address only part of the pedagogical issues we hoped to address and none of the political or administrative concerns.

A second pedagogical issue for us was our desire to provide all first-year students with integrated instruction in the use of technologies for writing and research. I mentioned earlier that technology has played a part in how we deliver composition instruction. For a number of years, we scheduled some sections of introductory composition in computer classrooms, and each year, we saw an increasing interest among our instructors in teaching in computer classrooms. We also recognized the curricular need to teach students in environments that are most like the ones they use and will continue to use as writers and researchers. However, the number of computer classrooms on campus is not adequate for all of our sections to meet in them for all their class sessions, and given the size of our program, it is unlikely that the number of computer classrooms will ever be sufficient. We recognize as well that there are many important aspects of teaching writing that do not require being in a computer classroom and perhaps may even be hampered by that environment. Face-to-face classroom discussion, for example, sometimes is more difficult to generate and maintain in a computer classroom, particularly if the space is not designed to allow students and instructors to actually face one another or see who is speaking (I refer here to the notorious "talking monitor" effect in many conventionally arranged computer classrooms). Our new course meets twice per week in conventional classrooms and once per week in computer classrooms, allowing all of the students in the course to have access to instruction and guided practice in using technologies, ranging from the use of the review features in MS Word for commenting on others' writing, to the various databases and search options available on our library's website, to critical evaluation of Web resources, to elements of document design and visual rhetoric, to the use of programs like PowerPoint for designing presentations of their work. By scheduling one class per week in a computer classroom, we maximized[12] the number of sections and students who could be accommodated in the available classes, though at what some may see as the cost of not scheduling any sections in these classrooms for all of their meetings.

Finally, a third pedagogical issue was how to increase the amount of time instructors could spend with individual or small groups of students. While all of our instructors held office hours regularly and most required conferences once or twice a semester, instructors and administrators shared the belief that students would benefit from more intensive discussion of their writing with their instructors. Many instructors have commented about the infrequency with which students take advantage of office hours to talk with them about plans for writing or revising papers, yet many also felt, and had had students tell them, that such opportunities to work closely have been extremely beneficial. In our new course, we addressed this by adding a conference-tutorial component, so that every student will be scheduled to meet on a regular basis with his or her instructor, and every instructor will have as part of her or his appointment to the course the opportunity and responsibility to meet with students regularly. We recognized as we discussed this component of our new course that we could not simply require conferences and not provide instructors with the means to hold them or students with credit for attending them. I will be addressing the political and administrative aspects of this particular change in the sections that follow.

Political Motivations

The pedagogical motivations for our new curriculum were our major consideration in changing how we deliver composition, but there were also political considerations. The political considerations cover a broad range of issues, from the economics of postsecondary instruction in the late twentieth and early twenty-first centuries to the more local issues of enrollment growth and the negotiations within the institution that were required before this new course could be approved.

Like many other postsecondary institutions, Purdue in the 1990s experienced a period of enormous growth. From an undergraduate student population of 29,311 in 1992,[13] Purdue grew to a university enrolling 30,908 undergraduates in the fall of 2002.[14] Enrollment continues to grow despite the administration's efforts to "control" it by increasing admissions requirements and, more recently, increasing tuition and fees.[15] Recently released data from the Office of Enrollment Management indicates that the number of first-year students for fall 2005 is 7,191, an increase of more than 750 students since fall 2000. As I explained earlier, the increased enrollment, along with Purdue's policy of accommodating students in entry-level required courses, led to increased demands for first-year composition courses that were not accompanied by increased resources for permanent instructors. Class sizes for first-year composition grew as administrators insisted that students who needed English 101 be accommodated and we became more and more reliant on adjunct instructors. As has been the case at many institutions, the administration's argument for hiring adjuncts instead of more permanent faculty was that enrollment growth was unanticipated, a temporary situation to be responded to with temporary measures. Such an argument is challenged by the fact that some of the adjuncts teaching in our department had done so for twenty years or longer. I need not spend much space to explain that these lecturers were underpaid, taught more sections (often twice as many) than tenure-track faculty, and had no status in the department.[16]

Those of us on the faculty in rhetoric and composition, particularly those of us with administrative responsibility for first-year composition, were becoming, in James Sledd's derogatory phrase, "boss compositionists."[17] Our efforts to hold the line on class size and on the number of classes offered were constantly being defeated, and as the university admitted more and more students, it became clear that business as usual in the delivery of composition could not continue. We simply would not be able to administer a composition program of the quality we knew students deserved if we were constantly faced with larger and larger classes and a staff to which we could make no commitments, nor expect to receive any from. We faced the unfortunate irony of having a nationally recognized graduate rhetoric program, writing lab, and teaching assistant mentoring program but teaching and learning conditions that we knew were worsening, even if not uncommon.

The politics of enrollment and funding could not be addressed by our arguments, but one means of addressing the situation that was in our control was the curriculum. If we could not accommodate the demand for first-year composition under our current curriculum, then we could try to change it. If the problem was in large part the number of students to be taught, we could find a way to decrease that number. While there are a number of ways to bring about this decrease, many were not acceptable—nor even considered. For example, we could have developed a placement test or a test-out procedure, or exemption policy, any one of which could have been constructed in a way that would reduce the numbers of students in first-year composition.[18] However, we believe that instruction in composition is valuable to students and that the number of students who could not benefit from such instruction is very small, particularly if the course is pedagogically sound and taught by instructors who are receiving or who have received good preparation and who are teaching under appropriately professional conditions, with a sound curriculum to deliver.

Under the circumstances described in the beginning of this chapter, with approximately two-thirds of the students at the university being required to take a two-semester sequence of composition, it became apparent that one way to reduce the aggregate number of students we were required to teach would be to stop teaching one of the courses. Such a change would significantly reduce the total number of composition courses we needed to teach, but it would still allow us to provide nearly all of the students entering the university with a composition course in their first year.

But simply eliminating one of the courses would not address either the pedagogical issues I outlined in the previous section or the political issues of working conditions discussed in the preceding paragraphs. In fact, eliminating the second-semester composition course and revising the curriculum of the first course would likely have meant only that we would reduce the number of teaching assistants and adjuncts since the administration could simply insist that we continue to offer the remaining composition course in sections no smaller than the current ones. In other words, the savings would be only economic and the benefits would be only to the administration.

We believed from the outset that a major curricular change would be worth the time and the work it would (and did and has continued to) require only if it improved both the working conditions for instructors and the learning conditions for students. As I explained in the discussion of pedagogy, several factors supported the move from a fairly conventional two-semester sequence to the one-semester course: the fact that about one-third of the first-year students were not required to take the course in which academic research and argument were taught, that only some students were scheduled in computer classrooms, and that the time instructors could spend with students in individual or small-group instruction was limited. We had already established a limit of twenty students per section in classes taught in computer classrooms, based partly on our recognition that instructors teaching in computer classrooms would need to be able to work closely with students who were learning unfamiliar technologies, but also because the computer classrooms available to us usually had fewer than twenty-five stations, and we knew that we needed to assume that at least one or two stations would not be functioning at any given time. With the precedent of twenty students as a limit for writing classes taught in computer classrooms, we agreed that we would argue for a similar limit for the new course. This class limit would also make it feasible for instructors to meet regularly with students in individual or small-group conferences, if we could work out an approach that would not overburden instructors and would provide students with credit for attending these conferences. Since a half-time teaching assistantship is defined as approximately twenty hours per week, we considered how much time an instructor would need to work with twenty students in a course that combined traditional classroom instruction, computer classroom instruction, and conferencing. Our estimate,[19] which included actual contact time, preparation time, and evaluation time, suggested two things. First, instructors could not possibly meet with every student each week, and second, the time demands for this course meant that instructors teaching it should be considered to be carrying a half-time appointment.

Our argument thus became one that combined our pedagogical and political motivations: the new composition course, because of its combination of three pedagogical approaches and the time demanded for them, had to be limited to twenty students, and it had to count as a half-time appointment for instructors. Teaching assistants who taught the new course would teach two sections per year instead of three, and each section would be limited to twenty students, instead of twenty-four to twenty-seven.[20] Instructors would meet with half of their students each week, either individually or in small groups, based on the instructor's determination of what would be most helpful to students, and this additional meeting for students along with the additional time demands for instructors was the basis of our assigning the course four credits rather than three.[21] A key argument for these changes was that the change from a two-semester to a one-semester sequence would eliminate the need to offer approximately two hundred sections of English 102 per year, but to make this change work, we would need to recoup part of the salary savings by reducing class size and redefining the teaching assignment. In fact, this change in delivery has not led to significant cost savings, but saving money was never a goal of ours as we developed the new course. Our goal was always how to deliver composition to students in the most responsible way we could.

Administrative Motivations, Considerations, and Processes

As I discuss the administrative motives for our curricular change, the overlap between institutional politics and administrative processes and decisions will be obvious. An early administrative motivation for our curricular change had to do with the increasing difficulty of finding qualified adjuncts during a period of rapid enrollment growth. Purdue is located in a community of approximately one hundred thousand people, a little more than one hour from Indianapolis and a little more than two hours from Chicago. Because we offer adjuncts one-semester, per-course contracts, we are not able to recruit people who live very far away, a situation that we share with many other colleges and universities located any distance from major population centers. We rely on people in the community, often spouses of faculty or graduate students, sometimes experienced high school English teachers, sometimes graduates of our own programs who continue to live in town. Reducing the number of sections of first-year composition we offered would thus help address this particular staffing issue: fewer sections would likely mean a reduced demand for adjuncts. And while the reduced class size and redefinition of the teaching assignment would not eliminate our need for adjuncts, it would serve the twofold benefit of reducing it so we could focus on hiring the very best qualified people and of improving the working conditions of those adjuncts who are part of our staff, thus connecting staffing, an administrative issue, with working conditions, a political issue, and class size, a pedagogical issue.

The process of making a curriculum change that affects every academic program in the university is obviously more complex than the process of changing the curriculum for a course that serves only students within a given department or school. Just how complex, however, we did not know. First, the concept of the new curriculum had to be discussed and approved by the Introductory Writing Committee of the Department of English. I introduced the idea to the committee in the fall of 1999, having first talked about it with a several colleagues who shared administrative responsibility for the program with me. The committee discussed the idea and developed a proposal. In December, that proposal was vetted with the head of the department and with our dean, herself a former English department head, since we realized that without their approval or support, the proposal could not move successfully through the administrative processes that were to follow.

In order to be approved, a curricular change that affects other programs has to be made known to those programs so they can comment on its impact. Since this change would affect every academic program, I wrote a letter to the administrator responsible for undergraduate education in each of Purdue's ten schools, outlining the changes and offering to provide more information and answer questions. I was asked to meet with the curriculum committees of some schools to discuss the new course, I received telephone calls or emails from people in other schools, and I heard nothing from people in some of the programs. In some cases, the responses were in the form of messages thanking me for providing the information; in others, I was presented with objections to the plan, which I then had to address (and, as I mentioned in a previous footnote, it was this kind of feedback that led us to change from our originally proposed five-credit course to a four-credit course). Since one of the Purdue regional campuses uses the same course number and structure as we do at West Lafayette, I also worked with the English department chair and WPA there to talk about how the change might impact their program.[22] Once these letters were sent (though not before all the responses were received or all the objections considered), we could prepare a formal proposal for discussion and a vote by the English department faculty. At the February 2000 faculty meeting, a number of questions were raised, including some about how the change in definition of a half-time teaching appointment for teaching assistants in this course would affect the teaching appointments in other courses. While it was clear that this administrative issue would have to be addressed, the department voted to support the change without insisting that it be addressed first.[23]

Following the department approval, the proposal had to be approved three more times, by both the Educational Policy and the Curriculum committees of the School of Liberal Arts, and finally by the School of Liberal Arts Faculty Senate. Normally, these three approvals could take place within the period of a semester, but such was not the case for this change. After the proposal was approved by the Department of English, I was asked to attend a meeting of the Course Availability Committee, people from across the university who discussed curricular needs, course offerings, and so on. At this meeting, I heard several objections, particularly from an associate dean of one large school, concerning the already existing demands on students' time, the tightness of their existing curriculum, the need for students to have more than one semester of writing instruction, and the problems she anticipated students having getting into professional schools. (This last argument, along with a concern about meeting requirements of accrediting associations, was one I heard several times. It was not an argument that I took lightly, but through the process of investigating these concerns, I found evidence that what had been presented to me as requirements for composition turned out to be requirements for instruction in written and oral communication that could be met in a variety of ways, through courses in the English department as well as in other departments.) While I listened to the arguments, took note of them, and later investigated them, I did not indicate whether I thought these arguments were persuasive enough to prevent our going forward with the proposal, nor did university guidelines demand that every objection be met or explicitly responded to. However, as our proposal moved its way through the committees in the school in the spring of 2000 before being sent to the school faculty senate, it became apparent that following the Course Availability Committee meeting, some attendees assumed their objections were so persuasive that the proposal would be withdrawn.

And that is when the dean of the large school and the dean of the School of Liberal Arts began to talk. It is also when the proposal's progress slowed. As the deans talked, I continued to make myself available to talk about the change, and the Introductory Writing Committee continued to iron out some of the details for implementing the new course. Finally, our dean, a strong supporter of the new course throughout the process, said that the proposal could be presented to the School of Liberal Arts Faculty Senate, first for discussion, and at a later meeting, for a vote. The proposal won approval in December 2001.

The preceding paragraphs discuss the formal process of faculty approval. Once that process was completed, the course became an official reality, but not an actual one. The delay in getting approval for the course, which we originally hoped would occur in spring 2000, meant that the year we always knew we would need to develop curriculum, provide a means of professional development support, and work out the scheduling logistics once the course was approved would not be 2001–2, as we'd originally hoped, but instead would be 2002–3. In the spring of 2002, we continued our conversations with the Office of Space Management and Scheduling (SMAS) and Information Technology at Purdue (ITaP) about our needs for computer classrooms and space for the individual and small-group conferences. While our changed curriculum certainly affects both of these administrative units of the university, we have found the people we have worked with in them, as well as in the Office of the Registrar, to be helpful and supportive. SMAS agreed to allow us to convert two classrooms that were used as offices for adjuncts into rooms dedicated to the conference component of the new course. Support from our dean provided funds for remodeling these classrooms, buying new furniture, and equipping them with computers. ITaP decided to convert a large, fifty-station computer lab in a nearby building into two smaller labs that are scheduled exclusively for composition courses from 7:30 A.M to 5:30 P.M. Monday through Friday. They also agreed to configure the computers in the conference rooms so they are identical to those in the classrooms and to connect them to their network, rather than to the School of Liberal Arts network, so that the interfaces are identical in the classrooms and the conference spaces. SMAS proposed several ways for the three components of the course to be scheduled, using its expertise at maximizing space use to suggest options we would have been unlikely to come up with on our own. While our conversations with these units required negotiation on both sides, we have been pleased to work with cooperative people interested in sharing their expertise, and we have certainly learned a lot about the role these administrative units play in how instruction is delivered to students and the differences between their perspectives and ours.

Delivering Composition at Purdue, Part III: Where We Are, Where We're Going

As I write in September 2005, we are two years into our new course, English 106. Our accelerated course, renumbered from English 103 to English 108 (a purely administrative move to suggest that the higher-numbered course is more advanced than the "regular" course), is still being offered, but English 100, our developmental writing course, is not being offered, since the demand for that course declined so that there were not enough students for even one section.

During the 2002–3 academic year, the Introductory Writing Committee articulated the previously implicit goals and outcomes for English 106, based on revisions of those of our current courses; formed working groups to develop several examples of syllabi for the course; and perhaps most importantly, organized workshops and orientations for current teaching assistants and adjuncts who taught the new course in fall 2003. We also continued to work with SMAS and ITaP on the details of scheduling the course and setting up the computer classrooms and conference rooms, all of which were ready for us when our classes began.

Though we have just begun to see what English 106 is, we believe that the pedagogical, political, and administrative work that has gone into its creation has been worthwhile. Most importantly, we believe that we have developed a course that provides students with a richer learning experience than we had been able to provide previously. We are pleased that we appear to have done this in a way that has improved the working conditions of teaching assistants and adjuncts who are the key deliverers of the course, reducing both class size and the number of classes these instructors will teach.[24] We are also pleased that this revision has generated significant interest in the composition program, from current instructors, from administrators, from advisers, and from faculty across the university. Anecdotal reports from instructors tell us that they are particularly pleased with the increased contact they have with students because of the required conferences. They believe they are able to address students' questions about their work more quickly and effectively than they did in the past, when they relied more on written comments and email exchanges with students to communicate with them.

The work on this course continues. The Introductory Writing Program is developing an approach to evaluating the course and that evaluation will certainly result in revisions and improvements. Instructors are testing the new syllabi and will certainly both revise them and develop new ones. Everyone involved in the development of the course and many of the instructors who are teaching it recognize that a change in the delivery of a course provides opportunities for research and learning in addition to improvements in how students learn.

The delivery of instruction can become routinized, particularly when instruction must be delivered to large numbers of students. Courses and programs can be taken for granted. While I do not mean to suggest that a major curricular change should be undertaken simply for the sake of change, it has become clear to us over the past three years that our own reflection on how we deliver composition and the reflection it has led to among others at our university has been generative and stimulating. We have looked hard and long at what we do, and in doing so have caused others in the university who are affected by this change to think more about the place of writing instruction in their students' education.

Notes

1. I use this phrase to signal the change in funding at most public universities. While at one time state legislatures provided the majority of the funding for public universities so that they could accurately be described as state supported, in the early twenty-first century, the funding pattern has changed so that tuition and private funding play a much more significant role in keeping universities operating. A department head in another department here at Purdue has, with tongue in cheek, begun to use the phrase "state located" to describe this change.

2. Throughout this chapter, I talk about what "we" have decided and "our" program. My use of first-person plural is quite deliberate. By "we," I mean the faculty, adjuncts,

and graduate teaching assistants who administer and govern the Introductory Writing Program by serving on the Introductory Writing Committee of the Department of English. But I also mean to convey the collaborative nature of writing program administration and my understanding and firm belief that no single writing program administrator (WPA) or departmental administrator can or should try to own a writing program. During my years as a WPA at Purdue, I have been particularly fortunate to serve with faculty colleagues like Linda Bergmann, Muriel Harris, Janice Lauer, Tony Silva, and Shirley Rose, all of whom have made and continue to make significant contributions to how composition is delivered here.

3. This approach to placement is described by B. Suddarth and S. E. Wirt in "Predicting College Placement Using Precollege Information." *College and University* 49 (1974): 186–94.

4. *Data Digest 2004–2005*. Purdue University, 2005, 28.

5. For a full description and history of this program, see my "When Teaching Assistants Teach Teaching Assistants to Teach: A Historical View of a Teacher Education Program," in *Preparing College Teachers of Writing: Histories, Theories, Programs, Practices*, ed. Betty P. Pytlik and Sarah Liggett, New York: Oxford UP, 2002, 40–49.

6. For my colleague Shirley Rose and myself, who have shared responsibility for administering the introductory writing program over the past several years, this has meant that in order to teach composition, which we both believe it is important for us to do, we have done so primarily during a summer session.

7. *Data Digest 2004–2005*. Purdue University, 2005, 19.

8. *Data Digest 2004–2005*. Purdue University, 2005, 23–24.

9. There is some indication of a change in these expectations. As the fall 2002 semester approached, we were authorized by our dean's office to close our advanced first-year composition course even though there were students on a waiting list for it. Because we were able to offer additional sections of this course in the spring, we did not create the same problem we would have if we had closed the first course in the sequence.

10. Such principles also apply in some configurations of writing across the curriculum, particularly linked-course programs, where the "content" instructor assumes the composition instructor will take care of all the writing instruction.

11. We did, however, install our first computer classroom dedicated to instruction in writing in 1985, so we are certainly among the "early adopters."

12. While I have separated the pedagogical, political, and administrative for the sake of this discussion, I want to emphasize that these motivations overlap in nearly every case. For example, the decision to schedule all sections of our class into computer classrooms once per week was certainly a pedagogically driven decision, but it was not without administrative or political implications and consequences. This decision, along with the decision to incorporate a conference-tutorial component in the course also discussed in this section, has meant significant interaction with other administrative units in the university, including Space Management and Scheduling and Information Technology. I will have more to say about these interactions in the section focusing on administrative concerns.

13. *Data Digest 2001–2002*, Purdue University, 2002, 18.

14. Holsapple, Matt. “Freshmen at Purdue Down, by Design.” *Journal and Courier* [Lafayette, IN] August 28, 2002. Accessed online at www.boilerstation.com/planet/stories/200208280purdue_planet1030511473.shtml.

15. I am, to some extent, oversimplifying a more complex situation. Under its new administration, Purdue responded to decreasing support from the state by increasing both tuition and fees this past year. Tuition was increased by more than 10 percent, but tuition at many universities across the country was increased by a similar percentage, primarily because of the impact of the recession on state funds, endowment income, and so on. Fees were increased by a flat one thousand dollars for all new students as a way of achieving two of the goals of the university’s recently adopted strategic plan: hiring of new faculty and increasing student financial aid. However, it is also reasonable to assume that increased costs might lead to decreased applications. It’s too early to tell if this is the case, since as often happens during economic hard times, applications actually increased this year.

16. In fact, unless the lecturers were spouses of faculty, they often were not even known by the faculty. A particularly unsettling example was when one of our long-term lecturers died several years ago and her death was announced to the department. Several faculty asked who this person whose death was being announced was.

17. For the origins of “boss compositionist,” see James Sledd, “Why the Wyoming Resolution Had to Be Emasculated: A History and a Quixoticisim.” *JAC* 11 (1991): 269–81.

18. This appears to be the strategy at some institutions, where very few students are actually placed in first-semester composition courses but instead fulfill the composition requirement in some other way. Neither of my own children, in fact, were required to take composition at the public research universities they attended; both were exempted on the basis of SAT-V scores and fulfilled the university writing requirement by taking writing-intensive courses later in their curriculum.

19. We conservatively estimated the time as follows: three hours per week in class (either conventional or computer); five hours per week in class preparation; seven hours per week reading and evaluating student writing; five hours per week conferencing with ten students for an average of thirty minutes per student. It seems likely to us that instructors will spend more time on class preparation, particularly the first time they teach this class; the estimate of seven hours per week reading and evaluating students’ work assumed that instructors would spend about twenty minutes per student per week. In developing this estimate, we tried to be realistic, but we also acknowledge that politically, it was important that the course not be estimated to demand more than the contracted twenty hours per week from a teaching assistant. As anyone who teaches knows, it’s possible to spend many, many hours preparing to teach and reading and evaluating student work, just as it’s possible to give short shrift to these activities and the students as well.

20. The director of composition, Shirley Rose, used a credit-hour equivalency formula to determine the appropriate course load for adjuncts. Full-time adjuncts teach twelve credits per semester, or four three-credit courses; those teaching the new course teach three of the new four-credit courses per semester for a full-time appointment; thus they, too, benefit from a smaller class size and a fewer total number of students per semester.

21. We initially proposed the course as a five-credit course, primarily to reflect the time demands on the instructors. However, it became clear in conversations with other

departments and schools that the increase in credit hours during a single semester was an obstacle. We were told that students already carried very large numbers of credit hours, and two additional credits would be too much. Since the concept of credit hour is tied to contact hours, and our major reason for increasing the number of credit hours was to support the case for a reduced teaching assignment for instructors, we offered the four-credit course as a compromise. As I'll discuss later, it was not a compromise that satisfied everyone.

22. Ultimately, their decision not to follow our new curriculum resulted in another round of administrative processes: since they preferred to maintain the current curriculum, we have had to change our course number because courses with the same number must carry the same number of credits if they are not explicitly variable-credit courses.

23. At that meeting, at which I presided over the discussion, I pointed out that the Introductory Writing Committee had no authority over the definition of a half-time teaching appointment, but that we were making a proposal for a new course and explaining what we believed the half-time appointment had to be in order for the course to be successful. Ultimately the decision of how to define half-time appointments was made by the head of the department (a position I now hold) in consultation with other departmental administrators. What has happened is that the director of composition and I outlined what we think makes sense as definitions for half time, based on a variety of scenarios mixing three- and four-credit courses, and teaching assistants have been assigned accordingly.

24. We recognize that we will have to be vigilant about the pressures to increase class size that we have faced for more than a decade and that these pressures may be strengenthed by a tighter university budget and increasing first-year enrollments.

Works Cited

Brereton, John C. *The Origins of Composition Studies in the American College, 1875–1925: A Documentary History*. Pittsburgh: U Pittsburgh P, 1995.

Data Digest 2001–2002. Purdue University, 2002.

Data Digest 2004–2005. Purdue University, 2005.

Holsapple, Matt. "Freshmen at Purdue Down, by Design." *Journal and Courier* [Lafayette, IN] August 28, 2002. Accessed online at www.boilerstation.com/planet/stories/200208280purdue_planet1030511473.shtml.

Sledd, James. "Why the Wyoming Resolution Had to Be Emasculated: A History and a Quixoticisim." *JAC* 11 (1991): 269–81.

Suddarth, B., and S. E. Wirt. "Predicting College Placement Using Precollege Information." *College and University* 49 (1974): 186–94.

Weiser, Irwin. "When Teaching Assistants Teach Teaching Assistants to Teach: A Historical View of a Teacher Education Program." In *Preparing College Teachers of Writing: Histories, Theories, Programs, Practices*. Ed. Betty P. Pytlik and Sarah Liggett. New York: Oxford UP, 2002, 40–49.

4

Getting Our Money's Worth
Delivering Composition at a Comprehensive State University

Joyce Magnotto Neff
Old Dominion University

In spite of my thirty years as a writing teacher, a writing program administrator, and a writing-across-the-curriculum advocate at both two-year and four-year institutions, I have never seriously questioned the financial balance sheet for first-year composition. It all seems routine: students pay tuition, the department counts its FTEs (full-time equivalent students), instructors draw paychecks, the semester ends, and we start all over again. On the other hand, perhaps it is not quite routine. I know that the engineering and science departments have bigger budgets than the English department, and in those disciplines the demand for faculty is greater than the supply. I know their faculty teach large first-year sections and fund their research with grants. I know that the chemistry department puts more than three hundred students into one lecture section of its first-year course and trains teaching assistants (TAs) and adjuncts to supervise the labs attached to the lecture. I know that the State Council for Higher Education in Virginia (SCHEV) devises faculty-to-student ratios to determine resources for each public college and university. Nevertheless, it took the writing of this chapter (plus a heated session with my writing group)[1] for me to put these facts together in new ways and to investigate more deeply the balance sheet for first-year composition. The result is a controversial proposal: Deliver first-year composition at comprehensive state universities the way other first-year courses such as biology, psychology, history, and sociology are delivered. Put three hundred students in a one-hour lecture section each week and divide them into small writing workshops led by TAs, adjuncts, and instructors for two hours each week. This approach enables

English departments to meet state funding formulas and to challenge insufficient budget allocations that undermine the teaching of writing. Before I am accused of ignoring decades of scholarship that advocates small classes and individual attention as superior ways to teach writing, I ask you to consider the evidence that follows.

The Financial Balance Sheet

I will begin with the balance sheet for composition instruction at Old Dominion University, a comprehensive state institution with more than 20,000 students. In the 2001–2 academic year, the English department taught 3,185 students in 139 sections of first-year composition (an average of 23 students per section, in keeping with the departmental cap). The demand for additional seats could not be met because there were neither more adjuncts nor larger classrooms available. The 139 sections (not including summer sections) generated $1,203,930 in tuition.[2] Seventy-eight sections were taught by part-time adjuncts who earned $2,040 per course (no benefits); 27 were taught by full-time instructors who earned $3,750 per course plus benefits; 14 by full-time lecturers who earned $5,000 per course plus benefits; 18 by MA teaching assistants who earned $2,000 per course (no benefits); and 2 by tenure-track faculty who earned salaries according to rank (approximately $6,500 per course plus benefits). Thus, salary costs (without benefits) totaled $379,370. The difference between tuition income and salary expense for 2001–2 was $824,560. For the spring 2003 and fall 2003 semesters, the department taught 3,542 students in 154 sections of first-year composition. Tuition income was $1,562,022 and salary expenses (without including the cost of benefits)[3] were $376,100, for a difference of $1,185,922. More on these numbers later.

Most state universities are bureaucracies. Funding decisions in bureaucracies are historically based, which usually means the original reason that funds were allocated has long been forgotten and may be irrelevant today. Furthermore, bureaucratic funding decisions rarely change without an increase in resources, a situation not seen during the recent recession. In Virginia, the State Council for Higher Education sets formulas for workload analysis. These formulas are reported as student-credit-hour-to-full-time-faculty ratios, which are discipline specific and depend on whether the courses are offered at the undergraduate or graduate level. The formulas were changed in 2001 without public debate. Under the old formula, each full-time faculty member in English was responsible for 240 student credit hours or eighty students per semester. The new formula raises the number of credit hours to 270 and the number of students to ninety for each English faculty member every semester. At the same time, the formula for some disciplines moved in the opposite direction. For example, in the physical sciences, the student-credit-hour ratio was lowered from 330 to 270 (SCHEV website). There is no allowance for sabbaticals or reassigned time for administrative duties, and there is no procedure for appeal once the state has set a funding level for a university. When the SCHEV formula is applied to Old Dominion, the College of Arts and Letters shows a surplus of faculty—English alone has ten more faculty than it "needs," according to the formula. Multiple small sections of first-year (FY) composition are one reason the English department fails the SCHEV test. To complicate matters, the particular classrooms assigned to English (many have twenty-five desks: none has more than forty-five) play a part in enrollment numbers. The associate dean of Arts and Letters admitted that she is unsure why certain classrooms are assigned to certain departments, but even if English wanted to raise caps on some of its courses, it could not do so because the fire marshal has set a maximum capacity for every classroom.[4]

Delivery of first-year composition under such conditions seems fixed until we take a second look at finances. The balance sheet for composition has two sides: revenue and expenses, and as noted earlier, at Old Dominion in 2003, tuition revenue for FY composition was $1,562,022, and salary expenses—including fringe benefits for full-time faculty—are $431,375. The $1,130,647 difference goes into a pool to pay for infrastructure, equipment, and administrative and indirect costs not only in the English department but across the university. As one administrator patiently told me, the costs for teaching and for equipment and materials are much higher in disciplines other than English. That's not surprising, given the low wages paid to contingent faculty in composition, but the fact I want to emphasize here is that the labor of composition faculty is subsidizing the delivery of other courses, not only in the English department but also across the university. The composition program provides first-year instruction to more than thirty-five hundred students and produces annual revenue of more than $1.5 million. Even when salary, benefits, and overhead expenses are deducted, the "profit" can be counted in the hundreds of thousands of dollars, if not in the $1 million range. The reality is that composition programs make money for universities but do not get to spend what they make.

Unfortunately, the second-class status of composition programs is not news. As early as 1912, Edwin Hopkins deplored the working conditions for composition teaching and, with an analogy to business management, determined that writing instruction would not be sufficiently funded until the public understood the resources needed to produce writers: "To require the best workman, even with the best tools, to finish an assigned task in one-half or one-third of the necessary time is to spoil the work or the workman or both" (6). Hopkins compares writing courses to laboratory courses and explains why composition is "a laboratory subject" that demands small numbers of students per instructor. He goes on to say that "no effort has been made to determine scientifically the necessary cost; it has perhaps been guessed at, or the English budget has been fixed according to convenience after other things were provided for" (6). Yet some simple math convinces me that composition does more than pay its own way. Why, then, do writing programs and English departments see so little of the profits resulting from their labor?

In several 1997 posts to the WPA email discussion list, Chris Anson discusses the financial ramifications of management systems that do not sufficiently fund writing programs. In one post he explains a new management system then under consideration at the University of Minnesota that *would* allow an academic unit to keep the revenue its courses generated. If the composition program keeps its tuition dollars, the delivery of writing courses changes considerably, as Anson points out:

> [A] revenue-based funding model might lead to a large increase in annual funding. We could then use those funds to increase pay for TAs, hire more tenure-track faculty to strengthen our teacher-development program, improve working conditions, get phones for instructors, add to our allocation of professional travel funds for TAs to give papers at conferences, put new initiatives into place, continue to resist hiring underpaid non-tenured teachers, and so on.

At comprehensive universities, composition programs are a catch-22 for English departments. On the one hand, English faculty are in the enviable position of having their courses selected as university-wide requirements. We have the opportunity to teach all students to be better writers and critical thinkers. On the other hand, traditional workload formulas are based on the belief that the teaching of a writing course requires the same amount of work as the teaching of any other course. By maintaining reasonable class sizes for composition courses, English departments defy bureaucratic staffing formulas and end up with workload ratios unacceptable to state regulatory agencies such as SCHEV. To make matters worse, the more students we teach, the more money there is to support faculty and students in science, engineering, and other disciplines, leaving us pleading for basic resources such as computers and cost-of-living raises for adjuncts. In the rest of this chapter, I explore this catch-22 and further develop and justify my proposal to change the way composition is delivered at comprehensive state universities. First I describe the traditional delivery approach. Then I analyze that approach fiscally and pedagogically. Next I propose a lecture-and-lab model of delivery, and I conclude by considering the benefits and risks of my proposal.

Delivering Composition Traditionally at One Comprehensive University

Old Dominion University is a comprehensive state university that enrolls 13,500 undergraduate and 6,500 graduate students; 1,400 are international students from more than hundred countries.[5] There are 603 full-time and 331 part-time faculty, for a 16-to-1 student-to-faculty ratio. The university is divided into six colleges, which offer sixty-six bachelor's, sixty-seven master's, and twenty-four doctoral programs (ODU Campus Facts). As is the case at many similar universities, ODU has a six-hour first-year composition requirement: the first semester focuses on expository writing and the second on argumentation and research. An alternative version of the second-semester course is called Introduction to Scientific and Technical Writing. Students meet the first three-hour requirement in a number of ways: passing the course; taking the CLEP English Composition with Essay exam; scoring 3 or higher on the AP test in English Language and Composition.[6] Students meet the second three-hour requirement by taking the course, passing a departmental challenge exam, or earning credits from tests such as DANTES (Defense Activity for Non-Traditional Education Support). Transfer credit from Virginia community colleges is standardized across the state, while transfer decisions for credits from four-year institutions are made by the director of composition. Each means of earning credit carries a different price tag for students, from more than four-hundred dollars for a three-credit course to less than eighty dollars for a departmental challenge exam.

Students can also earn their composition credits in honors sections or through learning communities, which were recently renamed "fast tracks." In these communities, students register for courses paired by topic. For example, "The Matrix" pairs English 110 with Philosophy 110. Students get to know their classmates when they take two or more courses together, and faculty do their best to connect the syllabi for the two courses. Developmental courses are delivered as writing workshops by the Writing Center, which is housed in Student Services rather than in an academic department. The Writing Center administers the placement essay and the exit exam of writing proficiency. Coordination between the center and the English department is not formalized, but the director of the center and the WPA consult with one another on a regular basis.

Composition has a traditional history at ODU. In the 1950s, the one-semester requirement focused on writing about literature. In the 1980s, the required course was unbound from literature so those who wished could use other types of readings. In 1998 the general education writing requirement was increased from three to six credits for all university students. The increase was spearheaded by the provost at the time, a sociologist who believed in writing across the disciplines. The English department resisted the change because of insufficient resources, but reluctantly agreed when it was promised additional positions to staff the new sections; that promise has never been fully realized.

Guidelines for ODU's general education writing courses spell out objectives, assessment criteria, and writing requirements. For the first-semester course the objective is

> to prepare students to be effective writers of the kinds of compositions they will be called on to produce during their college careers. By the end of the course, students should be more mature in their understanding and use of language, should develop efficient writing processes, should know the qualities of effective composition in a given rhetorical situation, and should be able to demonstrate those qualities in their own writing. (Guidelines, p 1)

The guidelines go on to list the evaluation criteria: "scope and focus, organization, development, perspective, rhetorical awareness, expressiveness, and mechanics." The course requires a minimum of five thousand words; up to fifteen hundred of those words may come from journal entries, preliminary writing, and in-class writing. One in-class paper, at least three formal papers, and a final exam are required. Faculty hold a minimum of two conferences with each student, and each student maintains a writing folder, which is submitted at the end of the semester and kept on file in the department for one year. The second composition course stresses "the principles of analysis and argumentation and the skills of paraphrase, summary, and synthesis, and culminates in the preparation of a fully-documented research paper" (Guidelines, 1). In 2000, the department instituted an attendance policy for writing courses. Any student absent for one-fourth of class time (eleven contact hours in a regular semester) receives an F for the course. Both semesters of composition are delivered in sections of twenty-three students with one instructor.[7]

Rethinking Traditional Delivery

In an ideal world, all university courses would be delivered in ways appropriate for their goals and their audiences. A writing course that depends heavily on application of principles, student-teacher-peer interaction, timely feedback, and opportunities for multiple trials would warrant a low student-to-faculty ratio, extended periods for learning, and opportunities for reflection on the learning process. A writing course for students who are diverse in age, preparation, class, ethnicity, and race would be flexible enough to meet individual needs. The instructor for each course would be a visible, stable member of the department, perhaps a tenure-track professor or an instructor from the "full-time teaching-intensive tract" that Michael Murphy suggests when he argues that we must "recognize as fact that *most* compositionists are not, have never been, and will not in the future be supported to do research; that the economic strictures on the field will always require that we be primarily a teaching discipline; and *that we work within those limits to professionalize faculty and instruction as thoroughly as possible*" (32, emphasis in original).

Composition programs at comprehensive state universities may not be ideal, but they are complex. They usually include placement and exit testing, tutorial services, various delivery methods for first-year courses, and numerous upper-division courses in everything from electronic writing to writing in the disciplines to writing internships. Programs are embedded in bureaucratic departmental, college, and university structures, so delivery decisions are made at any or all of these levels by a long list of players: state agencies, the provost, the university general education committee, the dean of the college, the department chair, the curriculum and instruction committee, the director of composition, the composition committee, the full- and part-time faculty, and sometimes, even the fire marshal. This list does not include those responsible for alternative methods of delivery such as an office of experiential learning or an office of testing. Delivery decisions are also implicated in scheduling, hiring, and evaluating faculty, mentoring teaching assistants, assigning classrooms, and assessing outcomes mandated by local and state regulations (for example, in 2001, SCHEV mandated exit testing of writing proficiency at all state colleges). Of special import to the delivery of composition at comprehensive universities are decisions about adjunct funding, faculty development, and program administration.

With so many players and so many decisions to be made, decision points can be fuzzy. Sometimes things are done a certain way because they have always been done that way (mentoring of TAs, for example). Other times a new chair or WPA will change an aspect of the delivery system because of program exigencies (no longer assigning TAs and their mentors to double-capacity rooms because the fifty-seat classrooms are reallocated to another department). Nevertheless, with so many sections of composition offered each semester and with the majority of those sections taught by MA teaching assistants and adjunct instructors, some type of management system is needed.

At Old Dominion, one individual, the director of composition, manages a staff of thirty or more. Course guidelines, policies, and paper trails both result from and sustain this management system. For example, the guidelines and policies for FY composition grew out of the course's status as a general education requirement, and they function administratively to standardize the curriculum and the outcomes across dozens of sections. Written guidelines and policies are handed out to instructors who are apt to be with us for a few semesters until they move on and new adjuncts take their places. The imprimatur of the department is stamped on the course through these documents, and instructors use the policies to keep students in line just as the policies are used to keep instructors in line (see Shor). Much of the oversight of the composition program depends on a paper trail of filed documents (syllabi, exams, teaching portfolios, and student writing folders), which gives the impression of sufficient administration. In reality, the director of composition, a non-tenure-track lecturer, has two course releases per semester out of a 4/4 course load. He supervises and trains instructors through summer and biweekly workshops, evaluates instruction, handles student complaints, settles disputed transfer credits, assesses CLEP and challenge exams, chairs the composition committee, and runs an annual conference for area high school and college writing teachers. The director does not manage the financial decisions related to his work. His many responsibilities include adding and staffing sections days before the semester begins, but he is not given authority to appropriate the funds that these added sections (or any other composition sections) bring in. The separation of financial decisions from pedagogical decisions contributes to the lose-lose situation that can arise in a department with a large first-year composition responsibility.

Can a Crisis Lead to Change?

In bureaucracies, delivery systems function methodically to perpetuate the status quo. Until there is a crisis, complaints are resolved inside the system, and major changes are avoided. At Old Dominion, the English department should have been able to handle an increase from a three-credit to a six-credit general education writing requirement phased in over two or three years as students entered under the new catalog, especially if the increase were accompanied by funding for more faculty. In 1998, some resources were available, but not in 1999 and 2000. In 2001, SCHEV raised its faculty workload formula as the state entered a deep recession, declaring there would be no raises for at least one year (that one year extended to three). In fall 2001, the director of composition had trouble staffing sections. An emergency instructor position was created the weekend before classes began because no more part-time adjuncts were available and sections would have to be canceled without the added full-time position. This crisis has repeated itself every semester since, as it does at other four-year and two-year colleges, with WPAs in the Tidewater region calling one another late every summer to find adjuncts willing to pick up sections at a second or third campus.[8]

Of course, as soon as a semester is under way, administrators face different crises (e.g., preparing for reaccredidation), and the bureaucratic routine lulls us into thinking things will be OK. Having weathered this cycle for so many years, as an adjunct, a full-time instructor, a tenure-track professor, a WPA, and a department chair, I, too, came to see the crisis of staffing composition sections as an inevitable, but temporary, part of the natural cycle of educational administration. Writing this chapter, however, has forced me to rethink my complicity in perpetuating a dysfunctional delivery system.

The change I propose is to deliver FY writing courses through a combination of one hour of lecture (with two hundred to three hundred students) and two hours of discussion/workshop/lab (twenty to twenty-five students) per week. An expert in rhetoric and composition would negotiate lecture topics, assignments, and grading responsibilities in consultation with instructors and teaching assistants, who would lead the discussion groups attached to the lecture section. At a school the size of Old Dominion, there would be five large lecture sections each semester. Both the design and the delivery of the course would be a collaborative effort (more about this later).

The financial balance sheet under such a system would change, too. Salary costs would increase by approximately $6,500 per lecture section because of higher costs for the lead faculty member. The university would realize less profit (about $91,000 less per year at ODU) from the cash cow of composition, but the English department would improve its showing on the state workload formula. The 10,500 annual credit hours generated by 3,500 composition students would be divided by 14 sections rather than by 154 sections, as is presently the case. Each of the lead faculty would show a workload of 750 student credit hours and

250 students per semester (without even counting his or her other teaching assignments), well above the state's goal. Or, as is more likely, the department could attribute one-third of the credit hours to the lead faculty and two-thirds to those who direct discussion sections. In this version the lead faculty, who would be responsible for one-third of direct teaching time, would show a semester workload of 250 credit hours, a much higher number than is currently possible with composition classes capped at twenty-three students. The remaining 500 student credit hours per course would be attributed to discussion-section faculty who are not TAs. The English department would more than satisfy state workload goals, but what about pedagogical goals?

The Benefits of a Design and Delivery Team

One benefit of the proposed lecture-and-discussion delivery system is its dependence on a collaborative design and delivery team. In disciplines other than English where separate lecture and labs are the norm, the lecture and lab faculty meet to plan and coordinate instruction. In contrast, English Studies favors lecture and discussion or lecture and workshop as a bound pair with one instructor designing and presenting the intertwined components. On a given day, the instructor might lecture on invention as a rhetorical concept, direct students through webbing or cubing, and ask students to share the ideas they have generated. The teacher works alone to plan and deliver all the lessons and assess all the student writing. In the team approach I am advocating, a lead teacher consults with ten to fifteen TAs, adjuncts, and instructors to plan, deliver, and assess the course. The lead teacher brings expertise in rhetoric and composition to a "design table" where other faculty contribute complementary expertise on high school and community college teaching, on workplace writing, on document design, on ESL, or on their lives as poets, novelists, and journalists. The collaborative approach to course design and delivery seems to me to be a natural outgrowth of our field's carefully established practices in collaborative writing and learning (Howard). Planning and delivering FY composition certainly meets Andrea Lunsford's description of tasks "that seem to call consistently for collaboration: high-order problem defining and solving; division of labor tasks, in which the job is simply too big for any one person; and division of expertise tasks" (quoted in Howard, 6).

A team approach has another benefit: the pedagogical modeling that can take place when a compositionist contributes to the design and delivery of every section of composition. As any WPA who has staffed classes at the last minute knows, small sections in themselves do not guarantee instruction by expert practitioners. At comprehensive state universities, the percentage of first-year students taught by experts in rhetoric and composition is—if the numbers at Old Dominion are any indication—unconscionably low. In 2001–2, only 2 sections out of 139 were taught by a PhD in rhetoric and composition, while 18 were taught by teaching assistants working on MAs in English (not in rhet/comp), 105 by part-time adjuncts and full-time instructors with MAs (rarely with an emphasis in rhet/comp), and 14 by lecturers with PhDs (none of whom has a specialty in rhetoric or composition). Thus, the overwhelming majority of those teaching FY composition are not compositionists and are not intending to become compositionists. This is not to deny their expertise as teachers or writers or literature specialists. Nor am I saying that they do not do their best under the worst of circumstances. But with the present delivery system of multiple small sections, faculty seldom co-create and team-teach courses, nor do they observe their colleagues' teaching on a regular basis. Composition studies, with its dual emphasis on theory and practice, has much to offer in the way of mentoring and modeling of teaching (see Yancey). Under the proposed delivery system with separate class hours dedicated to lecture and to workshops or labs, members of the design team can observe one another on a regular basis. The compositionist might present a lecture and a demonstration of rhetorical analysis while other members of the team observe or participate. Alternatively, a journalist might lead a writing workshop while others on the team observe or participate. At the very least, the design team will have discussed pedagogical practices in its planning meetings. Such modeling and mentoring are excellent forms of professional development for both novice and experienced teachers.

A corollary benefit of the proposal might be more respect for composition as a discipline. In its current service role, composition is unfairly assigned huge responsibilities; too many universities expect faculty in the first-year composition course to teach students to write (once and for all), to oversee the freshman experience, and to acclimate students to college (as the Jolliffe and Phelan chapter in this volume suggests). Faculty working collaboratively are more likely to set reasonable expectations for FY composition, and they can introduce students to the discipline in the same way the faculty in history or biology introduce students to those disciplines. As Edwin Hopkins argued ninety years ago, composition *is* a laboratory course. By teaching it as both lecture and workshop or lab, English departments should be able to make a stronger case for keeping more of the income that results from our labor. We may be able to calculate more accurately the hours spent responding to student writing, and we may be able to make the contribution of the WPA and the writing faculty visible to administrators who already value the lecture-and-lab model.

Is Lecture-and-Lab an Improvement?

Even though composition programs at comprehensive state universities are embedded in bureaucratic systems, faculty trained in composition theory and pedagogy are well situated to create better modes of delivery for first-year courses. Lecture-and-lab may not be the ideal delivery method for composition, but neither are small sections taught by underprepared and overworked adjuncts, many of whom at comprehensive state universities have not had the luxury of advanced graduate work in the field.[9] Furthermore, lecture-and-lab encourages experts in rhetoric and composition to practice what they preach: collaborative planning and teaching, mentoring, addressing multiple learning styles. Yes, there will be pitfalls, but without some reconsideration of delivery methods, English departments may lose more than the "unnecessary" teaching positions that bureaucrats claim exist when they apply their one-size-fits-all workload formulas (see, for example, Horner et al.; Laurence; Pratt; Murphy). As things stand, workload formulas hurt English departments that offer small classes. When the department works harder to offer more small classes, we dig the hole deeper. The repeated crisis in adjunct hiring and the increase in paper-based management are warning signs that the system is unhealthy.

In all bureaucracies, the push for conformity is strong. The 2001 mandate for assessment of writing abilities at Virginia colleges is a prime example. At the same time that SCHEV is requiring statewide writing assessment, it is advocating faster completion routes for degrees. We who are faculty at comprehensive state universities must calculate the balance sheets for composition at our institutions. We must investigate and expose financial and pedagogical profits and losses. If we find that our composition programs are generating revenue, we can argue forcefully for better ways to use the revenue, including pilot tests of delivery methods such as the lecture-and-lab I have proposed at Old Dominion. Testing alternate delivery systems is an important avenue for creating composition courses that satisfy state bureaucrats, please campus administrators, renew faculty, and support student writers.

Notes

1. Carl Whithaus and Joel English, valued colleagues, provided the feedback.

2. Tuition in 2001 was $126 per credit hour for in-state students. Thus, each of the 3,185 students paid a minimum of $378 per course for a minimum tuition total of $1,203,930.

3. In-state tuition increased to $147 per credit hour for the 2003 year; salaries did not increase.

4. Old Dominion is not alone in this space dilemma. Rising enrollments across Virginia in fall 2003 led to a headline in *The Virginian Pilot* that read: "A photo of big class at VA Tech attracts the fire marshal." When the *Roanoke Times* reported that students were sitting in the aisles and on the stairs in crowded classrooms, the fire marshal's office sent an inspector to investigate.

5. The Carnegie Foundation recently placed ODU in its "Doctoral Research Extensive" category. Three other universities in Virginia (University of Virginia, Virginia Tech, and George Mason) hold this distinction.

6. There is no statewide agreement on how AP credits will transfer in; nor is there a means for students to be exempted from the composition requirement at ODU if they transfer in after being exempted from composition at other universities.

7. The cap was lowered to nineteen students in 2005.

8. Murphy describes last-minute staffing in detail.

9. Pedagogically, small sections seem ideal, but lecture is not inherently evil, and research dollars are going into improving lecture delivery systems (Sinha).

Works Cited

Anson, Chris. WPA-L Archives 013235. Sept. 2, 2003. http://lists.asu.edu/archives/wpa-l.html.

"Blacksburg: A Photo of Big Class at VA Tech Attracts the Fire Marshal." *The Virginian Pilot* Sept. 12, 2003: B3.

Hopkins, Edwin. "Can Good Composition Teaching Be Done Under Present Conditions?" *English Journal* 1 (Jan. 1912): 1–9.

Horner, Bruce, Kelly Latchaw, Joseph Lenz, Jody Swilky, and David Wolf. "Excavating the Ruins of Undergraduate English." In *Beyond English Inc.: Curricular Reform in a Global Economy*. Ed. David Downing, Claude Mark Hurlbert, and Paula Mathieu. Portsmouth, NH: Boynton/Cook Heinemann, 2002, 75–92.

Howard, Rebecca Moore. "Collaborative Pedagogy." In *A Guide to Composition Pedagogies*. Ed. Gary Tate, Amy Rupiper, and Kurt Schick. New York: Oxford UP, 2001, 54–70.

Laurence, David. "The Latest Forecast." *ADE Bulletin* 131 (2002): 14–19.

Murphy, Michael. "New Faculty for a New University: Toward a Full-Time Teaching-Intensive Faculty Track in Composition." *CCC* 52:1 (2000): 14–42.

Old Dominion University. "Campus Facts." Sept. 10, 2003. www.odu.edu/webroot/orgs/IA/campusfacts.nsf/pages/campusfacts.

———. Guidelines for English 110C and English 111C: English Composition. Photocopied handout.

Pratt, Linda Ray. "In a Dark Wood: Finding a New Path to the Future of English." *ADE Bulletin* 131 (2002): 27–33.

SCHEV. Home page. Sept. 2, 2003. www.schev.edu/.

Shor, Ira. "Illegal Literacy." *Journal of Basic Writing* 19.1 (2000): 100–12.

Sinha, Vandana. "ODU Pushes Boundaries of Teaching Methods." *The Virginian Pilot* May 27, 2002: D1+.

Yancey, Kathleen B. "The Teaching Circle, the WPA, and the Work of Writing in the University." In *Kitchen Cooks, Plate Twirlers, and Troubadours: Writing Program Administrators Tell Their Stories*. Ed. Diana George. Portsmouth, NH: Boynton/Cook Heinemann, 1999, 129–38.

5

Delivering Composition at a Liberal Arts College
Making the Implicit Explicit

Carol Rutz
Carleton College

The liberal arts college—typically a private, nonprofit, coeducational, four-year school with five thousand or fewer students—represents a tiny slice of the post-secondary options available to college students. According to the 2000 Carnegie Foundation classification statistics, liberal arts colleges constitute only 5.8 percent of the higher-education opportunities in the United States, a small portion of all the students enrolled in two-year colleges, four-year universities, and for-profit institutions. Given this statistic, it is fair to ask why anyone should care how composition instruction is delivered at liberal arts colleges. The answer is that despite their small numbers, liberal arts colleges deliver writing instruction in ways that make them worthy sites for examination.

Liberal arts colleges tend to produce generalists who have spent their late adolescent years (eighteen to twenty-two) in a residential environment rich with developmental challenges. Upon graduation, those individuals may well choose to pursue a graduate or professional school degree. As their careers develop, a disproportionate number pursue careers in government, education, business, medicine, law, and other professions that influence public policy, including education policies (see, e.g., Bowen and Bok). For graduates of liberal arts colleges, a key result is their application of educational values to family, work, and civic settings. Written communication is a primary vehicle for the development and application of those values. However, in many selective liberal arts schools, composition is not an explicit feature of the curriculum; the assumption is that these select freshmen will not need it. Instead writing is integrated into the academic environment, with much of the apparatuses available at most universities to diagnose students' writing upon admission and offer appropriate writing instruction absent. Furthermore, many liberal arts colleges do not attempt to assess student writing, whether at the individual, course, or program level. Proficiency in writing is desired and valued, yet the teaching and learning that yields proficiency is left to a process that essentially combines faith in student maturation with osmosis. The implicit delivery of writing instruction becomes a complex and subtle undertaking.

For many liberal arts colleges, delivery of writing instruction occurs in the context of writing across the curriculum (WAC) or writing in the disciplines (WID), often culminating in a capstone senior thesis or comprehensive project in the major. Such a delivery system depends on the establishment and maintenance of a culture among faculty and students that esteems written communication in many forms for many purposes. Within such a culture, the chemist and the historian not only require students to write in their courses but respect the work their students will encounter throughout the curriculum. Not only are students exposed to various rhetorical demands, but their achievements across the curriculum are validated by the institution.

The challenge, therefore, is to distribute the responsibility—and the rewards—of writing instruction without creating a hierarchy of rhetorical merit: The ethnography or the geological field report must stand next to the critical analysis of a primary text as equally valid and valuable for student learning. The successful graduate counts on the whole curriculum and the support of her professors to provide the preparation she needs to complete her major, even if specific writing courses are not available to her.

Carleton College as a Case Study

Liberal arts colleges address the delivery challenge in a number of ways. In what follows, I offer the experience of Carleton College in Northfield, Minnesota (eighteen hundred students) as a case study. Carleton has recently employed portfolio assessment to revive a WAC program and improve the delivery of writing instruction.

My colleagues and I have written elsewhere[1] about Carleton's history as an early adopter of WAC. Briefly, a visionary dean in the mid-1970s addressed problems within a required first-year writing course by instituting writing instruction in some introductory courses outside of the English department. The writing requirement for graduation was valued by all faculty, but the English department was hard-pressed to provide the resources to make writing instruction available to all students. In response to the dean's invitation, faculty from disciplines such as classics, philosophy, history, and biology volunteered to spend part of a summer reading Aristotle's *Rhetoric* and other theoretical material in preparation for inserting direct instruction of writing into their courses. To ease the perceived burden implied by adding writing instruction to courses that traditionally were concerned with content coverage, faculty employed some special features: (1) the group of students who were pursuing their writing course in a non-English class was a subset of the whole class—usually six to ten students; (2) that subset was expected to do more work on writing than the rest of the class, through conferences with the instructor, revision, or extra writing projects; (3) instructors had access to upperclassmen trained as "rhetoric assistants,"[2] who would provide students with more feedback on their writing and help implement the instructor's goals for writing in the course; and (4) at the end of the course, the instructor submitted grades as usual, plus a yes-or-no decision on writing proficiency for the subset attempting to demonstrate proficiency.

This curricular innovation settled into the status quo within just a few years. Among other immediate effects, the distribution of writing instruction allowed the English department to offer sections of first-year writing on an elective basis, substituting topical seminars that remained sites for writing instruction under the new system. However, problems remained. Both faculty and students worried that standards for proficiency were undefined and subject to what faculty viewed as rigor and students considered whim. Some students found themselves judged proficient in an introductory course in say, history, yet unsuccessful as writers in subsequent courses in other fields. In contrast, some students attempted WAC courses in one discipline after another, seeking a professor who would be willing to certify them as proficient so they could graduate. Because they served so many purposes in the curriculum, ranging from general education to introduction to the major, the WAC courses lacked coordinated pedagogy or outcomes. Student complaints about inconsistency were disturbingly accurate but not easily addressed. Over a decade, informal and formal reviews of the writing program turned up anecdotal evidence of a decline in quality of student writing, complicated by the slow increase in the number of nonnative speakers of English in the student body. Frustration was abundant; solutions were not.

By the late 1990s, WAC courses began to be less devoted to writing *instruction* and more concerned with writing *assignments* that met the course goals and incidentally offered students a means of demonstrating proficiency. Few students enrolled in the one remaining elective writing course in the English department. These trends alarmed some faculty, who worried that writing instruction was being abandoned in favor of informal assessment. Simultaneously, a group of WAC faculty actively sought a means to reform the system of assessing writing within one course. The institution responded to both concerns by securing external funds[3] for faculty development to update local knowledge about both writing instruction and writing assessment. External funding supported visits from experts from the composition and writing assessment community who literally taught Carleton faculty and administration about current theories of instruction and assessment. Beginning in 1999, faculty worked with writing program staff to pilot a new method of writing assessment with two closely related goals: (1) direct assessment of student writing to determine proficiency and (2) establishment of a method to communicate with all faculty about students' writing experience.

A midcareer portfolio of writing collected by the end of the sophomore year surfaced as the preferred assessment instrument,[4] submitted at the end of the sophomore year when Carleton students declare a major. They are expected to have completed their distribution (general education) requirements, the language requirement, and so forth. Using the rhetorical demands of the major as a touchstone, faculty mused about the skills that sophomores should be able to demonstrate as they enter a major. Through focus groups, open meetings, and the normal governance process, a scheme for the sophomore portfolio emerged based on rhetorical tasks and framed by a reflective essay written especially for the portfolio.[5] Where possible, the specific assignment for each paper was requested as well.

Looking ahead to the rhetorical demands of the major, faculty settled on the following criteria to be met with three to five papers (ten to thirty pages) of the student's choosing: observation, analysis, interpretation, thesis-driven argument, identification and proper use of documented sources, and control of Standard American English. To underscore the WAC context and move away from the single-course approach to assessing writing proficiency, papers must be collected from at least two courses that represent at least two curricular divisions—arts and literature; humanities (history, philosophy, religion); social sciences; and mathematics and natural sciences. These criteria were defined broadly with the expectation that they would be modified as necessary during the pilot. Minor adjustments continue to be incorporated, but the general architecture suits the institutional context.

While the structure of the portfolio pilot developed fairly quickly, skepticism reigned in some quarters. Carleton's departmentally based culture makes collegewide reform challenging; maintaining a dialogue among divergent views while moving ahead with the pilot was not always easy. The saving grace was a basic WAC premise: students were already writing in nearly all of their courses, and everyone agreed that writing serves learning. Departments or individuals within departments who did not want to change their courses to accommodate specific writing instruction would still be indirect participants in the program. Every time a student chose a paper for the portfolio, that professor, that course, and that department were on record as generators of writing opportunities. For some faculty, this passive participation allowed them to take a wait-and-see attitude without committing themselves to a change that worried them. Imperfect as the existing system of writing instruction and assessment was, it also had the power of tradition behind it. Carleton insiders were accustomed to students fulfilling the writing requirement through one course, taught and assessed by a single instructor. The move to a portfolio seemed inefficient at best and an invitation to student rebellion at worst. For some, the prospect of assessing writing they had not assigned was nonsense and anathema. Better the devil they knew—imperfections and frustrations included—than a system that asked faculty to become amateur readers of disciplinary rhetorics rather than professing the disciplines they knew best.

As this debate simmered, external funds were used to support a suite of faculty development opportunities, including a speaker series, annual workshops on WAC pedagogy, annual workshops on portfolio assessment, summer curriculum development for courses that would generate assignments appropriate for the portfolio, and course releases for three faculty (one each in the humanities, the social sciences, and the natural sciences) to help administer the program. One early effect of this faculty development blitz was to shape faculty discourse about writing instruction and assessment in informed, theorized ways. By the time faculty were faced with the actual reading of student portfolios, they had solid experience with the language of assessment, the rhetorical tasks required of students, and some of the disciplinary variations that would come into play. For example, the physicist who worried about being qualified to assess a close reading of Chaucer learned how the portfolio reading experience differed from the reading of her own assignments. She also found ways to reassure her nonscientist colleagues that physicists appreciate clarity, economy, and grace as much as any humanist.

Volunteers from the class of 2004 answered an invitation to participate in a portfolio pilot, which produced about fifty portfolios for faculty to practice the assessment of a body of student work (as opposed to an individual assignment). Following the pilot year, the class of 2005 was required to submit portfolios; by the time they complied—at a rate of 96 percent!—faculty readers were ready for them. That first reading of nearly four hundred portfolios produced results that met the two initial goals of (1) direct assessment of student writing and (2) better communication among faculty about student writing. Results also validated the WAC curriculum, identified students who needed more work on their writing as they pursued a major, and provided data that informed further faculty development.

What We Have Learned About Delivery of Writing Instruction

Bearing in mind that Carleton's midcareer portfolio came into being amid a conflicted political climate, the early results, including those from two subsequent classes, show outcomes that range from the obvious to the startling. Not surprisingly, the faculty response to the results also covers a broad spectrum. For the rest of this chapter, I will discuss six outcomes, three that primarily address student learning and three that primarily touch on faculty development. Of course, all six of these outcomes have reciprocal effects, but for convenience, I will consider them separately.[6]

The Portfolio Documents Students' Experience as Writers

The nearly four hundred portfolios scored in June 2003 included papers from 302 different courses (multisection courses were counted as one) taught by 181 different faculty. That number exceeds our faculty FTE (full-time equivalent student), which indicates that students who enrolled in courses taught by visiting and other temporary instructors found suitable writing opportunities in those courses as well as those taught by regular, tenure-track faculty. All curricular divisions were well represented, with arts and literature (AL) leading the pack with 107 courses and 68 faculty; social sciences (SS) showing 92 courses and 38 faculty; humanities (HU) represented by 72 courses and 38 faculty; and math and natural science (NS) contributing 33 courses taught by 37 faculty. These data clearly demonstrate that WAC is functioning well at Carleton, a claim that had no empirical backing until now. We were particularly delighted to document the strong presence of writing assignments among NS courses and faculty.[7]

In terms of the criteria for the portfolio itself, students collect written work that demonstrates specific rhetorical tasks defined by Carleton faculty as essential to success in the major: observation, analysis, interpretation, documentation of sources, and use of a thesis-driven argument. Students' self-reported classification of their work on a summary sheet shows that these strategies occur in all distribution groups, often in combination within a given paper.

When sorted by distribution group, *observation* is almost absent in HU papers, common in AL and SS papers, and most strongly represented in NS papers. The humanities group consists of history, philosophy, and religion—three disciplines that traditionally do not depend heavily on fieldwork, which may account for the small number of observation papers in that curricular group. *Analysis* and *interpretation* are spread quite consistently throughout the curriculum, as is the *thesis-driven argument* with a significant exception: NS. This anomaly may be explained by assignments that are descriptive or that speak to a hypothesis. To students, the notion of hypothesis may be rhetorically different from the thesis they develop in nonscience papers. The use of *documented sources* is most present in HU and SS courses and least present in AL, which may be related to the frequency of assignments based on primary texts in AL courses. We rejoice that the recipe we concocted produces a respectable entrée. The beliefs we held about the rhetorical skills that faculty expected students to master by the end of the sophomore year are supported by the evidence students collected in their portfolios.

The Portfolio Yields a Finer Assessment of Student Writing

Carleton readers rate portfolios as "exemplary," "pass," or "needs work." Any portfolio rated exemplary or needs work is read at least twice, and many of those rated pass are reread as well to establish interrater reliability. Results for the class of 2005 show that 77 percent of the students earned pass; 15 percent earned exemplary; 7 percent earned needs work; and 1 percent were incomplete (not scored). Three-year averages show a slight tightening of standards: 78.8 percent have earned pass; 13.8 percent have earned exemplary, and 7.1 percent have earned needs work.

In the past, any student who graduated found a way to have his or her writing certified as proficient—with proficiency loosely defined within the context of one course. With the portfolio, the student has the responsibility to select and frame a set of papers that meets institutional criteria. The vast majority who succeed have a clear sense of what they have done well, which they often specify in their reflective essays. In addition, portfolios are returned to them, along with comments from readers. For those who earn exemplary ratings, the opening convocation in the fall offers them special recognition—an honor that has never before been available to underclass students. Finally, students whose portfolios are rated as needing work meet individually with staff in the writing program or the Write Place (Carleton's writing center) to address the problems noted by readers. Students resubmit within a term, and if they fail the portfolio a second time, their records are referred to the Academic Standing Committee for review. Under the (earlier) certification system, students were able to delay completion of the writing requirement until the eve of graduation. For several students each year, the challenge of the capstone project was the first clear indication to their major advisers that a problem with academic writing would be a barrier to their success. We hope that early identification—as they begin the major—will help students and their advisers prepare for writing in the major. Experience thus far supports this goal.

The Portfolio Offers Students an Opportunity to Reflect on Their Writing

Reflection, as an explicit feature of teaching and learning, does not occur too often in the Carleton curriculum. Consequently, the reflective essay required of students as part of the portfolio has inspired angst in many students. However, the student culture is rapidly adapting. For every cranky reflection that says, "Here's the writing you made me collect—enjoy it," there will be two or three that express surprise and appreciation concerning the benefits of reviewing and organizing one's own work with an eye toward impressing readers. The best evidence I can offer is a brochure that my student assistant composed one summer after helping to organize the portfolio reading. In his brochure titled "An Insider's Guide to the Sophomore Writing Portfolio," Keith Purrington writes, in Q-and-A form:

> **What in the world is this "reflective essay"? What should I write about in my essay?**
>
> It's a paper that you write specifically for the portfolio to introduce it to your readers. Ideally, your essay provides some insight into yourself as a writer. I know this sounds trite, but think of it as explaining to your audience how you relate to the task of writing—for school or on your own. Many of the essays then explain the reasons for including each piece in the portfolio and how the pieces satisfy the requirements. This can work if it is done elegantly, but many essays become formulaic at this point. The best essays integrate this explanation with

the thoughts about writing in general, or even forego explicitly addressing the rest of the portfolio, instead focusing on the student's writing and writing process. The most important thing is that the essay is genuinely about *you*. Readers really appreciate the more personal reflective essays, and the more your essay is about you, the more you will gain from writing it.

My other papers can speak for themselves. Why do I have to write a reflective essay?

The essay can be extremely important, especially if you want an "exemplary" score. The reflective essay probably gets read more carefully than any other paper in your portfolio, and many of the faculty readers commented that the essay can make or break the portfolio. The impression left by the introductory essay significantly informs the reading of the rest of the portfolio. If you want an exemplary rating, you will be best served by investing in the essay. Taking the time to write a good reflective piece has intrinsic benefits, too. By thinking about your own writing, you may become a more self-aware, and eventually, a better writer.

As student culture accommodates the portfolio, we expect to see the results of Keith's advice in an increasing number of reflective essays. Granted, reflection as a genre has its problems, which Kathleen Blake Yancey and others have noted in detail, but we are confident that Carleton students will approach this particular rhetorical situation with both persuasion and self-knowledge as filters.

The Portfolio Exposes Faculty to a Variety of Approaches to Writing

This outcome of the portfolio project is among the most obvious—and probably engendered the most anticipatory resistance. Faculty know what they're doing in their courses and departments. They know how their work figures into the institutional mission. They are not necessarily attuned to the practices in other departments; life is short and art is long. Having specialized in a discipline, why should a faculty member fiddle around with pedagogy in other disciplines? Thanks to the combination of WAC workshops, a speaker series, curriculum development grants, and the portfolio reading experience, an increasing number of Carleton faculty are expressing interest in their colleagues' methods of teaching and using writing in courses. Healthy interdisciplinary contamination has yielded two complementary results. On the one hand, faculty offer one another great ideas that are often adapted and improved in new contexts. On the other hand, faculty recognize that students will encounter many sophisticated writing assignments as they complete their degrees; no one course need bear the burden of teaching and assessing academic writing as a monolithic construct. In that sense, the worry about understanding and attending to various disciplinary approaches is replaced with relief. And respect.

The Portfolio Informs Faculty Development

In addition to the informal sharing, comparing, and collaboration connected to exposure to various writing approaches, the portfolio also gives rise to thoughtful pedagogical questions to drive faculty development activities. At Carleton, initial questions about students' experience with writing, the specific places in the curriculum that yield writing, and the quality of student writing as students enter the major now have answers based in data rather than anecdote. Furthermore, the faculty development program that has helped prepare for the portfolio has shown some specific results. As noted previously, external funding has supported workshops, a speaker series, and summer curriculum development grants. Early on, we identified a weak but statistically significant correlation between an individual's participation in faculty development events and the number of times a paper from one of his or her courses appeared in the class of 2005 portfolios ($r = .249, p < .001$). More recently, we note that faculty who have participated in four or more of these activities find a larger number of their own writing assignments represented in the portfolio ($p < .003$). Nonparticipating faculty are also represented; however, those who have sought out faculty development in writing across the curriculum apparently are offering their students writing experiences that both meet the portfolio's criteria and are valued enough by students to be included in the portfolio.[8]

As faculty have reworked introductory courses with the portfolio in mind, a campuswide lexicon is beginning to gain currency. Assignments employ the language of the portfolio and direct students toward mastery of the rhetorical tasks. Students are beginning to seek out opportunities to write rather than avoid writing until the capstone project.[9] Curriculum development grants have been used in some departments to assess writing throughout the department's offerings. At least three departments (classics, economics, and history) have revised their capstone projects to build specifically on the portfolio's tasks. Those efforts were cited in a successful proposal to extend external funding; the thrust of faculty development for the current grant period is writing in the major. Not all departments are progressing at the same pace; nevertheless, the work to date on the portfolio has made explicit what had been an implicit writing environment. With the advantage of clarity, better questions can be asked, and better answers can be articulated.[10]

The Portfolio Affirms the Effectiveness of Delivering Writing Instruction Through a WAC Model

This outcome links to the first one on the list, documenting student experience. In that respect, it does the work that assessment groupies like to tout: closing the feedback loop. For Carleton, portfolio assessment has demonstrated that writing occurs throughout the curriculum, that students successfully rise to the demands of many disciplinary situations, and that more than 90 percent of them write well enough to tackle the major with secure preparation as college writers. More important, those whose skills are not at the passing level receive individual instruction aimed at achieving a level of preparation rather than allowing them to avoid the pain and frustration of writing poorly or not at all.

Research at Eckerd College (Harrison) demonstrates that portfolio standards become more stringent over time. As noted earlier, we have begun to see that pattern emerge at Carleton; the WAC environment adjusts to support new students as academic writers at the appropriate level. The peer culture among students will convey the importance of academic writing as well as tips for success, à la the "Insider's Guide" and word on the street. Our students have already recognized that a portfolio of their best work, doubly vetted by classroom instructors and independent readers, is a powerful addition to their credentials as job seekers and applicants to professional schools. We expect the portfolio, which is currently a paper artifact, to migrate to the Web within a few years. Furthermore, we expect that portfolio results will assist the institution with its admission and retention programs by making institutional expectations for writing clear and understandable rather than murky and intimidating.

Feedback throughout the institution has already strengthened and redirected faculty development—closed that loop, as it were. Writing assessment has evolved from chronic complaints about a steady decline in student performance to active, creative change in teaching to foster learning. The most telling shift I have seen at Carleton over the past eight years has been the abandonment of any hint of student bashing—blaming students for what they do not know. My colleagues challenge themselves to create learning situations that work for students and generate products—many of them written products—that demonstrate learning. The portfolio has provided a medium for pedagogical discourse that reaches far beyond the particular assessment moment.

What About Other Liberal Arts Colleges?

Carleton's experience with writing assessment as a means to uncover and improve writing instruction—to make the implicit explicit—demonstrates that liberal arts colleges can benefit from a close examination of their writing cultures. If composition is delivered through a WAC or WID environment, Carleton's model may be particularly helpful. Even in cases where composition is embedded in a first-year seminar program or a dedicated first-year course, attention to student experience beyond that context will yield important and useful information. Of course, any liberal arts college that can (1) document student experience with writing; (2) assess individual student performance; (3) offer opportunities for students to reflect on their writing; (4) acquaint faculty with a variety of writing approaches; (5) inform faculty development programming; and (6) affirm and adjust the institution's method of delivering writing instruction is way ahead of Carleton and many sister schools.

The reverence for tradition at small schools can be an enormous barrier to change. However, all traditions are not equal. At Carleton, we have found that nurturing the traditions of commitment to education and civic leadership through WAC-based writing instruction and portfolio assessment has overcome a tradition of certification of (undefined) proficiency. Small schools can sustain long, dearly held traditions even as new ones are invented. The paradox is that a small, relatively closed community can revere ponderous traditions and simultaneously show lithe agility in seizing, adopting, and adapting a new idea. The key seems to be congruence with the institution's fundamental values. With that assurance in place, change can occur, even in as vexing and covert an arena as the delivery of writing instruction.

Notes

1. See Rutz, Hardy, and Condon.

2. The dean in question, Harriet Sheridan, took this innovation with her to Brown University, where the writing fellows continue to be celebrated as part of the writing instruction environment at Brown.

3. Carleton is grateful to the Bush Foundation of St. Paul, Monnesota, for its support for faculty development related to writing instruction and assessment.

4. Models from Eckerd College and Washington State University were particularly helpful. We owe heartfelt thanks to the writing program administrators of both institutions.

5. Instructions for students may be found at http://webapps.acs.carleton.edu/campus/writingprogram/portfolio/.

6. Statistics quoted herein refer to records of students who provided written permission to use their writing in research. The portfolios of those who refused permission are not included; however, the remaining sample is representative of the entire class of 2005 in gender and ethnicity. The same is true of data relating to the classes of 2006 and 2007.

7. Similar counts were recorded for portfolios read in the summers of 2004 and 2005.

8. See Rutz and Lauer-Glebov for details.

9. In my own courses, students increasingly report their desire to produce papers appropriate for the portfolio.

10. Of course, the portfolio is not the only vehicle for faculty development on campus. The Perlman Center for Teaching and Learning at Carleton has promoted faculty development in general for the past thirteen years, and the center's cosponsorship of the writing program's speaker series has helped create a value-added context for both programs. Through multiple exposures, faculty of all ranks have embraced faculty development as a venue to improve teaching and learning.

Works Cited

Bowen, William G., and Derek Bok. *The Shape of the River: Long-Term Consequences of Considering Race in College and University Admissions*. Princeton, NJ: Princeton UP, 1998.

Carnegie Foundation for the Advancement of Teaching Website. Classification tables. www.carnegiefoundation.org/Classification/CIHE2000/Tables.htm (accessed Dec. 30, 2003).

Harrison, Suzan. "Portfolios Across the Curriculum." *WPA: Writing Program Administrator* 19:1–2 (1995): 38–49.

Purrington, Keith. "An Insider's Guide to the Sophomore Writing Portfolio." Brochure for Carleton College. Also available at http://webapps.acs.carleton.edu/campus/writingprogram/portfolio/.

Rutz, Carol, Clara Shaw Hardy, and William Condon. "WAC for the Long Haul: A Tale of Hope." *WAC Journal* 13 (2002): 7–16.

Rutz, Carol, and Jacqulyn Lauer-Glebov. "Assessment and Innovation: One Darn Thing Leads to Another." *Assessing Writing* 10.2 (2005): 80–99.

Yancey, Kathleen Blake. *Reflection in the Writing Classroom*. Logan, UT: Utah State UP, 1998.

6

Keepin' It Real
Delivering College Composition at an HBCU

Teresa Redd
Howard University

Within the United States there are more than one hundred historically black colleges and universities (HBCUs). While litigation and immigration have altered the face of some HBCUs, most of these institutions still serve a predominantly African American student body and preserve the history and vitality of African American culture. Yet they are also situated within the dominant Euro-American culture. Consequently, they are what Mary Louise Pratt calls "contact zones"—"social spaces where cultures meet, clash, and grapple with each other, often in contexts of highly asymmetrical relations of power, such as colonialism, slavery, or their aftermath" (4).

Pratt's metaphor illuminates what transpires every day in composition classrooms at HBCUs, for within these classrooms African American culture and the tradition of college composition inevitably collide. Conflicts arise because the traditional Composition 101 curriculum prescribes a purpose, texts, rhetoric, and language that are rooted in the Euro-American values of the dominant culture in this country. Sometimes the conflicts are salient; at other times the influence of the dominant culture is so subtle that African American teachers and students may not notice the threat or contradictions.

To illustrate this problem, I explore four of the conflicts that composition students and teachers face at an HBCU: (1) literacy as an instrument for liberation versus literacy as a vehicle for social conformity, (2) African American texts versus the "Great Essays" canon, (3) African American rhetoric versus the conventions of academic discourse, and (4) African American English versus Standard Written English. Citing examples from Howard University, where

I have taught for twenty years, I will also describe how some HBCUs have sought to resolve these conflicts: While they have *con*formed to the curriculum in some ways, they have also *trans*formed it, delivering a distinct brand of freshman composition.

The Purpose: Liberation Versus Conformity

At an HBCU, the very purpose of Composition 101 is a source of conflict, although the conflict often goes unrecognized by those who have forgotten the history of African American literacy. From the perspective of African American history, the primary purpose of learning to read or write can be summed up in one word: freedom. Believing in the emancipatory power of literacy, African Americans such as Thomas Jones tried whenever they could to circumvent the laws against educating slaves. Jones explains:

> "I was a slave; and I knew that the whole community was in league to keep the poor slave in ignorance and chains. Yet I longed to be free, and to be able to move the minds of other men with my thoughts. It seemed to me now, that, if I could learn to read and write, this learning might—nay, I really thought it would—point out to me the way to freedom, influence, and real, secure happiness." (Webber 135)

The promise of freedom also motivated Frederick Douglass to learn to write: He mastered writing by copying the abbreviations that carpenters wrote on timber as they set aside pieces for shipbuilding (57). Writing enabled Douglass not only to forge travel passes for himself and other runaway slaves but, later, as a spokesman for the abolitionist movement, to pen some of the most scathing indictments of slavery ever written (94). His abolitionist writings represent an African American tradition of wielding words as weapons to attack racial injustice, the tradition of Ida B. Wells, W. E. B. DuBois, Amiri Baraka, and bell hooks. On the other hand, Douglass' *Narrative* represents an African American tradition of autobiography that celebrates physical or psychological liberation through literacy. This tradition boasts such remarkable narratives as Harriet Jacobs' "Incidents in the Life of a Slave Girl," Malcolm X's *Autobiography*, Richard Wright's *Black Boy*, and Nathan McCall's *Makes Me Wanna Holler*. Even when African Americans did not know how to write, runaway slaves appropriated the language and the scribes to commit their "emancipatory narratives" to paper (Mitchell). Like the autobiographies cited above, these works are what Pratt calls "autoethnographic" texts, for they "involve a selective collaboration with and appropriation of idioms of the . . . conqueror" in order to challenge the dominant culture's representation of the authors (5–6). As Thomas Fox recommends, "composition teachers need to see these texts as forming the 'social ground' from which African American students write" (300). But the tradition of Composition 101 can blind us, given that the purpose of literacy in the dominant culture is normally not liberation, but conformity.

Even before Paulo Freire, Henry Giroux, James Paul Gee, and others exposed the indoctrinating power of literacy education, some composition teachers understood that freshman composition is a particularly powerful vehicle for social conformity. Because it is a service course designed to prepare students for their academic careers and beyond, the university and the community exert tremendous pressure on freshman composition teachers as well as students to conform; typically, we do because we have so little status and power. Despite recent interest in fostering critical thinking and self-expression, the stuff of most freshman composition courses is rules and conventions. We teach grammar rules, spelling rules, punctuation rules, capitalization rules, you name it rules. We teach ready-made formulas for outlining, formatting, citing, and editing. When permitted, exploration and creative expression are usually confined to journals, ten-minute freewriting sessions, and online discussion boards. Even those of us who try hard to nurture self-expression and critical consciousness may find ourselves locked into departmental syllabi, required textbooks, or institutional exit exams that stymie our attempts. At its core, Composition 101 is an exercise in conformity, which, as I will demonstrate later, means that it promotes adherence to the white, Western, middle-class values of the American status quo.

So how have HBCUs responded to the conflicting purposes of literacy in Composition 101 and African American culture? Through the years, Howard has espoused the liberatory goals of literacy, particularly the freedom to define oneself and to shape one's destiny. For instance, Charles Eaton Burch, who taught English at Howard and Wilberforce during the Harlem Renaissance, welcomed student essays that denounced racism and critiqued the status quo (208). In his article "Freshman Papers in a Negro College," he observes, "There is the protest against a repeated injustice; there is a sad cry of despair and the confident note of hope. In their limited way, they reach out and speak to America; and sometimes to the British Empire" (208). As Scott Zaluda notes, Burch implied that African American students "should not be seen as passive receptors of knowledge but as actively engaged with transforming the university and the world" (245).

Today, Howard's departmental syllabus for freshman composition reflects that spirit of empowerment in its opening paragraph:

> The eloquence of the spoken word and writing—the art of language by line—are two of the most highly valued skills manifest in African-American culture. James Baldwin succinctly expresses the importance of these values when he tells us, "People evolve a language in order to describe and thus control their circumstances, or in order not to be submerged by a reality they cannot articulate." Language, after all, is the means by which African-American ancestors emancipated themselves from a "dwarfing, warping" reality imposed upon them (James Weldon Johnson). You are, therefore, heirs of a *literate* tradition that equates reading and writing with the emancipation of

> the self from internal limitations (caused by inexperience) and external oppression. It is a tradition that equates reading and writing with the expression of self-identity, self-possession, self-empowerment, and self-esteem. (1)

This tradition is reflected in the mission statements of other HBCU English departments as well. For instance, Spelman encourages its students to "explore their own identity through the contexts and perspectives of writers," and, above all, to realize "that language is power and that sisterhood depends on communication." Jarvis Christian College aims to develop "cultural awareness, self-awareness, multi-ethnic sensitivity, and personal enrichment . . . enabling students to assume leadership roles in society." Oakwood attempts to "provide an atmosphere for appreciation of oneself and affirmation of cultural diversity," while Southern prepares students "to demonstrate an awareness of and sensitivity to the problems of people in society" and to "seek solutions to those problems." In the meantime, South Carolina State tries to "engage [students] in the questioning process that would promote reflective decision-making and effective performance in an ethnically and culturally diverse society."

But do Howard and other HBCUs teach what they preach? Do they inspire and equip students to use writing to challenge the racial injustices and stereotypes that are reinforced by the traditional composition course? Only by examining the texts and rhetoric and language of freshman composition can we determine how well HBCUs have carried on the legacy of African American literacy while delivering Composition 101.

The Texts: Black Studies Versus "Great Essays"

Until the turn of this century, at HBCUs choosing mainly African American texts for composition classes was an act of defiance. Afraid to depart from the status quo, many HBCU English departments adopted traditional composition textbooks, textbooks that have ignored the very existence of an African American literate tradition. Composition 101 promulgated a "Great Essays" canon, in which African American authors rarely found a place next to the likes of George Orwell, E. B. White, Jonathan Swift, Ralph Waldo Emerson, and Virginia Woolf. For instance, in 1988, when I examined one of the most popular anthologies, *The Norton Reader, Shorter Edition* (Eastman), I found that fewer than 5 percent of the essays were written by blacks. In the current edition (Peterson, Brereton, and Hartman), the percentage has increased to 9 percent, but the editors still restrict the number of African American selections as if the book (like a neighborhood) might become too black.

By limiting the number of black authors and by identifying the ethnicity of only nonwhite or foreign-born writers, books like the *Norton Reader* silently promote a "whiteness" defined by Ann Louise Keating as "a pseudo-universal category that hides its specific values, epistemology, and other attributes under the guise of a nonracialized, supposedly colorless, 'human nature'" (916). Thus, unless it bills itself as a "multicultural" textbook, the typical composition anthology presents white authors and white experience as the norm. The result: When composition teacher Wendy Ryden questioned her class about two poems in an anthology, they replied that Langston Hughes' "Theme for English B" was just a poem about race while Robert Frost's "The Road Not Taken" was a "universal" poem written about a "person" considering two paths. Predictably, when asked what that person looked like, they described someone resembling "a white male model for an L. L. Bean catalogue" (Marshall and Ryden 249).

If white is normal, then, as Dorothy Perry Thompson points out, "whatever is not white becomes, syllogistically, not normal" ("Dabbling" 2). Consequently, when she ordered an all-black anthology for her racially mixed composition classes, even some black as well as white students felt the text was abnormal, one of the black students explaining that she had felt comfortable reading all-white texts taught by white teachers in high school. She remarked, "I didn't feel uncomfortable because I was used to it" (4).

One reason for the whiteness of composition texts is that the dominant culture has tended to characterize African Americans as an oral people. This characterization is misleading, as Elizabeth McHenry and Shirley Brice Heath have documented in their study of nineteenth-century African American religious texts, literary journals, and reading and writing clubs. "The denial or omission of these events and organizations," they observe, has permitted "the distancing and objectifying of African Americans while reserving designations such as 'literate' for the 'dominant' culture" (263). Granted, with the birth of black studies and multiculturalism, the dominant culture has acknowledged the existence of African American autobiography, poetry, and fiction. But how many Americans know about the nineteenth-century NACW (National Association of Colored Women), whose founding members "set out to encourage women across America to form their own clubs and societies to speak out and write about matters of race and gender" (267)? Who has heard of the *Colored American Magazine*, a collection of literary and political pieces that boasted a circulation of fifteen thousand in the early 1900s (272)?

Such nineteenth-century achievements prove that African Americans have established not only a literate tradition but an *essay* tradition. It has spawned volumes of collected essays by literary figures such as Richard Wright, Ralph Ellison, James Baldwin, Toni Morrison, Alice Walker, Ishmael Reed, and Haki Madhubuti; by public intellectuals such as W. E. B. DuBois, Cornel West, Michael Eric Dyson, Stephen Carter, bell hooks, Shelby Steele, Stanley Crouch, and Henry Louis Gates Jr.; by journalists such as Nathan McCall, Earl Ofari Hutchinson, and Farai Chideya. Yet this essay tradition is almost invisible in composition textbooks—even multicultural ones—for they scatter a few African American essays across the table of contents, breaking the thematic and stylistic ties that bind the works. As a result, the African American essays may seem out of place.

Not only is the African American essay tradition absent in most composition texts, but other types of African American writing are missing altogether, for example, Black Panther Party documents, whose content might offend a mainstream audience. Yet some daring teachers have successfully employed such texts to teach writing in addition to the critical-thinking skills we claim to foster. Gwendolyn Pough says of the Black Panther texts she taught, "they offered students an example of counter public discourse aimed at entering the public space. In addition, they offered an example of using that entrance into public space to make a disruption in the existing order—to create change" (470). Like Pratt's "testimonios," they are a product of the contact zone in which "autoethnography, critique, and resistance have reconnected with writing" (6).

Whether they hail from the Black Power Movement or the Harlem Renaissance, African American texts invite African American students to see themselves as writers, as heirs to a tradition of intellectual and rhetorical force. These texts show students how other African Americans have transmuted the materials of the dominant culture to forge tools, even weapons, in a process Pratt calls "transculturation" (9). As Thomas Fox argues, "teaching texts by African American authors teaches 'positions' of literacy (social and cultural positions) that go beyond learning to write like a white man, from Ishmael Reed's 'writin' is fightin' to writing for freedom as explored by Frederick Douglass" (300).

Some HBCU faculty have harnessed the power of these texts to teach composition. As early as 1931, two members of Howard's English department, Lorenzo Dow Turner and Eva B. Dykes, teamed up with a public school teacher, Otelia Cromwell, to publish an African American anthology for a college literature and composition course. *Readings from Negro Authors, for Schools and Colleges* consisted of speeches, essays, stories, plays, and poems by African American writers such as Frederick Douglass, Paul Laurence Dunbar, and Charles Chesnutt (including some, like Zora Neale Hurston, Georgia Douglas Johnson, Sterling Brown, and Carter G. Woodson, who had studied or taught at Howard). With its impressive collection of African American writing, the anthology invited African American students "to continually question the notion that a national language and literature had already been stabilized and could therefore serve as a standard for defining their culture and community" (Zaluda 247).

Sixty years later, after struggling with mainstream composition anthologies, Howard English faculty once again sought an Afrocentric alternative. Insisting that the current textbooks did not contain enough essays by or about blacks, they ordered a custom-made anthology for the first-semester composition course in expository writing: *Revelations: An Anthology of Expository Essays by and About Blacks* (Redd). Now in its fourth edition, the book features black men and women writing about the black experience. The sheer number of professional essays (fifty-eight) shows African American students that they are heirs to an essay tradition. Moreover, the book models the writing of autoethnographic texts. Through these texts, students can see how African

Americans have appropriated the dominant culture's idiom to challenge its representations of blacks:

- Ishmael Reed deconstructs the American myth of a homogeneous Western heritage ("America: The Multicultural Society").
- Ralph Ellison critiques "the fantasy of a blackless America" ("What America Would Be Like Without Blacks").
- Kwame Ture exposes the Western naming games that divide the African race ("Pan-Africanism").
- John Hope Franklin counters the image of the submissive slave ("Slave Resistance").
- Brent Staples interrogates the stereotype of the violent black male ("Black Men and Public Space").
- Claude Steele attacks the theory of black intellectual inferiority ("Race and the Schooling of Black Americans").

Since the release of *Revelations*, English faculty at Hampton and Grambling have published similar anthologies of black writing, but they feature poetry, fiction, and/or drama as well as essays. Margaret Giles Lee and Joyce Jarrett of Hampton, along with their coeditor Doreatha Drummond Mbalia, compiled *Heritage: African American Readings for Writing* "to illustrate the beauty and power" of the African American canon (xix). The editors of Grambling's anthology *Black Orpheus: Rhetoric and Readings* share this goal. Like the editors of *Heritage*, Ruby Lewis, Beatrice McKinsey, and Don Hoyt want to expose African American students to "the best of their literary heritage" (xi). "While we do not discourage our students from reading Shakespeare, Milton, and Keats," they explain, "we seek to enrich and broaden their experience so that we do not create the impression that either black literature is limited in its existence or that black literature has limited value in the academic environment" (xi). Thus, like their 1931 forerunner, all three contemporary anthologies demonstrate "the powerful ability of a marginalized subculture" to deliver "new canons and new models as well as new ways for student writers to go about defining them" (Zaluda 248).

The Rhetoric: African American Versus Western

In the composition contact zone, African American tradition clashes not only with the content of readings but also with the rhetorical form, for the rhetoric of Composition 101 is, for the most part, culturally biased. According to Marcia Farr and Gloria Nardini, "the style of discourse underlying writing instruction in this country . . . is grounded historically and culturally in the development of Western civilization" (4). This type of rhetoric values "rational, decontextualized, explicit, and carefully ordered" discourse (108). Therefore, writers schooled in this rhetoric carefully order ideas in structures such as lists, topical nets, hierarchies, and matrices (Calfee and Chambliss 364), and they compose "thesis-driven" essays, adopting an "objective, 'scientific' voice" (Heilker 78).

While even white students find aspects of this rhetoric unfamiliar (Bartholomae), African American students may find it more alien because it contrasts so dramatically with the traditional rhetoric of their community. As Geneva Smitherman, Molefi Asante, Claudia Mitchell-Kernan, Roger Abrahams, and others have documented, African Americans have inherited a rich rhetorical tradition, rooted in the cultures of Africa and cultivated in the streets and churches of black America. Asante calls this repertoire of rhetorical strategies "styling" (39). Although styling is primarily an oral tradition, some of its verbal arts—such as punning, rhyming, image making, and signifying—have enriched African American writing as well, especially since the 1960s when numerous African American writers started "modeling their work upon styles derived from Afro-American culture" (Turner 305).

Many African American students bring these rhetorical strategies into the composition classroom. Arnetha Ball found that, unlike other high school students, African American teenagers reported a "strong preference for using vernacular-based organizational patterns" in academic writing as well as in informal conversation ("Cultural Preference" 524). These patterns included "circumlocution" ("a series of implicitly associated topics with shifts that are lexically marked only by the use of *and*") and "narrative interspersion" ("a subpattern embedded within other patterns, in which the speaker or writer intersperses a narrative within expository text") (509–11). In another study of African American students' writing, Ball noticed formulaic patterns of repetition, intimate dialogue with the reader, storytelling as a transitional device, and popular African American idioms ("Textual Design" 281). Other researchers have discovered these or other culturally influenced features such as redundancy, preaching, folk sayings, wordplay, word coining, image making, indirection, alliteration, and rhyme (Campbell; Gilyard and Richardson; Noonan-Wagner; Smitherman "African American"; Redd; Thompson "Rescuing"; Troutman). Clearly, African American rhetoric is more emotional, intimate, indirect, and loosely structured than the rhetoric traditionally taught in Composition 101.

Given the conflicts between African American and Western rhetoric, how have HBCUs approached the teaching of rhetoric in composition classes? At Howard, African American rhetoric has remained marginalized. In the 1930s, '40s, '50s, and '60s, while Sterling Brown was exploring the folk art forms of African American discourse, such exploration was apparently confined to the literature classroom, and so it is today. Teachers are more likely to discuss "signifyin'" and folk sayings in their African American literature classes than in composition classes, and students are more likely to study blues, jazz, or rap structures in poetry workshops than in expository writing workshops. Perhaps teachers feel free to celebrate African American rhetoric in literature because, in literature, it has won the approval of the Nobel and Pulitzer prize committees.

Meanwhile, in composition classes, Western rhetoric reigns. For years, Howard's syllabus never mentioned African American styling, even though the department's anthology presented Geneva Smitherman's classification of African American rhetorical devices. Instead, the section of the syllabus titled "Styling Sentences" referred to Marie Waddell's twenty basic sentence patterns. It was only this year that the composition faculty received a list of African American styling patterns as well.

Likewise, in the Western tradition, the department still exhorts students to write decontextualized, rational, explicit, and carefully ordered essays. This emphasis is reflected in the department's grading criteria for an A paper: "Throughout the paper, ideas are logically ordered, well developed, and unified around the organizing principle enunciated in the thesis statement. . . . The transitions are artful; the phrasing is tight, fresh, and highly specific" (Syllabus, 8). Similar grading criteria appear in departmental syllabi from other HBCUs. For example, South Carolina State University's description of an A paper calls for "clearly ordered" essays with "fresh" and "concise" diction. Xavier's syllabus identifies the objective of the course as the writing of essays that possess a "clear central point communicated in direct, clear language and with adequate and pertinent support." While Lincoln's syllabus encourages faculty to assign "creative writing exercises" to stimulate students' interest, it states that "the traditional five paragraph essay structure, with thesis statement, topic sentences, introduction, and conclusion, should be emphasized."

By emphasizing Western rhetoric, freshman composition at these HBCUs initiates students into a discourse that can help them gain access to status and power in academe and beyond. Moreover, as Farr and Nardini point out, the Western "tradition of critical, reason-based discourse, especially one that emphasizes the appraisal of alternative points of view, can serve democratic principles well" (33). *But why not take advantage of African American rhetoric too?* I suspect that the virtual exclusion of African American rhetoric from these HBCU syllabi stems from a common perception that African American rhetoric cannot contribute to academic success. However, the results of the National Assessment of Educational Progress (NAEP) suggest otherwise: When 867 student essays were collected and rated by the NAEP, papers that displayed an African American rhetorical style earned higher NAEP scores than those that did not (Smitherman "African American" 185). Clearly, African American rhetoric deserves a place in the composition classroom, especially at HBCUs.

The Language: AAE Versus SWE

Of all of the conflicts between African American culture and Composition 101, no conflict is as violent as the one surrounding language. The conflict has truly produced a "war of words" in the contact zone, where proponents and opponents of African American English (AAE) have clashed and grappled with each other. Since the 1970s, proponents of AAE have demonstrated that it is a rich and rule-governed variety of language with its own grammar, phonology, and lexicon (e.g., Baugh; Labov; Rickford; Smitherman; Wolfram and Thomas). Yet despite their evidence, AAE remains stigmatized in the political arena, the workplace, and especially the freshman composition classroom.

Keith Gilyard and others attribute much of this bias to racism: As long as society denigrates African Americans, it will denigrate their language (70). However, while racism plays a critical role, class does as well. As Lynn Bloom argues, Composition 101 is particularly hostile toward AAE because "freshman composition is an unabashedly middle-class enterprise" (655). From Bloom's perspective, Composition 101 privileges Standard Written English (SWE) because it is a written variation of the dialect spoken by the American middle class. Since most college composition teachers are middle class, they tend to see not only AAE but other nonstandard dialects as unsightly deviations from the norm, that is, "unclean" language. So they "clean up" papers, ridding them of errors in spelling, grammar, and mechanics, or they attempt to "disinfect" the students themselves (656, 665).

One might assume that AAE would fare better at an HBCU. Yet, on linguistic issues, Howard has remained staunchly conservative. Referring to the 1920s, Zaluda reports, "For students at Howard and in segregated schools and colleges generally, using what the college catalogue called 'good English' meant practicing writing conventions sanctioned by Anglo-American society as a well as the 'standard of American speech'" espoused by the Progressives—"standardized, clear, unpretentious, moral speech and writing" (237). This concept of good English has persisted from the '20s until today. While linguists Lorenzo Dow Turner and Patricia Jones-Jackson were documenting the vitality of the African American Gullah dialect, while literature professors such as Stephen Henderson were introducing Howard students to the vernacular skill of Sonia Sanchez and Haki Madhubuti, composition teachers in Howard's English department were busily drilling their students on the intricacies of Standard Written English and continue to do so today.

A recent study I conducted at Howard reveals the reverence for Standard English in the freshman composition program. Most of the ten composition teachers I interviewed (half white, half black) referred to black English simply as a mode of communication belonging to African Americans, while they characterized Standard English as "the language of power," "the language that gets the mighty dollar," or "proper dress" ("'How I Got Ovah'" 8). Most said they identified AAE as an error in a student's paper unless it appeared in written dialogue, a journal entry, or sentences where the student was "making a point" (7). In their courses, even classroom speech revolved around Standard English. Although most of the African American teachers reported that they spoke AAE, they did not speak it in the classroom unless they were discussing examples from class readings (7).

Apparently, the students also expect to use only Standard English: Over the years, like A. Suresh Canagarajah, I have invited students to switch to AAE in online chat rooms, discussion boards, or email, hoping to construct "safe houses" for developing "shared understandings" of course material (Pratt 17). But relatively few students have taken advantage of these opportunities to employ AAE for academic purposes (Redd and Massey 250–51).

Howard's stance toward SWE and AAE is not unusual. Syllabi and mission statements indicate that Standard English sets the standard at many other HBCUs (e.g., Bowie State University, Lincoln University, and Fort Valley State University). Why is there so much emphasis on Standard English at these institutions? Lisa Delpit identifies three reasons when she explains why so many African American parents and students are concerned about the "superficial features" of academic discourse. "First," she observes, "they know that members of society need access to dominant discourses to (legally) have access to economic power. Second, they know that such discourses can be and have been acquired in classrooms because they know individuals who have done so" (552). But Delpit considers the third reason the most important: "they know that individuals have the ability to transform dominant discourses for liberatory purposes—to engage in what Henry Louis Gates calls 'changing the joke and slipping the yoke'" (552). Delpit maintains that teachers can help African American students transform academic discourse by (1) acknowledging and validating AAE, (2) teaching students about African Americans who have used the "language of the master" for emancipatory ends, and (3) openly discussing the linguistic prejudice of American society. Although the students may already be aware of society's unjust "discourse-stacking," Delpit contends that "the open acknowledgment of it in the very institution that facilitates the sorting process is liberating in itself" (554).

This type of acknowledgment is already occurring in most of Howard's freshman composition classes, but it is not a teacher-led discussion of linguistic oppression. Rather, students debate the status of AAE and SWE as they discuss and write about the "Mother Tongue" unit of *Revelations*. Within that unit, they weigh the arguments of linguists who explicate the rules of AAE and the *rule* of SWE. But the students also consider the counterarguments of prominent journalists. Other HBCU anthologies invite debate by presenting both essays and literary examples. For example, Hampton's *Heritage* contains a short chapter on black language, along with rap lyrics and a wealth of short stories pulsating with the vernacular—works by John Edgar Wideman, Toni Cade Bambara, Sonia Sanchez, Paul Laurence Dunbar, Toni Morrison, and Zora Neale Hurston.

Despite such attention to AAE, it is hard to find essays in these books that show students how African Americans can *rewrite academic language*, endowing it with a distinctively African American flavor—in other words, how to invent an African American Standard English (AASE). The notion of an AASE is worth exploring. First of all, as Smitherman (*Black Talk*) and Baldwin remind us, AAE has already transformed some of the everyday vocabulary of mainstream American English. (Just consider how the AAE phrases *chill out* and *give me five* have "crossed over.") Second, Martin Luther King Jr. and other African American preachers have been speaking AASE for years: they have deftly interwoven AAE and the spoken standard to move, instruct, and entertain their African American congregations. Recently, Michael Eric Dyson and Cornel West have carried this tradition into academic circles, dazzling both blacks and whites with their skillful oratory. There are also academics in the literacy field who have advocated a *written* AASE, though they disagree about what it might look like. On the one hand, Henry Evans would inject into SWE Afrocentric words, terms such as *endarkening* instead of *enlightening* (281). On the other hand, Mary Hoover has proposed a "Standard Black English" consisting of "standard grammar enhanced with elements of black style, speech events, and vocabulary" (205). As for Geneva Smitherman (*Talkin and Testifyin*) and Keith Gilyard (*Let's Flip*), each has wrought his or her own brand of AASE by blending into SWE elements of AAE grammar as well as the vocabulary and rhetoric. By infusing academic language with such features—instead of merely delivering the standard—HBCU teachers could engage composition students in the type of transculturation Pratt has described.

Conclusion

The foregoing analysis suggests that Howard, along with several other HBCUs, has negotiated some of the conflicts in the freshman composition classroom by transforming the curriculum, but chiefly by altering content rather than form.

In keeping with the historic purpose of African American literacy, Howard's composition program offers African American students an opportunity to use reading and writing to think through issues of importance to themselves and the African American community. As the preface to *Revelations* declares, by placing an Afrocentric text at the center of the composition curriculum, Howard has made "writing a process of revelation, an act of liberation" (Redd xx).

However, Howard's composition program is hardly a hotbed of black radical thought. After all, like most HBCUs, Howard is not an economically independent institution: it has always relied upon the federal government for a substantial portion of its budget, and therefore it is mindful of its image within the dominant culture. Moreover, though it is historically black, it is not *all*-black. In the English department, in particular, a large proportion of the composition faculty is not of African descent, and even those who are might not be steeped in the African American folk tradition or "down wit the program" of black liberation.

It is not surprising, then, that the English department continues to adhere to the rhetorical and linguistic conventions of the traditional Composition 101, as so many other HBCU departments do. And it is easy to justify this type of conformity at marginalized institutions that strive to empower their students.

As Marcia Farr and Gloria Nardini concede, "some uses of essayist [academic] literacy are socially, economically, and politically powerful, and it is vitally important that students from all backgrounds have equal access to the power such uses confer" (114). By focusing on the academic essay and SWE, the department tries to equip African American students with writing skills that they will need for their careers in academe and beyond even if they can think critically and creatively. Most of our faculty believe, as Delpit does, that "if minority people are to effect the change which will allow them to truly progress we must insist on 'skills' *within the context of* critical and creative thinking" (384).

I concur. But at Howard and many other HBCUs, composition teachers could do more to help students transform the discourse of the dominant culture, *for true power lies not only in the mastery of the game but the ability to change the rules*. As Pratt observes, "while subordinate peoples do not usually control what emanates from the dominant culture, they do determine to varying extents what gets absorbed into their own and what it gets used for" (9). We can help students "select and invent from materials transmitted" by the dominant culture (9). For instance, we can show students how to enrich their academic essays with African American metaphors and lyrical devices as we use African American rhetoric to help students write successful academic prose. Without our encouragement, many African American students might hesitate to draw upon this resource when writing school assignments, fearing that we will admonish them for using colloquialisms or straying from the topic (Ball "Text Design"; Redd "Untapped"). That would be tragic. Whether we are speaking in class or writing comments on students' papers, we must value the resources our students bring to school. Otherwise, how can we nurture them as writers? How can we even *recognize* a Frederick Douglass if one shows up in our classroom?

In composition programs at HBCUs, that's what we should "be about"—nurturing Douglasses. We can nurture them if we deliver a brand of first-year composition that empowers African American students not only to "invent the university," as David Bartholomae says but to invent themselves as African American writers—through autoethnography, critique, resistance, transculturation, and bilingualism. By teaching these "literate arts of the contact zone" (Pratt 11), HBCUs can help African American students "keep it real" in Comp 101.

Works Cited

Abrahams, Roger D. *Talking Black*. Rowley, MA: Newbury House, 1976.

Asante, Molefi Kete. *The Afrocentric Idea*. Philadelphia: Temple UP, 1987.

Baldwin, James. "If Black English Isn't a Language, Then Tell Me, What Is?" *The New York Times* Aug. 27, 1979. Aug. 16, 2002. Accessed online at http://partners.nytimes.com/books/98/03/29/specials/baldwin-english.html.

Ball, Arnetha. "Cultural Preference and the Expository Writing of African-American Adolescents." *Written Communication* 9 (1992): 501–32.

———. "Text Design Patterns in the Writing of Urban African American Students: Teaching to the Cultural Strengths of Students in Multicultural Settings." *Urban Education* 30 (1995): 253–89.

Bartholomae, David. "Inventing the University." *Journal of Basic Writing* 5 (1986): 4–23.

Baugh, John. *Out of the Mouths of Slaves: African American Language and Educational Malpractice*. Austin: U of Texas P, 1999.

Bloom, Lynn. "Freshman Composition as a Middle-Class Enterprise." *College English* 58 (1996): 654–75.

Bowie State University. "Freshman Composition." Sept. 3, 2001. www.bowiestate.edu/academics/english/freshcomp/index.htm. April 29, 2002.

Brown, Sterling. *Southern Road*. New York: Harcourt, Brace, 1932.

Burch, Charles Eaton. "Freshman Papers in a Negro College." *Crisis* 22 (1921): 208–10.

Calfee, R. C., and M. J. Chambliss. "The Structural Design Features of Large Texts." *Educational Psychologist* 22 (1987): 357–78.

Campbell, Kermit. "The *Signifying Monkey* Revisited: Vernacular Discourse and African American Personal Narratives." *JAC* 14 (1994). August 14, 2002. Accessed online at http://jac.gsu.edu/plaintoc.htm.

Canagarajah, A. Suresh. "Safe Houses in the Contact Zone: Coping Strategies of African-American Students in the Academy." *College Composition and Communication* 48 (1997): 173–96.

Cromwell, Otelia, Lorenzo Dow Turner, and Eva B. Dykes. *Readings from Negro Authors, for Schools and Colleges*. New York: Harcourt, 1931.

Delpit, Lisa. "The Politics of Teaching Literate Discourse." In *Other People's Children: Cultural Conflict in the Classsroom*. New York: New P, 1995, 152–66.

Douglass, Frederick. *Narrative of the Life of Frederick Douglass: An American Slave, Written by Himself*. New York: Signet, 1968.

Eastman, Arthur. *The Norton Reader: An Anthology of Expository Prose*. New York: W. W. Norton, 1988.

Evans, Henry. "An Afrocentric Multicultural Writing Project." In *Writing in Multicultural Settings*. Ed. Carol Severino, Juan Guerra, and Johnnella Butler. New York: Modern Language Association, 1997, 273–86.

Farr, Marcia, and Gloria Nardini. "Essayist Literacy and Sociolinguistic Difference." In *Assessment of Writing: Politics, Policies, and Practices*. Ed. Edward White, William Lutz, and Sandra Kamusikiri. New York: Modern Language Association, 1996, 109–19.

Fort Valley State University. "Department of Languages." www.fac.fvsu.edu/as/la/home2.htm. April 29, 2002.

Fox, Thomas. "Repositioning the Profession: Teaching Writing to African American Students." *JAC* 12 (1992): 291–301.

Freire, Paulo. *Pedagogy of the Oppressed*. New York: Continuum, 1990.

Frost, Robert. "The Road Not Taken." In *Poems of Mountain Interval*. New York: Henry Holt, 1921.

Gee, James Paul. "Literacy, Discourse, and Linguistics: Essays by James Paul Gee" [special issue]. *Journal of Education* 171 (1989).

Gilyard, Keith. *Let's Flip the Script: An African American Discourse on Language, Literature and Learning*. Detroit: Wayne State UP, 1996.

Gilyard, Keith, and Elaine Richardson. "Students' Right to Possibility: Basic Writing and African American Rhetoric." In *Insurrections: Approaches to Resistance in Composition Studies*. Ed. Andrea Greenbaum. Albany, NY: SUNY P, 2001, 37–51.

Giroux, Henry. "Introduction: Literacy, Difference, and the Politics of Border Crossing." In *Rewriting Literacy*. Ed. C. Mitchell, and K. Weiler. New York: Bergin and Garvey, 1991: ix–xvi.

Heilker, Paul. "Official Feasts and Carnivals: Student Writing and Public Ritual." *Teaching English in the Two-Year College* 29 (2001): 77–84.

Henderson, Stephen, ed. *Understanding the New Black Poetry: Black Speech and Black Music as Poetic References*. New York: Morrow Quill Paperbacks, 1973.

Hoover, Mary. "The Nairobi Day School: An African American Independent School, 1966–1984." *Journal of Negro Education* 61 (1992): 201–10.

Hughes, Langston. "Theme for English B." In *The Collected Poems of Langston Hughes*. New York: Knopf and Vintage, 1995.

Hurston, Zora Neale. *Dust Tracks on a Road*. 1942. New York: Perennial-Harper, 1991.

Jacobs, Harriet. "Incidents in the Life of a Slave Girl." In *The Classic Slave Narratives*. Ed. Henry Louis Gates. New York: Mentor Penguin, 1987.

Jarvis Christian College. "Literature and Languages." www.jarvis.edu/acadaffairs/arts&sci.pdf. April 29, 2002.

Jones-Jackson, Patricia. *When Roots Die: Endangered Traditions on the Sea Islands*. Athens: U of Georgia P, 1989.

Keating, Ann Louise. "Interrogating 'Whiteness': (De) Constructing Race." *College English* 57 (1995): 901–18.

Kochman, Thomas, ed. *Rappin' and Stylin' Out: Communication in Urban Black America*. Chicago: University of Illinois P, 1972.

Labov, William. *Language in the Inner City: Studies in the Black English Vernacular*. Philadelphia: U of Pennsylvania P, 1972.

Lee, Margaret Giles, Joyce M. Jarrett, Doreatha Drummond Mbalia, eds. *Heritage: African American Readings for Writing*. 2d ed. Upper Saddle River, NJ: Prentice Hall, 2002.

Lewis, Ruby M., Beatrice McKinsey, and Don Hoyt. *Black Orpheus: Rhetoric and Readings*. 2d ed. Boston: Pearson, 2002.

Lincoln University. "The Composition Program." www.lincoln.edu/english/english composition.html. April 29, 2002.

Malcolm X. *The Autobiography of Malcolm X*. New York: Ballantine, 1965.

Marshall, Ian, and Wendy Ryden. "Interrogating the Monologue: Making Whiteness Visible." *College Composition and Communication* 52 (2000): 240–59.

McCall, Nathan. *Makes Me Wanna Holler*. New York: Vintage, 1994.

McHenry, Elizabeth, and Shirley Brice Heath. "The Literate and the Literary: African Americans as Writers and Readers: 1830–1940." *Written Communication* 11.4 (1994): 419–44.

Mitchell, Angelyn. *The Freedom to Remember*. New Brunswick, NJ: Rutgers UP, 2002.

Mitchell-Kernan, Claudia. *Language Behavior in a Black Urban Community*. Monograph of the Language-Behavior Lab, No. 2. Berkeley: U of California, Berkeley, 1971.

Noonan-Wagner, Desley. "Black Writers in the Classroom: A Question of Language Experience, Not Grammar." Paper presented at the convention of the Conference on College Composition and Communication, Washington, DC, March 1980. ERIC ED189599.

Oakwood College. "English and Communications." www.oakwood.edu/english/1.htm. April 29, 2002.

Peterson, Linda H., John C. Brereton, and Joan E. Hartman, eds. *The Norton Reader, Shorter Edition*. 10th ed. New York: W. W. Norton, 1999.

Pough, Gwendolyn. "Empowering Rhetoric: Black Students Writing Black Panthers." *College Composition and Communication* 53 (2002): 466–86.

Pratt, Mary Louise. "Arts of the Contact Zone." 1990. In *Professing in the Contact Zone: Bringing Theory and Practice Together*. Ed. Janice M. Wolff. Urbana, IL: National Council of Teachers of English, 2002, 1–18.

Redd, Teresa. "'How I Got Ovah': Success Stories of African American Composition Students, Part II." Paper presented at the annual convention of the Conference on College Composition and Communication, Denver, CO, 2001. ERIC ED455537. 2002.

———, ed. *Revelations: An Anthology of Expository Essays by and About Blacks*. 4th ed. Boston: Pearson, 2002.

———. "Untapped Resources: 'Styling' in Black Students' Writing for Black Audiences." In *Composing Social Identity in Written Language*. Ed. Donald L. Rubin. Hillsdale, NJ: Lawrence Erlbaum, 1995, 221–40.

Redd, Teresa, and Victoria Massey. "Race on the Superhighway: How E-Mail Affects African American Student Writers." *Journal of Advanced Composition* 17.2 (1997): 245–66.

Rickford, John. *African American Vernacular English: Features, Evolution, Educational Implications*. Malden, MA, and Oxford: Blackwell, 1999.

Smitherman, Geneva. "African American Student Writers in the NAEP, 1969–88 and 'The Blacker the Berry, the Sweeter the Juice.'" *Talkin That Talk: Language, Culture, and Education in African America*. London: Routledge, 2000, 163–91.

———. *Black Talk: Words and Phrases from the Hood to the Amen Corner*. Rev. ed. New York: Houghton Mifflin, 2000.

———. *Talkin and Testifyin: The Language of Black America*. Detroit: Wayne State UP, 1977.

South Carolina State University. "English 150." www.scu.edu/academics/s_art&hu/commandlang/courses/e150.htm. April 29, 2002.

Southern University. "College of Arts and Humanities—Department of English." June 28, 2000. www.subr.edu/artshuman/english.pdf. April 29, 2002.

Spelman College. "English Department." http://www.spelman.edu/english/index.html. April 29, 2002.

Syllabus for Freshman Composition. Handout.

Thompson, Dorothy Perry. "Dabbling in the Abnormal: Blackening the T's (Text, Topics, and Teacher) in the Composition Classroom." Paper presented at the annual meeting of the Conference on College Composition and Communication, Phoenix, AZ, 1997.

———. "Rescuing the Failed, Filed Away, and Forgotten: African Americans and Eurocentricity in Academic Argument." In *Perspectives on Written Argument*. Ed. Deborah Berrill. Creskill, NJ: Hampton P, 1996, 221–40.

Troutman, Denise. "Whose Voice Is It Anyway? Marked Features in the Writing of Black English Speakers." In *Writing in Multicultural Settings*. Ed. Carol Severino, Juan Guerra, Johnnella Butler. New York: Modern Language Association, 1997, 27–39.

Turner, Darwin T. "Black Experience, Black Literature, Black Students, and the English Classroom." In *Tapping Potential: English and Language Arts for the Black Learner*. Ed. Charlotte K. Brooks. Urbana, IL: NCTE, 1985, 297–307.

Turner, Lorenzo Dow. *Africanisms in the Gullah Dialect*. 1949. Ann Arbor: U of Michigan P, 1973.

Waddell, Marie L., Robert M. Esch, and Roberta R. Walker. *The Art of Styling Sentences: 20 Patterns for Success*. 2d ed. Woodbury, NY: Barron's, 1983.

Webber, Thomas L. *Deep Like the Rivers: Education in the Slave Quarter Community 1831–1865*. New York: W. W. Norton, 1978.

Wolfram, Walter, and Erik Thomas. *The Development of African American English*. Oxford: Blackwell, 2002.

Wright, Richard. *Black Boy: A Record of Childhood and Youth*. 1945. New York: Harper and Row, 1966.

Xavier University. "English 1010." Resource Handbook. 2000. www.xula.edu/EnglishDept.html. April 29, 2002.

Zaluda, Scott. "Lost Voices of the Harlem Renaissance: Writing Assigned at Howard University, 1919–31." *College Composition and Communication* 50 (1998): 232–57.

7

Advanced Placement, Not Advanced Exemption

Challenges for High Schools, Colleges, and Universities

David A. Jolliffe
University of Arkansas
Bernard Phelan
Homewood-Flossmoor High School

There are no doubt hundreds of thousands of people—students, parents, teachers, and administrators—in the United States and abroad who think that taking a high school course in preparation for the Advanced Placement (AP) English examination and achieving a high score on the exam represent an alternative method of delivering traditional, introductory college writing instruction. We, the coauthors of this chapter, are not among them.

From our positions as "insiders" in several camps—high school English classes, university writing programs, inservice teacher seminars, even the Advanced Placement Program itself—we maintain that parents, students, administrators, and faculty at the high school and college levels need to recognize that the name of the program is Advanced *Placement*, not Advanced *Exemption*. The Advanced Placement Program, in our view, challenges high schools to develop and teach demanding courses in which students learn to read and analyze the rhetorical effectiveness of texts of all genres—not solely fiction, poetry, and drama—and to write strong, cogent, and persuasive arguments. Such courses can be most appropriately seen as *transitions* from high school reading and writing instruction to the same at the college level. Moreover, the Advanced Placement Program, in our view, challenges colleges and universities to develop and staff with trained faculty a variety of courses stressing close reading and careful rhetorical analysis, a sequence into which a first-year student can enter at different places depending on the abilities he or she has demonstrated through taking high school courses, scoring well on examinations, and presenting any other credentials that the college or university might request.

The genre of our chapter is an exploratory essay, the name one of us (Jolliffe *Inquiry and Genre*) has given to a type of text that emerges from James Kinneavy's synoptic view of Thomas S. Kuhn's design for exploration in *The Structure of Scientific Revolutions*. In *A Theory of Discourse*, Kinneavy shows how Kuhn portrays revolutionary scientists moving through four steps: initially accepting current dogma, sensing anomalies in it, asserting the present as a moment of crisis when the anomalous dogma should be countered, and then searching for a new paradigm (101–2). Similarly, our chapter will initially rehearse the existing dogma about AP English—what the exams and preparatory courses are and why so many people (mistakenly, we believe) perceive AP as an alternative method of delivering college writing instruction. We will then examine the limitations and drawbacks of this status quo thinking, pointing out problems in the status quo that we label *curricular*, *developmental*, and *attitudinal*. Finally, we will propose new ways of thinking about the relationship between AP English and college writing courses and programs.

We must, however, offer personal disclaimers from the outset. Both of us are involved with, and support in various ways, the AP English Program. Both of us have served as readers and table leaders for the scoring of the AP English Language and Composition examination; both of us have led workshops for high school teachers interested in developing courses that would prepare students for the AP English exams. One of us (Phelan) is a veteran teacher of such courses and formerly served as AP coordinator at the high school where he taught. Perhaps more vitally, he has also been an elected trustee of the College Board, the not-for-profit organization that "owns" the Advanced Placement Program and employs the Educational Testing Service (ETS) to develop and score the examinations. The other of us (Jolliffe) has been a member of the ETS committee that creates the AP English examinations. He has also been a question leader for the AP English Language and Composition scoring, and in 2003 he began serving a four-year term as the chief reader for this examination. In short, we believe in and promote the AP English Program. Because we also believe in the ultimate benefit—to high school students and curricula, to AP English, and to college and university writing programs—of rethinking the AP–college English relationship, we take the positions sketched out in this chapter. In doing so, we speak for ourselves, not for the Educational Testing Service, the AP Program, or the College Board.

Current Dogma: What Is AP English, and Why Do People Perceive It as They Do?

Status quo thinking about AP English rests on several misconceptions, widely held by teachers, parents, and administrators. Many of these stakeholders are misinformed about what the AP English exams are, what courses students might take to prepare for them, who creates the exams, what kinds of questions are on them, and what successful performance on them is supposed to signify.[1]

First of all, the exams: A great many teachers, at both the high school and the college level, think there is just one AP English exam. Contrary to this belief, AP English consists not of a single examination but instead of two examinations, the AP English *Literature* and Composition Examination and the AP English *Language* and Composition Examination. A great many colleges and universities offer a waiver of first-year composition to students who perform well on either of these exams, so a quick look at both of them is germane to the argument.

The two AP English examinations are similar in structure, both consisting of an hour's worth of multiple-choice questions and three essay questions, with forty minutes allotted to respond to each. The AP English Literature and Composition exam's multiple-choice questions test a student's ability to read poetry and fiction closely. Its three essay prompts call for students to write compositions that analyze the style and structure of fiction and poetry and explicate important themes manifest in novels and plays. On the AP English Language and Composition exam, the multiple-choice questions test a student's ability to read nonfiction prose closely. Its three essay prompts call for students to write compositions that analyze the rhetorical structure, technique, and style of prose passages and develop strong, cogent arguments of their own.

Many people mistakenly assume there is some standardized, certified AP course that students must take to prepare for the examination. There is no such thing. The College Board does issue publications and sponsor workshops and institutes that promote various designs for courses that prepare students to perform well on one or both of the exams, but there is no official AP course or AP reading list.

A third misperception is that some nameless, faceless ETS staffers create the exams. Contrary to some teachers' beliefs (see, for example, Jones), the AP English exams are not created by ETS psychometricians, but instead are generated by a six-member test-development committee: three high school teachers and three college or university faculty members, who are appointed to four-year terms by ETS and are paid for their work. ETS staff professionals assist this committee, as do two university faculty members, one for English Literature and Composition and the other for English Language and Composition, who serve as the chief readers—that is, the supervisors and administrators—when the completed exams are evaluated.

Because they are familiar with other kinds of standardized exams that essentially test reading comprehension and grammatical knowledge, many teachers, students, and parents misunderstand the kinds of questions, both multiple-choice and essay, that one finds on the AP English examinations. The test-development committee tries to generate multiple-choice questions that are designed neither to trick students into guessing the "correct" answer from several ambiguous choices nor to require students to manipulate a sentence's syntax and speculate about its consequently changed meaning. Instead, multiple-choice questions require students to identify how the structure and style of a text are congruent with and generate its meaning. Within the committee, the common way of thinking about the multiple-choice questions is this: If you were teaching the passage upon which the questions are based, where in the passage would you ask the students to pause and consider what the author is doing in terms of rhetorical appeal, organization and structure, diction, figurative language, syntax, and so on, and *why*? At each of these "pausing points" in the anatomy of a text, a well-constructed multiple-choice question can test a student's close reading, his or her ability to understand the *what* and the *why* of an author's choices. Consider, for example, the following material from an AP English Language and Composition exam that has been released by the College Board. The student is given a passage of about five hundred words from an 1821 essay by William Hazlitt. Here are the first three sentences of this passage:

> It is not easy to write a familiar style. Many people mistake a familiar for a vulgar style, and suppose that to write without affectation is to write at random. On the contrary, there is nothing than requires more precision, and, if I may so say, purity of expression, than the style I am speaking of. (16, quoted in *Advanced Placement Course Description*, 2002)

The passage, of course, continues in this Hazlittean vein, and after reading it, the student is asked to answer ten multiple-choice questions. Here is a representative sample:

> Which of the following best describes the rhetorical function of the second sentence in the passage?
> A. It makes an appeal to authority.
> B. It restates the thesis of the passage.
> C. It expresses the causal relationship between morality and writing style.
> D. It provides a specific example for the preceding generalization.
> E. It presents a misconception that the author will correct. (18)

There is nothing tricky here—the answer is E. The student does not need to guess at the gist or manipulate syntax or call upon any body of arcane knowledge. The student simply needs to read the passage and determine what rhetorical moves—strategies of topical development, organization, and style—the author is making at various points in the text.

Some critics of the AP Program are troubled by what they see as an undue emphasis on close reading in an exam that is designed to show a student's preparedness to take advanced writing courses in college. We are unapologetic about the emphasis on reading in the AP English exams. Indeed, one of us maintains that the teaching of critical reading is the most neglected aspect of contemporary college composition instruction (Jolliffe "Who Is Teaching"). The teaching of reading tends to drop off the educational radar screen, in fact, after middle school, when courses called reading get phased out of the curriculum. Many high school teachers and college writing instructors simply assume that students know how to read closely and critically, just because the students have made it to high school or college. One of the chief benefits of any curriculum that purports to prepare students to succeed on either AP English exam is that it *must* pay careful, diligent attention to teaching students how to read challenging texts. While we do not necessarily advocate that high school and college instructors incorporate multiple-choice questioning in their pedagogy (we see the multiple-choice questions on the AP English exams as a necessary evil, prompted by the fact that several hundred thousand students take these exams yearly), we do recommend that high school and college composition teachers attend to the principles of teaching close reading that are inherent in the multiple-choice sections of the tests—principles that lead a student to attend carefully to the ways a writer develops key ideas and points, appeals to readers, and makes strategic decisions involving genre, organization, structure, and style. Like learning to write, learning to read, we believe, is a lifelong education, one that a student must take up at successive levels of study, even through graduate school. To put it bluntly, we believe that if high school and college writing instructors are not teaching reading, then they are not really teaching writing.

Just as there are misconceptions about the multiple-choice questions on the AP Engish exams, so are the essay questions often misunderstood. The essay questions, in the test-development committee's thinking, ought to resemble the kinds of short in-class compositions students might do in a first-year college course. For the English Literature and Composition exam, the test-development committee tries to produce essay questions similar to those that might generate a brief paper in a literature-and-composition course. For the English Language and Composition exam, the committee tries for questions similar to those that would prompt analytic and argumentative papers in mainstream first-year composition courses.

Everyone involved with the AP English program acknowledges that not all writing is impromptu and that writers generally do their best work when they have time to process their compositions. At both the test-development committee meetings and the sessions at which the exams are scored, therefore, participating faculty members agree that the students' essays in response to these prompts will be first drafts and may not represent the level of writing ability a student could display if he or she were permitted to revise. Scorers are openly encouraged to look for sources of promise in the students' texts—to give them credit for what they *can* do with each prompt in forty minutes. (Issues of scope and security—nearly 450,000 students took the two AP English exams in 2004—make it difficult to envision a testing situation that would allow students to revise a text that they had drafted prior to the examination date.)

The procedures for scoring the exams are also misunderstood, often to the point of being the subject of a great deal of oral legend. The most egregious misperceptions about the scoring involve rumors of coercion and "groupthink" manipulation. While the multiple-choice sections of the exams are machine-scored, the students' essays are evaluated at one-week sessions, known simply as "the readings," conducted for the past several years at a large convention center in Daytona Beach, Florida. There is one reading for AP English Language and Composition and one for AP English Literature and Composition. At these readings, high school teachers and college and university faculty members who have applied to be appointed as readers, or "faculty consultants," evaluate the students' essays. For their work, readers receive transportation, lodging and meals for the week, and a stipend. To be appointed as a reader, a person must have taught a high school course related to AP English for at least three years or have taught a first-year college English course for at least three years.

At the readings, there are three rooms of readers, one for each essay question; thus, a reader typically evaluates compositions written in response to the same prompt all week. Readers work at tables of eight, generally comprising both high school and college-level instructors. Each table is supervised by a table leader, a person who has previously demonstrated some expertise as a reader, and each of the three reading rooms is overseen by a question leader.

The document that focuses the work of the reading is the scoring guide, a set of nine-point rubrics, one for each essay question, developed initially by the chief reader and then successively vetted and revised, first by the question leaders and later by the table leaders—about seventy for the English Language and Composition examination and more than one hundred for English Literature and Composition. To some assessment specialists, a nine-point rubric may seem excessively robust; essentially, however, it is a four-point scale with some modifications. Each rubric provides paragraph-long descriptions of the types of papers that receive an 8 for excellent work, a 6 for adequate work, a 4 for inadequate work, and a 2 for work that shows little or no success. The other scores are similarly described in relation to these four points: A 9 is a stronger version of an 8, a 7 a stronger version of a 6, a 3 a weaker version of a 4, and a 1 a weaker version of a 2. A 5 is a paper that could potentially be a 6 but is limited or unfocused in its development.

Prior to the reading, the chief reader, question leaders, and table leaders examine hundreds of pieces of student work and select an array of compositions—generally about eighty for each question—that they agree show the range of performance, from 1 to 9, in response to the prompt. These sample essays become the package of training papers that readers consult during the reading. As with all large-scale direct assessments, the goal is to achieve consensus of judgment among the readers. On the first day of the reading, therefore, guided by the question leader and table leaders, readers read and discuss the prompt, study the scoring guide carefully, and then read and discuss thoroughly two or three sets of range-finder papers. The readers generally begin scoring "live" essays on the afternoon of the first day, but regularly during the week, the question leader and table leaders pause the enterprise and ask readers to score additional sample papers and then discuss and justify their scores. Conversations about these scores, both in the room as a whole and at individual tables, help readers forge a consensus about standards. Idiosyncratic, outlying scorers are not, contrary to legend, called to the front of the room for a confrontation with the question leader or singled out for early dismissal.

While each live student essay is officially read by only one scorer, for about the first two days of the reading, table leaders do nothing but "back-read" (i.e., provide a second reading for) the papers evaluated by readers at their tables. Table leaders then have the opportunity to talk, quietly and individually, with any reader who may be failing to achieve consensus and to suggest modifications in the reader's judgments. Such back-readings and discrete, private discussions can continue periodically during the remainder of the reading.

By the end of the reading, each student's three essays have been scored from 1 to 9, and his or her multiple-choice answers have been graded. Using a formula that weights the scores on the essays at 55 percent and the multiple-choice score at 45 percent, each student's examination is given a composite score. After the reading ends, the chief readers and ETS staffers convert these composite scores into five categories, which amount to the final scores on the exam. The College Board recommends that colleges and universities interpret these five scores as follows: A 5 is "extremely well qualified" to receive college credit, a 4 is "well qualified," a 3 is "qualified," a 2 is "possibly qualified," and a 1 receives "no recommendation."

This interpretation leads to what we consider the most problematic misperception about AP English. Because many parents, students, school administrators, high school teachers, and university administrators equate college writing instruction solely with freshman English, stakeholders in all these categories can tend to see AP English as a method to *avoid* college writing courses rather than as a means to *place into* a writing course that is appropriately challenging for a student's level of reading and writing ability. The College Board, unfortunately, feeds this misperception in its official publications. Its booklet titled *Advanced Placement Program Course Description: English Language and Composition, Literature and Composition* (May 2002) offers from the outset these three paragraphs, worth quoting in full:

> Many American colleges begin with a course in expository writing for a year, a semester, or a shorter period, followed by a course in introductory readings in literature. Subsequently, students may take advanced courses in language, rhetoric, and expository writing or in literature.

> Students who elect courses in the first area typically focus their reading on discursive prose that ranges across the disciplines of the sciences as well as the arts. Those who elect advanced courses in literature generally study major authors, periods, genres, or themes: their reading typically concentrates on imaginative literature—poetry, fiction, and drama.
>
> The AP English Development Committee therefore offers parallel examinations: one in Language and Composition and one in Literature and Composition. The committee intends them both to be of equal rigor in keeping with the standards of quality of the AP Program, and it recommends that students taking either course or examination receive similar treatment by the college granting credit or exemption or both. That is, although the specific college courses that AP credit will satisfy differ from college to college, *each examination represents a year's college-level work. Therefore, the* amount *of credit that may be given for each examination is the same: up to two semesters of credit for the appropriate grade on either examination.* (3; emphasis added)

If, in the public's perception, college writing instruction is seen as a monolith that exists as one or two courses in the first-year curriculum rather than an important moment in a student's *lifelong* learning of reading and writing, then AP English can be seen as a way to get around this monolith—it can be seen, in the term this collection unpacks, as an alternative method of delivering first-year writing. We are troubled by this perception.

Anomalies in the Current Dogma: Problems with the Status Quo

As AP English insiders dedicated to improving the program, we are sensitive not only to the aforementioned public misperceptions about it but also to the critiques leveled against it from within high school and college English departments. In a 1989 collection titled *Advanced Placement English: Theory, Politics, and Pedagogy*, for example, David Foster takes AP English to task because, in his view, the program forces high school teachers to forego a full, process-oriented writing curriculum in favor of test preparation. As Foster puts it, "AP courses taught primarily to help students learn to write in the exam formats will cheat them out of the benefits of the writing process" (13). In a pair of articles in *English Journal* in 2001, Joseph Jones similarly decries the way the AP English exams force teachers to "teach to the test" (54), and Jeffrey Markham laments that the pressure of preparing students to take the exams produces an overemphasis on teaching close reading and an underemphasis on eliciting students' affective responses to literature. In our view, these critiques focus on just one of three problematic aspects of the current situation involving AP English. Let us label these three aspects as *curricular, developmental,* and *attitudinal.* In this section, we will examine them one by one, and later in the chapter we will suggest new ways of thinking about them.

As Foster, Jones, and Markham suggest, AP English can generate *curricular* quagmires, involving both content and method, in high school courses where students are preparing to take the exams. Here is one source of the content area problem: Because there is no such thing as a single, established, certified AP English curriculum, teachers can decide to teach anything in their courses that they are prepared to do, that their district or state requires them to do, or that they believe will prepare their students to perform well on the exams, and each of these decisions holds potential problems. Most high school teachers, in general, are prepared to teach imaginative literature—fiction, poetry, and drama. Indeed, their schools, districts, and states often require that they teach primarily literature-based curriculums (see Applebee and the chapters by Farris and Bodmer in this volume). While a course that focuses solely on reading and writing about fiction, poetry, and drama may help students perform well on the AP English Literature and Composition exam, it ultimately offers a limited perspective of the study of English (note, for example, Robert Scholes' call for English to be the study of texts rather than the study of literature), and it provides little support for students who hope to perform well on AP English Language and Composition, which focuses almost exclusively on nonfiction prose and is essentially a test of students' knowledge of rhetorical theory and ability to perform rhetorical analysis. Yet most students who take the AP Language and Composition exam prepare for it in a class that examines canonical literature, often from a thematic, "great ideas" perspective, rather than from a rhetorically oriented, analytic one. In short, a great many students take a class in one content area and then take a test, the AP English Language and Composition exam, that examines a different content area.

The methodological problems stem both from the current nature of the AP English exams and from the aforementioned lack of content area preparation on the part of teachers. The exams rely on multiple-choice questions and impromptu essay questions, both tools that are staples of standardized tests but that have fallen out of use and favor in English courses. While we support the emphasis on close reading in the AP English exams, we venture that relatively few teachers teach it. Similarly, given the ubiquity of process-oriented teaching in high school and college English courses (though for a contrasting view, see Yancey's conclusion to this volume), we venture that few teachers sense an inherent need for students to compose impromptu essays, and even fewer teachers strive to have students see connections between writing impromptu compositions and producing full, process-developed compositions. Therefore, since the type of multiple-choice questions and the kinds of impromptu writing assignments one finds on the AP English exams are not, in general, inherently congruent with most high school and college English teachers' pedagogy, teachers can respond to these testing tools in one of two ways. They can focus too heavily on them as test-preparation exercises—trying, in essence, to psych out the test writers, to figure out what ETS "wants," to come up with some mechanistic, reductive formula to score high on the multiple-choice questions and essays. This proclivity has given rise to a veritable cottage industry—a private enterprise, not sanctioned by the College Board or ETS—of test-preparation books, teacher seminars, even videos and CDs. In addition, teachers can dismiss multiple-choice questions and impromptu essays (and, by extension, the AP English exams) as disconnected from, and therefore irrelevant to, "real" English teaching, as Foster, Jones, and Markham do.

We call the second problematic aspect of the current AP English situation *developmental* because it derives from this unfortunate fact: A great many students who take the AP English Language and Composition exam as high school juniors or seniors miss the opportunity to study rhetoric and composition, to improve their already strong but still nascent reading and writing abilities, at precisely the time they need to do so—when they are beginning to encounter more difficult and challenging subjects to read and write about in college. Several studies in developmental psychology, succinctly reviewed by Karen Spear and Gretchen Flesher in their chapter in *Advanced Placement English: Theory, Pedagogy, Politics*, demonstrate two salient conclusions: (1) writing abilities continue to develop as writers mature, and (2) as proficient writers encounter more complex topics, their writing ability "initially decreases to the point where [they] find themselves unable to do in a new assignment what they had previously accomplished with ease" (27). In other words, an education in writing needs always to be a *continuing* education. If, as we noted in the previous section, colleges and universities (along with the students who attend them and their parents, counselors, and teachers) equate college writing instruction solely with first-year composition, and if AP is marketed as a way to avoid first-year composition, then this developmental problem becomes particularly pernicious. Doing well on the AP English exams can take students out of writing courses at precisely the moment they need one. It is worth noting that Spear and Flesher advocate different levels of mainstream and advanced writing instruction, an idea that we support and amplify later in this chapter.

A final problematic aspect of the current situation involving AP English can be labeled as *attitudinal*, and it is manifested in two ways. The first way affects students who do not waive first-year English: Many of these students have completed a rigorous, challenging high school English course (and there are some *very* good courses being taught under the local banner of AP English), taken one of the examinations, but then scored in the lower range and consequently have not waived first-year English. These students can represent a challenge to whoever ends up teaching them in their initial college course, especially if it is at a large university. In many cases, these students' high school English teacher was experienced, confident, and innovative, and the course was demanding; in many of these same cases, the students' first college instructor may be a teaching assistant who is working on a degree and learning the ropes of teaching critical reading and effective writing for the first time ever. To these students, first-year English can seem, well, a letdown, and all the problems attendant to letdowns—disappointment, frustration, anger, uncooperativeness—might ensue. The second way affects those students who do waive first-year English. Because first-year English is, for better or worse, an American educational rite of passage, a great deal of formal and informal socialization into the college and university culture happens in these classes. Doing well on the AP English exams can take students away from opportunities to acclimate to their new intellectual homes.

A Time for Change

Given the public misperceptions of AP English and the problems currently attendant to it, readers might wonder why we, the coauthors of this chapter, remain dedicated to working with the program and to improving the relationship between AP English and college-level writing programs and English departments. The answers are three: First, neither AP English nor introductory college English and writing programs are going to disappear. These two entities serve students at a crucial juncture in their educational lives; understanding and cooperation on both sides of the high school–college divide can only ease this transition. Second, the AP Program as a whole is growing, and if problems exist in any part of it, these problems need to be addressed before they are exacerbated by growth. The College Board's 2001 monograph, *Access to Excellence: A Report of the Commission on the Future of the Advanced Placement Program*, noting that "43 percent of American high schools do not offer AP courses, and many participating schools offer only a few courses" (3), lists growth as the first of its five major recommendations: It signals the College Board's goal to "focus on expanding access to AP in underserved schools and for underserved populations, while continuing to maintain AP's high quality" (21). Third, and most importantly, we believe there are major benefits for students inherent in the AP English program, benefits that can only be strengthened by improving the program. Let us simply list these benefits serially and then expand on several of them in a description of a very good high school English course that would both prepare students to succeed on the AP English Language and Composition exam and help them effect a solid transition to college-level courses in reading and writing. We maintain that, in its best courses, AP English

- Adds rigor, sometimes otherwise wanting, to the high school English curriculum.
- Emphasizes close reading and rhetorical analysis of texts instead of simply comprehending the major themes embodied in them.
- Emphasizes the importance of studying a variety of genres, not solely fiction, poetry, and drama.
- Stresses the importance of attending to underheard voices in historical periods and in contemporary writing.

- Provides solid instruction in analyzing others' arguments and producing one's own effective arguments.
- Offers students an incentive to perform well in high school that they might otherwise lack.
- Provides students with one artifact, one piece of evidence among many, that colleges and universities might examine for admission and placement decisions.

A Direction for Change: An Ideal High School English AP Course

We propose eventually to conclude this chapter in true exploratory-essay fashion by offering a series of challenges—alternatives to the problematic status quo—to high school English teachers, to college and university writing program and English department administrators, and to the College Board. Let us anticipate this conclusion by unpacking one of the recommendations right now. If AP English is going to provide students with courses that not only help them succeed on one of the examinations but also prepare them to take more advanced courses involving reading and writing in college, then high school English teachers and course designers must create curricula that move beyond the traditional three high school English activities: surveying the great works of literature, introducing expository writing, and teaching grammar and usage rules and skills. What follows is a description of an ideal high school class that one of us (Phelan) regularly provides to participants in his workshops for new and experienced teachers of courses that would do just that:

> It is not easy to describe an ideal AP course that would prepare students for advanced work in reading and writing in college. Syllabi are as plentiful as teachers. The AP Program offers, intelligently, no prescription as to content and curriculum. Such an ideal course, nevertheless, would be marked by certain crucial features. One key feature, perhaps the central feature, would be the attention to close reading of multiple kinds of texts. The word *reading* often suggests that the act of reading is a one-size-fits-all template. Further, people think that such a skill is mastered early—decoding—then simply applied uniformly for the rest of one's life. Reading, instead, needs to be viewed as developmental and plural: . . . reading really means readings. Reading a cereal box is not the same thing as reading a John Irving novel. Reading a train schedule differs from reading a poem. We recognize such differences readily at the level of content. We are less likely to admit to consciousness that the act of reading differs because we, as experienced readers, switch modes of apprehension intuitively. Those of us who read well because of good habits acquired, perhaps consciously, perhaps inadvertently, forget that we did learn them, and that there was a time that we did not read as well as we do now.

In an AP course a teacher, then, must be a reading teacher. But what does this mean? It means that we must pay attention to the uniqueness of text and find a way to talk about that uniqueness. One possible way to see and discuss the particularity of a text is to work with a metaphor: language landscape. We should ask students, when encountering a new text, to think of themselves as being dropped onto an unknown planet. Their job is to describe to each other and the teacher the features of that new planet. Is it warm? Is it cold? Is it flat, rolling, mountainous? Is it wet? Dry? Rocky? Verdant? In other words, what features characterize the previously unknown planet? Such an approach to new text—and the pedagogical subtext, the placement of varied and unusual texts in front of students—allows students to move away from what all teachers see with some frequency: flat-liner reading. Flat-liners read in such a way that all text is literal and linear. They remain on the surface of words, never getting to the richness of subtext, inference, and intertextuality. Many of us have had the experience of asking a student a question, then asking the student if he or she has read the text. The students most often answer yes. What are we to conclude? The student made eye contact with the page, but did not do what we would call reading. This more complex version of what we call reading is what we need to teach students consciously. We need to provide them with language to talk about these new planets, as well as to take that flat line and have it become a wave with subtext, inference, omission, and expectation. We need to teach people who read to be readers.

Writing clearly will be the other necessary feature of an ideal AP course. Rather than just thinking about the types of essays and specific assignments, though, we should consider two things: intentionality and connection to reading. Let's look at intentionality first since it includes connection to reading under its umbrella.

Students seldom understand intention. They tend to think of prose as being manufactured. Certainly, it does not strike them as the work of someone without whom the text simply wouldn't exist. Students believe that teachers have storehouses of materials, endless books and Xeroxed packets, which we inflict on students for specified periods of time. This belief, that texts are made or found objects rather than rhetorical entities, written in response to a real human exigence, lies at the heart of intentionality. Students draw a ready corollary: if these texts are not intentional, neither are their texts, the pieces of writing they generate for class. They are avoiding two things: responsibility and risk. Students see prose as manufactured because it relieves them of the rhetorical and argumentative responsibility for their own work. All of us are aware of the students' gestures that signal this: sliding a paper into the middle of the stack (as if this will prevent us from detecting authorship), using illegible handwriting, and lavishing immense attention on the formatting of the cover page. Substitute tasks and subterfuges abound. What question are they avoiding facing? Can you think? At the same time, the student is minimizing risk by engaging in compensatory behavior.

What then should writing look like in an ideal AP course? Students should demonstrate that they can think, show voice, adopt a clear rhetorical stance, articulate and develop an argument, analyze argument and rhetoric, and provide evidence of an emerging, stylistic maturity. Any student who can do all these things, and read varied texts in an analogously sophisticated way, is ready for a more advanced composition course.

Recommendations and Challenges

As *Access to Excellence* and other College Board publications frequently proclaim, the AP Program hopes to offer a model of curricular and pedagogical rigor in American high schools. If all high school English classes, not just AP, took it as their goal to teach students to read all kinds of texts rhetorically and analytically and to write with intention and force, then great progress could be made toward achieving a stronger degree of intellectual rigor and challenge. The problems involved with seeing AP English as an alternative method of delivering first-year writing instruction are clear by now. A great many high school teachers need to learn how to teach the types of courses described previously, courses that would fully prepare students to demonstrate their abilities to do the kinds of close, rhetorical reading and intentional, forceful writing that more advanced college work (not to mention responsible participation in the polis) demands. The AP English exams, as they are currently constructed with multiple-choice questions and impromptu essays, may not adequately test these abilities. The high school students themselves, no matter how proficient they are as high school–level readers and writers, are likely to need reading and writing instruction that will help them cope with the more complex intellectual tasks that their college courses place in front of them.

If AP English is to serve a legitimate role in preparing high school students to do successful work in more advanced college courses that require close reading and strong writing, four sets of stakeholders need to change. First, high schools need to develop courses (and faculty to teach them) that effectively teach rhetorical theory, analysis, and production. High school English teachers, particularly in AP-related courses, need to be teachers of reading and writing. Second, the College Board, and its contractor, ETS, need to listen carefully to excellent teachers at the high school and college levels, and to writing program administrators and composition scholars at the college and university level, about how the AP English exams need to change if they are to reflect what is really taught in first-year courses that students might waive if they do well on the exams. Third, the public—particularly parents of college-bound students, guidance counselors, and administrators at the secondary and postsecondary levels—need to rethink their notions of college-level writing instruction as something that happens only in the first-year curriculum and that then inoculates the students against faulty reading and poor writing for the rest of their college careers. Fourth, and perhaps most challenging, colleges and universities need to create a variety of appropriate courses where students can begin their college-level coursework in reading and writing. The one-size-fits-all model of freshman comp, regnant in American colleges and universities for a century now, has outlived its relevance. Colleges and universities need to make first-year English courses more demanding and, consequently, less likely to be seen—by students, parents, administrators, and the public at large—as something that can be avoided.

Note

1. Interested parties may, of course, find answers to all these questions by reading about the Advanced Placement Program at the College Board's website: www.collegeboard.com.

Works Cited

Applebee, Arthur. *Curriculum as Conversation: Transforming Traditions of Teaching and Learning*. Chicago: U of Chicago P, 1996.

College Board. *Access to Excellence: A Report of the Commission on the Future of the Advanced Placement Program*. New York: College Entrance Examination Board, 2001.

———. *Advanced Placement Program Course Description, English Literature and Composition, English Language and Composition*. New York: College Entrance Examination Board, 2002.

Foster, David. "The Theory of AP English: A Critique." In *Advanced Placement English: Theory, Politics, and Pedagogy*. Ed. Gary A. Olson, Elizabeth Metzger, and Evelyn Ashton-Jones. Portsmouth, NH: Heinemann, 1989, 3–24.

Jolliffe, David A. *Inquiry and Genre: Writing to Learn in College*. Boston: Allyn and Bacon, 1998.

———. "Who Is Teaching Composition Students to Read and How Are They Doing It?" *Composition Studies* 21 (2003): 127–142.

Jones, Joseph. "Recomposing the AP English Exam." *English Journal* 91.1 (2001): 51–56.

Kinneavy, James L. *A Theory of Discourse*. Englewood Cliffs, NJ: Prentice-Hall, 1971.

Markham, Jeffrey C. "Hidden Dangers of the AP English Exams." *English Journal* 91.1 (2001): 18–19.

Scholes, Robert. *The Rise and Fall of English: Reconstructing English as a Discipline*. New Haven, CT: Yale UP, 1999.

Spear, Karen, and Gretchen Flesher. "Continuities in Cognitive Development: AP Students and College Writing." In *Advanced Placement English: Theory, Politics, and Pedagogy*. Ed. Gary A. Olson, Elizabeth Metzger, and Evelyn Ashton-Jones. Portsmouth, NH: Heinemann, 1989, 25–51.

8

The Space Between
Dual-Credit Programs as Brokering, Community Building, and Professionalization

Christine Farris
Indiana University

A few summers ago at the annual Council of Writing Program Administrators (WPA) conference, I was part of a roundtable concerned with the impact on the profession of dual-credit courses, that is, courses taught in high school for which qualified students can also receive college credit. Several speakers described with alarm the efforts of their state higher education systems to outsource or launder college composition credits through the high schools, including slapdash arrangements lacking adequate instructor preparation or a standardized college-level syllabus. We could all appreciate the slippery slope dual-credit programs might provide profit-seeking administrators. In the interest of contrast more than apology for the downside of dual credit, I described my school's Advance College Project (ACP), a twenty-year-old cooperative program between Indiana University and ninety selected high schools in Indiana, Michigan, and Ohio. The program offers college credit to about fifteen hundred seniors a year who enroll in IU English, math, chemistry, psychology, and history courses offered in their high schools by teachers who are funded to participate with IU faculty in a summer seminar, fall and spring colloquia, and classroom site visits. For the last decade, I have taught the thirty-five hour seminar that introduces selected high school teachers to current methods in college composition and strategies for teaching the IU English department's first-year course, emphasizing analytical reading and writing. I also hold a composition colloquium in the fall that brings fifty or more of the English teachers in the

ACP back to campus for follow-up sessions to share pedagogical concerns and materials we've developed.

While students' reasons for taking a dual-credit composition course have to do with getting a head start on college credit and the academic work that will be expected of them, my reasons for working with a program that is technically outside my job description have to do with the bridging of high school and college English—a connection I have come to believe affects nearly everything we do and hope for as teachers of writing.

Dual-Enrollment Arrangements as Delivery of College Composition

Questions about delivery of dual-credit composition courses are inevitably tied to questions surrounding the delivery of all composition courses in the context of conditions at particular institutions. When writing program administrators whose programs rely on instruction provided by graduate teaching assistants who receive stipends based not on their teaching experience but on their scholarly potential have to defend the integrity of a composition curriculum, they know instruction in their program is only as good as each instructor's ability to deliver it. Programs dependent on contingent teaching labor can find themselves unable to meet the demand for sections of first-year composition, particularly when institutions increase the number of undergraduate admissions at the same time graduate programs providing teaching assistantships are shrinking. Faced in August with full sections of comp to which no instructor has been assigned, WPAs often hire last-minute replacements who may lack the background and preparation of the regular teaching staff. While failure (or refusal) to staff additional sections of composition may precipitate discussion of the need for more permanent budgeted lines in composition, unstaffed sections may also call higher administrative attention to a program's failure to generate maximum revenue within the current institutional configuration of first-year composition. If the English department can't come up with enough instructors, maybe there are other departments or new programs that can deliver lucrative courses required of all first-year students. No one knows better than writing program administrators, as Joyce Neff demonstrates, the extent to which required first-year composition in research universities delivers financially. In providing support for graduate students and in freeing a relatively large tenure-stream faculty to engage in specialized teaching and research, composition makes possible what Sharon Crowley refers to as English's "institutional base from which to operate an academic empire" (18), often with enough revenue remaining to float the rest of the liberal arts. In short, it's all market driven—the labor saving, the cost cutting, the replaceable workers. It's all corporate.

Comfortable before a group of fellow WPAs at the summer conference, many of whom face delivery dilemmas, I admitted to relief that the incoming freshman class that fall included a sufficient number of students who had already completed our dual-credit version of composition in their high schools before arriving on campus. A fellow roundtable discussant was appalled, insisting that nothing could substitute for the experience of students in his program's first-year course on campus. While I had no doubt as to the soundness of his curriculum or the rigor of his teaching assistants' preparation, I asked if he could guarantee the quality of what was taught in all sections of composition simply because instructors had attended an orientation workshop, taken a proseminar, or followed a common syllabus. Although I will defend the quality of TAs' teaching any time and anywhere, especially given their status, wages, and working conditions, I still have to ask, is the instruction provided by someone still engaged in graduate study, relatively new to teaching, and perhaps uninterested in composition automatically superior to that delivered by an experienced high school English teacher with some investment in how eighteen-year-olds think and write?

Maybe it's a matter of honor among WPAs, but generally we are the first to admit that what is taught is not always what is learned. Of course, the same can be said of dual-credit courses; what is delivered is still in question. Just because we pore over notebooks full of materials in a workshop for a week does not mean high school teachers provide all that I would hope for in a college-level writing course. In the last several years, however, rather than focus on what might prove that the two courses—on campus and off—are equivalent, or fixate on what makes the two versions of the course different, I have tried to pay more attention to how the composition courses taught in *both* sites might be strengthened as a result of a collaboration between the faculty, the TAs, and the high school teachers who work every day with the students we will see on campus in less than a year. Such collaboration was the focus of a recent endeavor that brought together first-year, advanced, and graduate-level composition courses and the reflective practice of preservice, high school, and college teachers. I will report on this project in my conclusion, but first, some context for my decision that dual-credit arrangements alone will not build a strong enough bridge between high school and college writing.

Over the last decade, my colleagues and I have worked to improve the delivery of the composition course our university offers for college credit in the high schools. We particularly wanted to avoid the dual-credit arrangement composition specialists fear, in which a university merely signs off on the curriculum of high school teachers it believes are doing a good enough job teaching "the basics" that professors would like to see addressed before students come to college. To undertake more than this, however, in my collaboration with experienced secondary teachers, I have had to work through some longstanding institutional assumptions that elide the important differences between high school and college—including the notion that any outreach by postsecondary institutions to high schools is automatically a smart and necessary thing. Or that because dual-credit teachers are experienced practitioners, university English faculty need only allude to lesson plans and strategies rather than model them as we would for instructors new to a particular course on campus. Over the years I have found it necessary to work more with what it means that we teach not just in different locations, as Paul Bodmer explains in the next chapter, but also in different cultural sites. The positions secondary English teachers occupy in their institutions, the sources of their authority with students and colleagues, and their attitudes toward the university intersect with old and new knowledge about the teaching of writing and have to be taken into consideration as we negotiate ownership of a dual-credit composition course that finally is *not* the same course as it is delivered into different sites.

Understandably, economics is also a factor in the delivery of this shared enterprise. IU's dual-credit program operates on the assumption that experienced teachers with master's degrees require a week of further professionalization in their subject area, for which they are paid a stipend plus travel, hotel, and meal expenses. (Many dual-credit programs assume teachers need even less preparation.) Instead of additional salary, the high school teachers with whom I work accept the "privilege" of adjunct faculty status and the opportunity to use real college texts and teach one or two of their classes every year to the top college-bound seniors. Since dual-credit programs typically do not and cannot hire, fire, or pay high school instructors, there is an understandable reluctance to be too critical of their pedagogy. Site visits to the schools provide an opportunity to observe classroom interaction, examine student papers, and discuss the challenges of implementing a college course in the high school setting. For these exchanges to be productive and not merely pro forma, though, site visitors ideally should have recent experience with the composition curriculum, if not with secondary teaching. Several years ago, the number of dual-credit composition offerings had grown too large for me to make all the site visits around the state, even with the help of half a dozen other English department faculty, most of whom, except for me, had not taught composition, much less high school, in a very long time, if ever. While the high school teachers welcomed the visits and chats with some of the very faculty they had known as students, they sometimes felt more annointed than professionally engaged in dialogue about pedagogy. There came a point when I felt that I could continue my involvement with the program only if we started taking the follow-up professionalization of teachers more seriously. I did not, however, just want to lay down more rules and restrictions. As is the case with the graduate instructors I supervise on campus, the teachers could be a community of peers who reflect on the changes they make in their teaching, in the process making for a stronger common curriculum than one constantly imposed and evaluated from above. Thus, I encouraged the ACP office to hire several of our very best retired ACP high school teachers to make many of the site visits and teach a section of the first-year composition course on campus, where they confer and collaborate with the faculty and graduate student instructors of the course. In recent years, based on their experience and, in one case, doctoral study in both English education and composition studies, we collectively developed an advanced composition course specifically for preservice secondary English teachers seeking certification. It is important that we share where the field of composition has taken us in the years since many of the teachers got their degrees and their high school positions and, at the same time, that we offer a content area composition course for new secondary teachers that attempts to unify English and language education writing pedagogy. We have managed to go from what felt like a top-down dissemination of the university course to the high schools toward a delivery shared among specialists, many of whom are familiar with English teaching in both sites.

The Role of Changes in Curriculum in Dual Enrollment

What has made this collaborative enterprise more complex is the extent to which the campus version of the first-year composition course has become increasingly focused on academic reading and writing across the curriculum. Key features of the process approach informed the curriculum of our dual-credit composition course in its early years, just as it did the course on campus, and traces understandably remain in that half of those teaching today were originally trained in that model twenty years ago. It was assumed that teachers needed to be brought up to speed on the so-called paradigm shift from product to process and urged to assign drafts, use peer writing groups, and de-emphasize form and correctness. While some veterans of the early days of the dual-credit program have recalled for me their enthusiastic embrace of the academic reading and writing approach adopted fifteen years ago, a good number admit their conversion took some time as the program's original, more expressivist emphasis was consistent with the role writing already played in their own lives or with the student-centered philosophy to which they were exposed in some of their education methods courses. In short, delivering the college-level course to the teachers who were to deliver it to the high school students used to be a simpler matter.

About twenty-five years ago, innovations in K–12 and college-level writing were more in sync. For instance, when I first taught K–12 English in an alternative school, the James Moffett I discovered in *Big Rock Candy Mountain: The Education Supplement to the Whole Earth Catalogue,* advocating a developmental sequence based on the distance between writer and audience, was the same James Moffett discussed at a conference I attended on composing at State University of New York-Buffalo when I worked as a poet in the New York City schools, and the same James Moffett I would later read in my first graduate seminar in composition theory. For a time, English at all levels shared a zeal for the process-not-product movement rooted variously in progressive politics, humanistic psychology, and cognitive research, resulting in what Bartholomae has called a celebration of the individual as fundamentally (or ideally) congruent with culture and history ("Writing with Teachers" 486). Hand in hand with the belief that solutions to more meaningful and effective writing lay in the processes of the individual mind was the assumption that conversion to the process model resided in the individual teacher, who (re)discovers herself as a writer and then replicates that discovery in her students. Connections between the improvement of student writing and teachers' own writing practices remain in college composition, but receive greater emphasis in K–12 initiatives like the National Writing Project and in English education methods courses (see Romano).

In the 1980s efforts to decenter authority in the classroom and not get in the way of students' efforts to express themselves, à la Donald Murray, replaced school writing that lacked personal and intellectual consequences, that is, the bullet-proof five-paragraph theme and the battleship term paper that sails into port at the end of the semester. Acknowledging, however, as does David Bartholomae, that "there is no writing that is writing without teachers" just as "there is no writing done in the academy that is not academic writing" ("Writing with Teachers" 481), my predecessor Barry Kroll expertly guided both the campus and the dual-credit program toward a new emphasis on academic writing that called for students to locate their positions in relation to the ideas of experts by moving them through a sequence of analysis, synthesis, and evaluative assignments tied to exploration of topics typical of disciplines across the curriculum. At first, this shift to a reading-and-writing-with-sources course was not so easily assimilated by all the high school teachers. Teachers whose chief capital lay in facilitating self-discovery through writing, in conveying a love of literature, or in the surveillance of form and correctness struggled to find their footing.

Perhaps because the process model allowed us to tap into awareness of our own writing habits (stages of drafting and revision, finding a voice), it was easier to sell and more comfortable to teach than trying to make visible the moves that successful academic writers inside the academy seem to intuit or imitate on their own. For a long time, many of the high school teachers adapted to the academic writing approach by focusing mainly on stages of the writing process or on students' manipulation of sources. Appropriate quotation, paraphrasing, and citation—all important skills, to be sure—got more attention in class and in the evaluation of papers than did students' critical involvement with the ideas in the readings taken from disciplinary or professional conversations. On my site visits to the high school classrooms, I observed a good number of teachers leading classroom discussion of complex issues based on the readings having to do with obedience to authority, gender roles, or genetic engineering, but few engaged the class in rhetorical or ideological analysis of the essays themselves. Good college-level writing, I believe, grows from work on both the interpretation and the construction of texts, and both are necessary if students are to understand the positions they are taking and the writing they are producing as "located in the perspective afforded by prior texts" (Bartholomae "Inventing" 596).

Instead of facilitating conversations with the ideas in texts, many of the high school teachers I observed engaged in what Sharon Sperry calls "brokering" for the university, assigning writing in order to dispense warnings about the writing that is yet to come from college professors whom some teachers construct as tougher, less merciful versions of themselves. The brokering position enabled some ACP teachers to draw on their prior teaching strengths as well as lore concerning error, proper format, and late papers, while others capitalized more on the contrast they imagined between personal and academic writing: "In high school, you have been writing about your experiences and opinions, but in college, it's all about other people's ideas; they're not going to care what you think. From now on, never use the personal pronoun *I*." In fact, just as in college, the weakest student papers I saw were those that cut and pasted together facts or received opinions, those in which students were unable to get out in front of their sources with an earned position of their own. Several summers of workshops finally convinced me that, while it is valuable to model student papers that do and don't grapple with complexity, that do or don't do a good job of weighing evidence or analyzing and synthesizing sources, these activities are apparently not enough to turn around hard-core notions of good writing and experienced teachers' roles in the production of it. Why were teachers perceiving only a portion of what we meant by academic writing? What, if anything, does the site in which the course is delivered have to do with that misperception?

Inventing the University Collaboratively

I finally came to the conclusion that because most of the high school teachers had been away from the university for a while, what they were missing were opportunities to engage in academic inquiry themselves in order to view the work of the university in that way. The dichotomizing of personal and academic writing, for instance, betrays a lack of awareness (or a forgetting) of what academics and professionals do when they make and debate knowledge and forge new but situated positions. On campus, we talk all the time of how one reads and writes not just to master material but to question, to refine and complicate ideas, and to join ongoing conversations in fields in which reasonable people can disagree. But what does that look and feel like?

Unlike most of our faculty colleagues and graduate teaching assistants, who readily branch out from mastery of texts and skills to ways of negotiating with one's culture and with other observers of that culture, the high school teachers are often reluctant to extend their authority beyond what they consider their traditional area, English, pure and simple. At first, some are anxious about teaching the readings from the required anthology (Behrens and Rosen's *Writing and Reading Across the Curriculum*) or assembling their own topical units, believing they lack expert knowledge on issues like gender roles and business ethics. I can appreciate that delivering information about good writing or delivering interpretations of *The Scarlet Letter* permits them a greater sense of authority than simulating nonliterary inquiry in the way that composition is delivered now. After all, the public perception of what makes for good writing and what works of literature mean is what has given postsecondary English a place to stand in the university as well.

Of course, when I say to the high school teachers, "Let's construct a classroom environment that invites the best sort of inquiry in college, and let's make the writing reflect that inquiry," perhaps I too am inventing a university—an ideal one that would locate the positions of students and teachers in a dialogue with the knowledge of experts in ways that, frankly, many colleagues in disciplines across the campus never do when they assign writing. Still, why settle for less? Why not try for even more than what the university expects? High school teachers can and do deliver more. In one summer seminar a teacher from a tiny rural high school told us that she now felt that introducing her students to the notion that writing is part of the way in which members of various professions make sense of competing theories for analyzing and solving messy problems would be the greatest gift she could give them, not just for college but for life. She chose to put together a unit on moral and ethical decision making because she felt her "sheltered" students needed to critically examine the reasons for their beliefs (for similar reasoning, see Meiland, "The Difference Between High School and College"). This sort of decision making on the part of the teachers alters what it is that they have authority over. They aren't our brokers and salespeople, but professionals. Nevertheless, many teachers, old and new, will teach as they are taught. So I decided in *my* delivery to concentrate less on the production of what can become overly prescribed assignments for papers and more on how to get students invested in academic inquiry. In short, if we want these teachers to invite inquiry—and if what we deliver is inevitably what they will attempt to deliver—we have to show them by inviting it ourselves.

We found that we could not just tell teachers how disciplinary conversations work; instead we now spend more workshop time investigating issues and texts that are perhaps new to all of us. In our last summer seminar, we explored controversies surrounding weight and body image in America, writing and sharing critiques, analyzing passages in articles from a variety of fields on the subject as well as scenes in Hollywood films like *Shallow Hal*. Rather than simply walk through the criteria for the trend-analysis paper assignment, framed by some theoretical essays on trend spotting (Gladwell), we explored together several trends that tap into particular cultural myths—including the Cinderella makeover as represented in a plethora of TV shows and films featuring plastic surgery, wardrobe consultation, and home improvement. A teacher who for some time was assigning a pretty standard five-paragraph "causes of a trend" paper that was light on analysis came to life, responding to the question "Why is this obsession with becoming someone else happening now?" with the suggestion that because Americans are frustrated in efforts to control the world situation, they have turned to a fixation on controlling personal image. "Like anorexia, it's about control," she said, "not the imitation of fashion models or the worship of pop stars."

Finally, a different mode of delivery—engaging in inquiry themselves—has to replace teachers' outmoded or nostalgic invention of the university as concerned only with deadlines, Fs for errors, professors who would have no time or patience to search for your thesis, or who won't care what you think. As a result of our changing focus in the summer and fall seminars, I have begun to see more writing as an ongoing activity in classrooms that take students' critical investigation of ideas as their subject matter. I still felt, however, that in order for teachers to exercise even more authority over the course, we needed to level the playing field by further professionalizing rather than patronizing them. For a long time I had thought it was important to let them in on more of the recent work in composition studies, a disciplinary conversation they could join for real in order to debate, resist, and negotiate what it is that we teach.

A Summer Session's Enhancement Grant for a "Bridging High School and College Writing" project made it possible last year for me to integrate a graduate course in composition pedagogy for English graduate students and returning high school teachers with an advanced expository writing course for preservice English teachers and two sections of first-year composition taught by two selected ACP teachers. The students in both the graduate and the preservice teacher courses read current composition theory and research relevant to the connection between high school and college writing in an effort to find common ground. Joseph Harris' *A Teaching Subject*, Victor Villanueva's *Cross-Talk* anthology, and Robert Tremmel and William Broz's *Teaching Writing Teachers of High School English and First-Year Composition* were useful for getting a diverse group of teachers and teachers-to-be talking about their literacy histories, writing processes, and experiences with academic writing on both sides of the desk. We focused particularly on the relationship between the writer's self and other voices and texts in academic writing with Harris' historical and theoretical categories of growth, voice, process, error, and community framing our discussion. I taught the graduate course and Ted Leahey, a retired high school teacher now conducting site visits and teaching composition on campus, taught the advanced writing course for the preservice teachers. We both required the students in our classes to read some of the same essays as the first-year students and to try their hand at writing several of the papers. In addition, our students constructed teaching portfolios that included reflective teaching statements, annotated redesigned writing assignments, and a case study of a student or phenomenon in one of the two sections of first-year composition. In addition, students in the 500- and 300-level courses took on several of the first-year composition students for tutoring on one of the paper assignments, which they later redesigned in light of what they learned. When they were not engaged in ethnographic observation, our students led several class sessions in the first-year courses, putting into practice strategies for finding an analytical focus, using evidence, or conversing with sources from the composition textbook with which we were all familiar on and off campus, *Writing Analytically*, edited by David Rosenwasser and Jill Stephen. Once a week, the 300- and 500-level classes met together, giving us an opportunity to discuss readings, evaluate sample papers, and discuss student writing problems and progress with the two teachers of the first-year composition courses who were also graduate students in my course.

Taking Stock

At this writing, we have only begun to take stock of what we all learned from this valuable collaboration. Returning ACP high school teachers were able to study up close on-campus college students' experiences with writing in the course and with writing in their other college courses at the same time that they were bringing some composition theory to their reexamination of practice. Because of access to the preservice teachers' discussion and final portfolios, we learned that they valued sustained attention to the teaching of writing, which they felt they were not getting in their methods courses, and the opportunity to examine students' difficulties with writing in light of composition theory and the writing they were themselves producing for the class. Perhaps most impressive are the returning high school teachers' case studies. One examined attitudes toward analytical writing of older returning students compared with traditional students in the first-year course; another looked at whether students with a professed religious commitment had more difficulty writing about religion than those without it.

In sum, we have all learned—processes and texts—that will help us reshape and deliver the high school and the on-campus composition courses. The teacher research on questions that arose in their practice underscores how we all contribute to the making of knowledge in composition, how we all practice not just writing, as the National Writing Project has long advocated, but critical inquiry, and how we all, including those of us on campus, still have much to learn from one another.

Works Cited

Bartholomae, David. "Inventing the University." In *When a Writer Can't Write: Studies in Writer's Block and Other Composing Process Problems.* Ed. Mike Rose. New York: Guilford, 1985, 134–165. Reprinted in Villanueva, 589–619.

———. "Writing with Teachers: A Conversation with Peter Elbow." CCC 46.1 (1995): 62–71. Reprinted in Villanueva, 479–88.

"Because Writing Matters: Key Points." National Writing Project. www.writingproject.org/pressroom/writingmatters/keypoints.html. Oct. 26, 2003.

Behrens, Laurence, and Leonard J. Rosen. *Writing and Reading Across the Curriculum.* 8th ed. Longman, 2003.

Crowley, Sharon. *Composition in the University: Historical and Polemical Essays.* Pittsburgh: U of Pittsburgh P, 1998.

Gladwell, Malcolm. *The Tipping Point: How Little Things Can Make a Big Difference,* Boston: Little, Brown, 2002.

Harris, Joseph. *A Teaching Subject: Composition Since 1966*. Upper Saddle River, NJ: Prentice-Hall, 1997.

Meiland, Jack W. *College Thinking: How to Get the Best Out of College*. New York: New American Library, 1981.

Moffett, James. *A Student-Centered Language Arts Curriculum, K–13*. Boston: Houghton, 1968.

Romano, Tom. "Teaching Writing Through Multigenre Papers." In *Teaching Writers of High School English and First-Year Composition*. Ed. R. Tremmel and W. Broz. Portsmouth, NH: Boynton/Cook, 2002.

Rosenwasser, David, and Jill Stephen. *Writing Analytically*. 3rd ed. Boston, MA: Heinle, 2003.

Sperry, Sharon Lynn. "Constructing College Writers: High School Composition Teachers as Cultural Brokers." Ph.D. diss. Indiana University, 1997.

Tremmel, Robert, and William Broz., eds. *Teaching Writing Teachers of High School English and First-Year Composition*. Portsmouth, NH: Boynton/Cook, 2002.

Villanueva, Victor, ed. *Cross-Talk in Comp Theory: A Reader*. Urbana, IL: NCTE, 1997.

9

Is It Pedagogical or Administrative?

Administering Distance Delivery to High Schools

Paul Bodmer
National Council of Teachers of English

When my campus began offering courses delivered over interactive television from our campus to area high schools as a way for high school students to accelerate their education, our vice president of instruction insisted that we were not changing the courses, only the delivery system. If delivery means being transported and if what is being transported is a fixed commodity, as in the case of a loaf of bread delivered by bicycle or station wagon, then my vice president was right—the delivery system does not matter.

For much of education, that is perhaps so. The professor owns the content, the information, and he or she delivers that information to the student—in the form of a lecture, a book, or a video, each one a means of delivery based on the assumption that knowledge can be not only banked but indeed *transported*, like a commodity, from one vessel to another. Put another way, knowledge is a bulk of material that can be absorbed or assimilated by a person who can be tested to see what percent of that knowledge has been absorbed. By and large, that is the view held by both public and academy. To verify this claim, walk over to the newest classroom building on your campus and count the number of rooms designed primarily for presentations or lectures, from large halls to small classrooms. The majority of rooms will have student desks facing one wall, and that wall will have some kind of focal point, whiteboard or chalkboard or projection screen, punctuated by a lectern of some sort. The message: Knowledge is a commodity that can be delivered to an audience. Making knowledge is not the domain of the student; it is the domain of the professor outside of the classroom who will bring it in and deliver it.

One problem with that view of knowledge is that it ignores any process of knowledge acquisition and knowledge making. Composition studies has shown us over the past half century that writing is not a commodity to be transferred, or transported from one vessel to another—delivered, as it were—but rather a process that each individual must learn as part of his or her affective, social, and cognitive development. As Chris Anson reminds us:

> The teaching of writing, unlike some other disciplines, is founded on the assumption that students learn well by reading and writing with each other, sharing perspectives, and finding some level of trust as collaborators in their mutual development. Teaching in such contexts is interpersonal and interactive, necessitating small class size and a positive relationship between the teacher and the students. (269)

What compositionists have discovered is that the location, the stimulus, the community in which this occurs all affect the learning process. Knowledge is made in the classroom through the interactive work of the teacher and the students. In such an environment, learning is dialogic (Stock 24) and results in the student's purposeful construction of meaning. It takes place in a controlled environment, is dependent on the interaction with teacher and other students, and is dependent on access to community. Changing any variable changes the outcome. While many of the structural elements of the institution are taken as a matter of course, and the assumptions about their validity have been proven over time, changing the delivery impacts those assumptions.

Assumptions about a first-year college composition course traditionally taught on campus in a two- to three-meetings-per-week sequence for a full term are assumed in Chris Anson's description of composition. At my institution, the English department was committed to these assumptions about first-year college composition:

- Learning to write and the act of writing are processes of making meaning out of ideas and images that the writer must struggle to comprehend and organize into a meaningful whole.
- Writing facility and writing itself are best developed through a community of colleagues who will join in grappling with the writer's question, and the writer will need to learn to negotiate with self and colleagues in that act of discovery; completing a writing is an act of negotiation between the writer and an audience, whether that audience is composed of peers or superiors.
- Creating an interactive community requires certain elements of size and congeniality.
- The instructor is crucial in establishing what is the most relevant material for that particular community to experience.
- Students must have access to material that will help them in their exploration.

Introducing first-year college composition to an interactive television audience in local high schools changes, dramatically, those five assumptions about the course. Specifically, adapting a college course for high school students changes assumptions about the campus culture and course integrity through the traditional or accepted expectations of

- class size
- student cohort, including expectations of similar environmental experiences such as classroom atmosphere, campus activities, and college readiness
- department and faculty control of course curriculum, content, and material
- ability to access resources for academic searches.

Background

I was the English department chair at a small community college in the American West when we began delivering first-year college composition to rural high schools within a fifty-mile radius of our campus. The delivery was to be through interactive television (ITV). Most of the high schools had an enrollment of fewer than two hundred students in grades 9–12. Most of the high school students saw this as an opportunity to take college courses while still in high school in order to accelerate their college careers. Over the same network, in addition to English, we offered history, mathematics, business management, economics, and psychology courses.

My story begins when our dean of instruction informed several of the department chairs that we would need to schedule a faculty member into the newly completed ITV classroom as each of our departments would be expected to deliver our beginning-level course to area high schools. We had been hearing rumors about the new ITV classroom and its potential use, but there had been no campus meetings to evaluate the effectiveness or needs of the system.[1] Our vice president of academic affairs talked loudly and consistently about its role as a different delivery system.

We had already developed partnerships with the local high schools, allowing high school students to enroll in our on-campus courses. As an English instructor, I had taught several classes that included high school students electing to take my first-year college composition course. I had always found that after the first few weeks of trepidation, the high school students were accepted as equals by the other students, and the class proceeded with no problems. Our naïve perception was that this new venture of including high school students in the college classroom, connected electronically, was but an extension of already accepted practice, much as the newly touted phrase "distance education" had been with us in the form of correspondence courses for much of the previous century. The difference was that this allowed an interactive and more immediate component to the correspondence course model, and we thought that it would allow us and the students to interact across barriers of space, reinforcing our belief that our courses were more than "read the book, and/or listen to the lecture and repeat what you read or heard on the test."

We had a studio ITV classroom on our campus for our traditional students and studio ITV classrooms in the area high schools. Each of the studio classrooms had two monitors. One monitor showed the teacher and the other monitor displayed whichever student was talking. The camera was voice-activated to focus on the noisiest student, but the instructor could pan the camera out to view the whole classroom at once. Demonstrations of the new ITV classrooms had focused on the marvels of the technology, and we were swept up in the view that this new development in extending our campus would be an answer for the long distances and sparse population in the American West. Technology would solve our problems of access and would allow us to teach our students, not just talk to them.

Almost all the English faculty used computers in instruction, and many had been experimenting with augmenting class work with discussion lists and email exchanges.[2] I talked to two of the English faculty who were technologically savvy and interested in computers and instruction, and one whom I will call Bill agreed to initiate the program. The other, Sally,[3] eventually taught over the network as well, so the experiences I will relate happened to both of them.

The instructors for the course enthusiastically entered into preparation, learning the mechanics of working in front of a camera, exploring ways of presenting materials over the network, and planning for a variety of classroom activities to help the students at the remote studio sites interact with the students in the on-campus studio site. All went smoothly until the first day of class.

Campus Culture

In a stand-and-deliver or banking-model classroom, where delivery is more important than learning, class size is determined by room size. Composition instruction, with its large paper load for faculty, and with the changing nature of composition instruction that includes considerable classroom interaction and discussion, has resulted in class sizes and student loads that are not dependent on room size, but on an appropriate size to accomplish the classroom activities. The position statements of both the National Council of Teachers of English and the Conference on College Composition and Communication indicate that no more that twenty students should be in a writing class and that no English faculty should teach more than sixty writing students per term (*Statement on Class Size*; *Statements of Principles and Standards*). At our campus we had established a maximum enrollment number of twenty-three students per composition class. While the number is higher than that recognized by CCCC and NCTE, we knew from normal attrition rates that our class sizes would average twenty students per class by the middle of the semester. When I had presented a copy of the CCCC statement to our dean during our negotiations for class size, he had informed me that the CCCC statement was a university statement, and as a community college, we had different assignments—we were not to do research, we were to teach—therefore, the number would be higher. In the final analysis, we were pleased with the class size set at no more than twenty-three students.

Bill checked his mailbox the day before classes and found he did not have any printouts or class rosters for the ITV class, but all his other classes were full. When he called the ITV administrator, he was told that the ITV rosters were not ready yet and would not be until the first day of class when all the students at the remote sites were officially registered. Bill was not to worry, though, as the courses were scheduled, and he would have students. When he walked into his class of 23 students on the first day, all the desks were filled. The system technician said that all the remote sites were up and ready, and when Bill looked at the monitors, he found that site A had 15 high school students, site B had 20, and site C had only 12, for a total of 70 students, plus his regular four on-campus sections with 23 in each. In other words, rather than the 115-student normal load for our campus (five sections of English), he now had 162 students, and he needed to contend with a completely different kind of preparation for his one first-year composition class with *70* students.

Because the computer system recognized each classroom site as a separate class, each had a maximum enrollment of twenty-three. In courses where the mode of delivery is simply lecture, the ITV classrooms can be infinitely expandable, but in classrooms where teaching and learning is dialogic, size must be controlled. In making this change, we had not recognized that the negotiation for the delivery system to accommodate interactive classrooms also meant negotiation with the registration system.

We had other problems as well. By the time Sally taught the ITV course, for example, we had solved the numbers problem by placing a cap of twenty-three students on all sites for the same course. Sally had decided that the best way to do peer response groups would be to have groups at each remote site. She walked into class the first day and had a studio class of twelve students, five students at high school site A, three at site B, and one at site C. The total number of twenty-one was fine, but the one student at site C would not have a group on site. To accommodate multiple sites, we had to consider other issues as well. We knew that groups of three to five would work effectively, for instance, but the groups had always been able to spend some time getting comfortable with each other. To set up one or more groups that would work together over the ITV network while other groups were working in the classrooms would cause a problem in monitoring the groups as well as in disrupting the group activities.

What we discovered is that we would need to negotiate maximum and minimum numbers for sites. If, as my vice president was wont to say, it is just a different delivery system, we needed to recognize that delivery in teaching and learning delivers the whole environment of students and teachers engaged in interactive dialogic growth.

Preparedness for College Work

Our institution is open admissions, but we have assessment and placement. Using the ACT test, we place students quite accurately into three different categories. Those who score below 12 on the ACT must enroll in a precollege writing class. Those who score 13 to 21 can enroll in the regular first-year college writing class but must concurrently enroll in a writing lab that will meet for one hour a week. This course is administered by the writing center. Those who score 22 and above enroll in the first-year writing course without the necessity of a lab. They may, however, use the writing center as much as they want. All students do a writing sample the first week of classes, and the instructor makes recommendations for re-placement, if necessary. This system works very well for our on-campus students, all of whom have been required to take the ACT test for admittance.

Because high school students are not required to take the ACT test, and requiring them to do so would delay the start of the program for at least a year and would be an added expense for the high school students, the administrators who negotiated with the area high schools agreed to excuse the high school students from the admissions assessment, relying instead on the recommendation of the high school principal to select only those students the principal deemed ready for college work.

The principal at one of the remote sites convinced our dean that all his high school students were exemplary students and certainly would score in the top percentage bracket of college-bound students. In one class, a student simply was not progressing, and the student's writing samples amply demonstrated that, had this student gone through our assessment program, he would not have been placed in the regular first-year college composition course. Moreover, there was no support system in the area high school—no writing center, no tutors, no help. And the instructor agonized over the failing student because dropping him would have made him the only one in the high school class who was not taking college composition.

These problems—of class size and student preparation—were caused by lack of anticipation of how ITV would change the classroom, but they were easily solved by clarifying our admissions standards and class-size requirements.

Student Culture

The transition from high school to college marks an important divide. Whether attending a residential or commuter campus, students attending the campus share in that campus environment. They are college students. In most cases when high school students attend classes on our campus, they quickly become part of the student cohort because they compete evenly, and they often do not mention or elaborate on the high school world. They are, for all intents and purposes, college students.

Those observations don't hold true for the ITV experience. Sally's course, for instance, began well. The high school students at the remote sites were reticent at first, but Sally did several exercises that relieved their anxiety and encouraged them to interact with students in the on-campus studio. Then she noticed an interesting dynamic: The on-campus studio students were becoming reluctant to participate. When they did, there were slight but noticeable put-downs of the students at remote sites. Apparently, the on-campus college students resented the high school students, particularly when the high school students were doing quite well. Sally visited with the high school counselor and found that the high school students scored much higher on the entrance exams than the on-campus college students.[4] In addition, our freshmen wanted to be regular college students, not in a class with high school students, so when they found that the high school students were doing better than they were, they retaliated in the only way they could, by trying to diminish and sabotage the high school students' efforts.

Again, in a stand-and-deliver teaching framework where students never know who else is in the class, this is not a problem. But when we are creating interactive, dialogic communities, the composition of the community, the culture, is a dynamic that directly impacts student involvement. If the teaching-learning dynamic is dependent on the college culture, then we need to discover how to give the college experience to students at the remote site. More importantly, and much more difficult, is creating an experience that mitigates the high school–college divide. The students at the remote site are not part of the college community, and in this instance they were reminded of that quite powerfully.

Course Integrity

Many first-year college composition courses introduce students to academic inquiry by requiring them to do some writing from sources. Traditionally, that has been accomplished through the campus library. The Internet has provided an alternative way of searching, and as more information becomes available online, institutions are able to expand their own resource base.

If the course is delivered to a small, rural high school with a very limited library and limited online searching available to the students, another administrative problem occurs. Technology is solving this problem as more material becomes available online. However, the lack of access to typical print sources such as journals and professional books limits students' abilities, with the result that they arrive on a college campus having taken courses that we assume will prepare them for academic work, but not having received the assumed preparation.

Another problem concerns the curriculum. At my institution, the college determines the curriculum through the Faculty Senate Curriculum Committee, which approves all programs for the college. It is the department's responsibility to develop and approve the syllabi for each course in the curriculum, and it is the faculty member's responsibility to develop the methodology and materials to teach the course. The faculty member uses her or his academic knowledge and skill to develop the materials to teach the curriculum. The bottom line is that the faculty member is given a great deal of latitude in choosing which materials would be most appropriate for the most effective learning.

A common assumption in this model of teaching and learning is that college students are adults. Even though legally many are not, we treat them as such. They are expected to engage fully in conversations and discussions of controversial topics in politics, religion, history, biology (including evolution and sexuality), economics, and philosophy—in short, to be fully functioning adults who will be challenged by the ideas put forth in the academy.

Because students in their traditional coursework have been located on a physical campus, whether residential or commuter, they are expected to be a part of that particular campus culture—research institution, comprehensive university, liberal arts college, two-year college—and as such, they bring their various interests and abilities to our classrooms, sharing in that same atmosphere and accepting each other as part of that community. One institution with its set of regulations is the home for all of the students, all the students are college students, and all will participate in that culture. And in fact, new faculty learn to negotiate the particulars of the campus culture, as do the first-year college students.

As this volume makes clear (see especially Redd, for example), the campus culture bears a direct relationship to the classroom culture, of course. Earlier in this chapter, I mentioned that one of the assumptions about writing instruction that our campus used was the practice of students working with fellow students to investigate, explore, and negotiate meaning in their work. One typical assignment was to have the students write against another text, in most cases a text with which the whole class was familiar. We tried to use material that would challenge our students, both in comprehension and concepts. We used a variety of texts and textual forms, and as we moved to ITV instruction, one particular instructor had decided to use a film. He could show it over the network for class viewing and discussion. Because the class periods are an absolute fifty minutes in length (the system is designed to shut down on a common clock between periods to accommodate a full day's schedule), he selected a ninety-minute film with the intent of showing it in two class periods.

The video started and just after the first scene opened, one site went blank. The instructor, assuming a technical problem, asked, "What happened?" One of the students from the remote site replied that the principal had walked by, had seen what they were watching, and had pulled the plug on the machine, remarking as he did that students were there for an education, not to watch filth. The instructor signaled the technician on our campus to pull the video so that all the sites were now visible on the monitors. The students wanted to know what was going to happen. All the instructor could say was he would investigate, and he dismissed the class.

The instructor related the problem to me as department chair and left my office. I was in the process of developing the letter to the high school principal about academic freedom when the call from the vice president's office came in. I was to report to the president's office right away about one of my problem faculty members. When I got to the vice president's office, I was told that I needed to watch a video to see what kind of filth my instructor was showing to high school students. I refused to watch the video and asked what this was about. I was told that one of *my* faculty members was showing pornography to high school students, and that we could not be accused of corrupting minors, particularly because this was a legislative year. I asked about the circumstances and rationale for whatever was being shown, and I heard the administrative version of what the instructor had told me earlier. In addition, the vice president of academic affairs informed me that the high school principal had called him and told him that one of our instructors was showing pornography, and he would not allow his high school students to watch pornography, so he turned off the machine.

This turned out to be a major event on our campus over the next few days, culminating in a meeting between the president, the vice president, department chairs, and faculty who had taught over ITV. The administrative view was that we needed to be careful about the image we were presenting. Several faculty members from other disciplines chimed in that they were careful to not choose inappropriate material, which finally brought us to the heart of the problem—what is appropriate in a college classroom with legal adults may not be appropriate in a college classroom with legal minors without the approval of the minors' guardians.

Several factors frame this issue. The first factor, of course, is the nature of the video, *Kids*, an R-rated film that had come out in the early 1990s. The instructor had viewed it, and he had talked to a couple of his students from the previous year who were at the same showing. His discussions with his former students convinced him that it would be ideal for raising questions about the world of adolescents. One of the early scenes, with actors costumed only in underwear kissing passionately, was the scene causing the high school principal to pull the plug. Interestingly, while the principal was incensed, most of us on college campuses would not think twice about screening material for students, whether they are under or over eighteen. All our students are expected to be adults in an adult world. If we choose to use an R-rated video for class discussion (such as most any movie, including contemporary presentations of Shakespeare), we use it. If we discuss a piece of literature with a joyful proliferation of cursing in it, so be it.

The second factor in this case is that administrators and faculty from other disciplines were invited into the discussion of material for a composition classroom and allowed to make judgment calls on what is appropriate in someone else's discipline. Ultimately, we were able to turn the discussion to the major issue, which is the issue of nonadult students in college courses and the effect that has on the syllabus—and ultimately on the curriculum.

The third factor, and the major one, is that the high school principal was controlling the syllabus in a college course. The high school principal was determining what was appropriate material for engaging college students in challenging discussions. And there were other cases. In another English instructor's ITV classroom, for example, the faculty member asked her students to turn in song lyrics for discussion. She reproduced them and returned them to the school. One of the students chose lyrics with the F-word in it; a principal saw it and pulled the student papers. End of assignment. End of day's work. Lesson plan destroyed.

What happened at our institution happened because we were very eager—perhaps too eager?—to try a new delivery system, and we had not fully explored the consequences of that system. Most of the supporters of the ITV delivery of courses to high school were still thinking of delivery systems as inert—what counts is the text, and any voice, any face, any medium can produce it. We were discovering what happens when delivery involves a different environment with different controls on that environment. In our case, we lost control of the environment, and because we lost that, we lost the curriculum—at least temporarily.

Conclusions

The problems described here are both pedagogical and administrative. It is the department chair or the program administrator, the one most familiar with the appropriate curriculum and pedagogy for instructing in her or his discipline, who will need to confront these issues. It is she or he who must contend with the dean, the vice president of instruction, the president, and other academic officers to ensure that the particular demands of that curriculum are supported by the institutional structure. The problems that we encountered had to be solved structurally. What we learned is that while the initial agreement and negotiation with the partner high school is negotiated at administrative levels that seldom include a department chair, when the department is asked to teach on this delivery system, we need to negotiate to establish procedures and practices for our courses to succeed. Our standards for teaching English over the ITV network, developed later, include the following:

- Class size must be clearly and effectively negotiated to ensure that instructors are not overloaded with students and that the student population at each site will be able to work with the course activities. We follow campus practice so that maximum size is established at the total of twenty-three students for each section of the course, regardless of the number of sites. We initially tried a minimum number limit, but the instructor decided she would waive that and have small groups of five students interact electronically if she were allowed to travel to the remote sites to honor each group of students equally.[5]

- Appropriate assessment and placement must follow the campus procedures. We allow into the remote sites only students who have scored 22 or above on the ACT.
- Recognition that all the students are *college* students is essential. We developed a consent form that each student's guardian had to sign that allowed that student, even though under the legal age of eighteen, to read, view, and discuss college-level materials. The parents and guardians were much more receptive to this than the high school administrators, but a certain amount of education about academic freedom is essential at this point. This is an excellent opportunity, by the way, for educating both high school administrators who will advise their students on college work and parents about the purposes and culture of higher education.
- Academic search processes must be established that are consistent with good academic searches. In some cases, a field trip to the college library by the remote students is one way of accomplishing a familiarity with academic searching.

Delivery does matter, and the problems it raises are both curricular and pedagogical. It is crucial that the administrative practices and procedures are in place to ensure that, at best, the delivery system enhances the experience, and at worst, it does not detract from the educational experience. From the outset of this chapter, I have emphasized that the culture of the classroom is a major factor in first-year college composition. Technology can solve some of the problems for delivering courses to distant high schools—that is, we can regulate class size, student preparedness through admissions processes, and student access to resources. We can also ensure that it is indeed a college course, with appropriate college material, that is delivered. What is not easily solvable is creating the college experience that is associated with a campus culture when we join two different educational levels. ITV classes between two different institutions of higher education often do not experience much trouble, because the students recognize that they are in similar institutions—they are part of the same culture. But attempting to bridge the divide between high school and college in the same classroom is much more problematic: the cultures are different.

Finally, it is the culture that we are delivering.

Notes

1. While all in academe would like to perpetuate the image of a powerful faculty who exert their academic freedom and control their own courses, the reality is most often less than that. In this case, the president wanted to be the first in the state to have strong ITV courses, the vice president of academic affairs and his dean of instruction were eager to be the administrators who championed the action, and many of us were willing to try a system that would ensure stable enrollments in a declining or stagnant economy. All those forces made it worthwhile to try the new system.

2. This was the time period when Web pages were not common and discussion lists were still somewhat cumbersome. The faculty who were experimenting with this found it much more time intensive than planned because of technical failures.

3. The names are pseudonyms.

4. This is not an aberration or coincidence. Our classes fill during registration on a first-come, first-served basis. Prime classroom times and regular classroom offerings always fill first. Registration order is determined by application order. The most serious and competent students apply first and receive early registration dates. The last students to register, as a general rule, are those least prepared for college work. Our ITV on-campus classes were offered during prime time, but because they were not a normal college class, they were not selected by the better students. Many of the on-campus students enrolled in the class had tested into first-year composition with the added requirement of the lab course. On the other hand, all of the students from the area high schools had tested in the top category and were qualified for first-year college composition without a lab course. We found this pattern was consistent during the time that I was department chair.

5. To try to honor all students as regular college students in a college classroom, the instructor traveled to the remote sites on a rotating basis. This partially deflected the notion that there is a campus class and that the other sites include merely visitors who might gain something by listening in.

Works Cited

Anson, Chris M. "Distant Voices: Teaching and Writing in a Culture of Change." *College English* 61 (1999): 261–80.

Statement of Principles and Standards for the Postsecondary Teaching of Writing. Urbana, IL: Conference on College Composition and Communication, 1989.

Statement on Class Size and Teacher Workload: College. Urbana, IL: National Council of Teachers of English, 1987.

Stock, Patricia Lambert. *The Dialogic Curriculum.* Portsmouth, NH: Boynton/Cook, 1995.

10

Design, Delivery, and Narcolepsy

Todd Taylor
University of North Carolina

Compositionists might have enjoyed Maxine Hairston's refreshing "Winds of Change," but, for most laypeople, the scene remains the same. College composition is delivered by an English prof (or graduate student) in a four-walled classroom to (often) recent high school graduates who submit essays.

Of course, the job of any specialist is to interrogate preconceived or superficial perspectives. So, when each of the chapters and authors in this collection turns over the rock of college composition delivery, previously concealed things scurry in all directions. Joe Harris reveals that one of the nation's leading writing programs is composed, by design, of instructors primarily from outside English studies. Becky Rickly tells us that students in her program meet online and not face-to-face a majority of the time; Joliffe and Phelan, Farris, and Bodmer each discuss how college composition is increasingly being delivered in high school. Marvin Diogenes and Andrea Lunsford declare that the academic essay might be on the way out at Stanford. Yancey and Redd remind us that the historically homogenous identity of the college student has shifted greatly over the last fifty years.

Each of these chapters describes prominent current practices that make strange the previously uninteresting question Who is delivering college composition to whom within what context? Most of the chapters focus on new kinds of teachers delivering new concepts of college composition to new kinds of students in new places. Consequently, instead of discussing composition delivery in terms of new faces and places, in this chapter, I want to pay attention to the more familiar scene of the typical teacher in a typical classroom with typical students (all the while admitting that the term *typical* should be contested). Following Martin Jacobi's lead, I also intend to return to the traditional sense of the term *delivery*, emphasizing the materiality and physicality of rhetorical acts—in this case, the body language of instructors and students operating in the architectural space of a four-walled, institutional classroom. I argue that college composition delivery shapes and is shaped by the physicality of its inhabitants.

Teachers do not often discuss writing instruction in terms of architecture and design. We might use these terms metaphorically, as in "the WPA is the *architect* of the writing program" or "she *designed* a wonderful syllabus for Composition 101." This chapter intends to use *design* more literally by trying to map or blueprint the most prominent ergonomic features of the way bodies behave in live, material settings. As the chapter title suggests, classroom narcolepsy can serve as a device to explore issues of delivery and design, since one of things that student bodies sometimes do is fall asleep in class, literally. I begin this consideration, then, by using Clifford Geertz as an imaginary auditor or design consultant for our classrooms, asking what features he might notice in a hypothetical ethnography of composition delivery. I then use Donald Norman's *Design of Everyday Things* as a way to support what must initially seem like two audacious ideas: (1) we have much to learn from students who fall asleep in class, and (2) from a design perspective, writing instruction is delivered more effectively in writing centers than in composition classrooms.

The Nature of the Composition Classroom

Clifford Geertz's well-known essay "Deep Play: Notes on a Balinese Cockfight" recounts his experiences as an anthropologist trying to understand the Balinese through one of their most prominent cultural obsessions: cockfighting. The climax of the story finds Geertz and his wife fleeing the authorities as they raid another illegal afternoon of poultry gaming. As an American anthropologist, Geertz is in no real danger of arrest, but he flees anyway, partly through instinct but mostly because of his desire to "go native" as essential to understanding Bali. What might we learn if Geertz were to conduct an ethnography of the contemporary composition classroom? How strange and exotic might composition teaching seem to the outside world? More importantly, what deep structures, what deep-seated ideas and values might an outsider identify that seem to govern our operation, especially inasmuch as we might be unconscious to or silent about powerful undercurrents?

Geertz's use of the term *deep play* comes from Jeremy Bentham, who defined it as an obsessive investment in an activity for which the apparent reward is irrationally out of proportion with its liabilities. The Balinese's deep investment in cockfighting revealed much about their culture. What might be revealed in a similar study of college comp? What powerful undercurrents shape the culture of college composition delivery? What issues, anxieties, and motivations are deeply embedded in how writing is taught, experienced, and received? How are our pedagogical designs shaped by deep structures, deep play? What makes students and teachers tick, and how do our deeper impulses manifest in lesson plans for delivering writing instruction? For example, one of my deepest and greatest anxieties about teaching is the fear of students falling asleep in class. Thus, Geertz might accurately observe that I deliver composition in ways to keep students awake. Fortunately, students don't apparently go unconscious in my classes as often as in other classes I have observed (or fallen asleep in myself)—probably because I'm so hyperconscious about the problem. But, how did I get this way, especially since I can't remember a single discussion about sleeping students in either my graduate training or the published research in rhetoric and composition? How could it be that academic narcolepsy is so important to the way I deliver instruction, yet nobody seems to talk about it much, if at all?

Students fall asleep in class, all of the time. The process-oriented, active-learning delivery methods that most compositionists currently endorse offer a de facto cure for classroom narcolepsy, even though little to none of our research directly acknowledges the familiar phenomenon of drooping eyelids, bobbing heads, and (sometimes) drooling lips. We should examine more carefully some of our unrealistic constructions of our students and their behavior, using in-class narcolepsy as a primary example of the things we have yet to admit and address openly. From this perspective, composition's active-learning, workshop-oriented pedagogies can be described as a style of educational delivery that literally aims to keep students awake. Online classrooms, dual-enrollment programs, new generations of students and teachers, and so on each profoundly reshape composition delivery. Such programmatic issues and topics regularly come to the surface in professional conversations—at conferences, in online discussions, in local meetings, through scholarship, in this collection, and occasionally in the press. These are essential considerations. But there is also much to be learned from a less telescopic and more microscopic perspective on the way composition has been delivered since Hairston's "Winds of Change" blew through. I have in mind a consideration of something analogous to the quantum-mechanics of composition delivery. Like subatomic particles whose behaviors defy initial expectations, how strange might the bodies moving in the space of the composition classroom appear if we examined them radically close up?

The Design of Everyday Teaching

Yancey's opening chapter establishes a vocabulary for questions of college composition delivery. One of her most prominent terms is *site*, and many of these chapters explore different or emerging locations of delivery—some literal, some figurative, some virtual. Yet, compositionists lack the kind of detailed vocabulary that architects or designers have for discussing physical sites, for analyzing the ergonomics of instructional delivery. Thus, it helps to consider a basic vocabulary of design.

Design is most canonically defined in terms of its elements and principles. The lists vary, depending upon whom you ask, but the elements of design generally include line, shape, direction, size, texture, color, and value. As established and useful as the elements of design might be, discussions about the principles of design are more interesting and relevant to composition studies, perhaps because such principles are explicitly rhetorical—they always discuss how a designer should create an artifact to "work" for an audience. Thus, it may be no surprise to learn that while there may be reasonable agreement on the specific *elements* of visual design (like those we enjoy regarding the elements of language), opinions differ widely on the specific *principles* of visual design. Linda Goin, for example, lists balance, contrast, direction, economy, emphasis, proportion, rhythm, and unity as the principles of design for all "design disciplines including . . . writing." Clement Mok and Vic Zauderer write,

> To design is to solve a problem. . . . You must understand the problem, define the goals, plan the steps, and generate a solution. Clearly defining the problem is intricately tied to understanding. Planning involves developing a clear approach and process for solving the problem. Only then can you look at execution.

Goin's taxonomy seems more aesthetic, while Mok and Zauderer are more industrial or functional.

Visual design theorists and artists have a lot of experience and advanced sensibilities when it comes to working with the tactile, with the material. Our first assumption might be that such experience binds visual designers too tightly to aesthetics, to the beauty of something as opposed to its function. However, the vast majority of things designed, seen, and used are not museum pieces; the *functions* of everyday things are often more important than their mere *looks,* a point particularly important to the delivery of composition. If we could get Clifford Geertz to study the delivery of college composition, the primary object he would consider would not be our published scholarship (like you're reading now) or our syllabi, but rather our classrooms and courses, in all of their three-dimensionality. Our documents, our essays and course materials, may be rarified (although important) like museum pieces, compared with what we might actually see when we watch composition being delivered live, in a classroom or online. What sort of things would Geertz, Goin, Muk, or Zauderer *see* when composition is delivered? What forms of balance, contrast, direction, economy, emphasis, proportion, rhythm, and unity would be visible in our teaching? What apparent classroom problems, goals, steps, and solutions reveal the deep structures of college writing instruction at the beginning of the twenty-first century? How do the ergonomics of delivery both reflect and reshape pedagogical design?

My thesis here is that a study of the tactile design of typical, contemporary composition classrooms reveals that one of the primary problems our pedagogical delivery systems aim to address is that of keeping students focused and on task, as revealed most literally in attempts to keep them awake. And, whereas design concepts like unity and economy might apply to curricular design within more abstract discussions, I'm more interested at present in looking at the composition classroom as a very common, everyday object. In fact, the composition classroom may be one of the very most common, everyday academic "objects" on college campuses. Thus, I'm more interested in design principles that aim to apprehend commonplace objects than those that are more likely to have emerged from the study of fine art.

Donald Norman's research on design has studied doorknobs, faucets, telephones, and instruction manuals. He was called upon to evaluate what went wrong at the control panels of the Three-Mile Island nuclear plant, and he works for Apple Computer. His book, *The Design of Everyday Things*, is required reading in many design communities. And, of course, Norman has his own set of essential design principles. According to him, a good design must provide users with (1) an effective conceptual model, (2) reliable feedback, (3) limited pitfalls, and (4) positive affordances. Norman is also adamant that a failed design for a commonplace object is the fault of the designer, not the user, since everyday things, by definition, should be designed for mainstream use. He writes:

> Affordances provide strong clues to the operation of things. Plates are for pushing. Knobs are for turning. Slots are for inserting things into. Balls are for throwing or bouncing. When affordances are taken advantage of, the user knows what to do just by looking: no picture, label, or instruction is required. Complex things may require explanation, but simple things should not. When some things need pictures, labels or instructions, the design has failed. (9)

In other words, a good design is transparent in the sense that almost anyone can apprehend at first glance how it works and what they are to do—the apparatus, the mechanism, should not interfere with the work to be accomplished or the problem to be solved.

What might Norman see if he studied the design of the everyday writing classroom? Would he see affordances that give strong clues to the students as to how to operate within the pedagogical design? Are the mechanisms—physical ones (chalkboards and textbooks) as well as pedagogical ones (group work and dialogue)—well suited to their ostensible purposes? Is composition being delivered effectively? Those answers would depend, of course, on what kinds of courses one observed, and when. Consider, for instance, the so-called current-traditional, or proscenium, classroom. What might Norman's design principles teach us about a current-traditional class meeting?

If one were to undertake the kind of tactile, kinesthetic examination of a composition classroom that I call for, in which the observer focuses most intently on the literal actions of bodies in space, what would she see? Current-traditional delivery would feature an instructor standing alone, at the front of the class, broadcasting a lecture, while students sat in rows facing the front of the class, trying to listen intently and talking rarely, while all the participants moved their eyes between the player(s) facing them and the words on the pages in front of them. In contrast, in the contemporary classroom, students spend time in a variety of physical orientations and activities. Sometimes they face the front of the space while the instructor or another student speaks. Compared with a straight lecture, this delivery is marked by frequent interchanges between a main speaker and the audience. A prominent feature of this design is that students and instructors occupy a variety of arrangements, often within a single class meeting. Students typically work in small groups, reading, talking, and writing amongst themselves, while instructors cruise throughout the room. Students in the new design also often work quietly and individually in addition to doing group work. It's thus clear why the current-traditional approach is called teacher centered while contemporary delivery is termed student centered.

How might these very different orchestrations of student bodies be understood in terms of Norman's design principles? With current-traditional delivery, the instructor might, at best, explain to the students verbally or in a printed syllabus that by listening to lectures and by reading and writing about acclaimed literature, the students will themselves become better writers. It seems unlikely that such instructors would specifically articulate to their students this *conceptual model* of the enterprise of the current-traditional course, but it is clear that model is in play. It seems more likely that the teacher in this case would simply hand out a reading list and start lecturing. *Feedback* in this design would emerge minimally in terms of live questions from the students and answers from the professor about the lectures, but the primary form of feedback from the users (the students) to the designer (the instructor) would be the papers that students wrote, which the instructor would evaluate in terms of whether they demonstrated that the student had indeed been listening to the lectures, completing the assigned readings, and assimilating the entire experience as demonstrated through writing proficiency (as reflected largely in terms of lack of error). This design asserts that by *constraining* the students only to the elevated, refined speech of the instructor and the language of the literary artist, the curriculum (and the instructor as its agent) will help improve student writing for lack of exposure to corrupt forms of literacy. Students are afforded the opportunity to perform appropriately within this design, and these *affordances* are assumed to be apparent by the nature of the examples contained in the instructor and the literature.

So, according to Norman's principles, is the current-traditional course an effective everyday design? It may very well be, if the problem is that students do not listen to or obey their teachers. But, if the design problem is delivering composition in a way that improves student writing, then at least twenty years of linguistic and composition research demonstrates that the teacher-centered design does not work, much as one of those chic glass hotel doors with no indication of where or how to open the thing fails. In fact, the design is so poor in terms of the everyday task of teaching writing that one must question whether the current-traditional approach is intended for common use or highly specialized application—whether or not the current-traditional paradigm is an everyday thing at all. Like the chic glass doors, the current-traditional design *is* an effective design for giving access to those already in the know, precisely because both offer the novice faulty conceptual models (is it a wall or an opening?) and a lack of effective constraint, feedback, and affordances (only those who already know can work the thing, and thing itself offers no real information about its proper operation).

In contrast, a student-centered delivery seems to follow Norman's advice for the effective design of everyday things. Foremost, a student-centered course follows Norman's admonition that a poor everyday design is the fault of the designer, not the user. If the student can't use the course effectively, the design must change. The conceptual model for the writing-workshop class is contained and apparent within the design itself: students will become better writers by practicing writing, not by talking about writing in abstraction. The constraints match the model: if the student is constrained by the pedagogical design to write and revise repeatedly, she will gain experience and improve. Since multiple revision of student writing based upon live feedback is the core activity of the workshop classroom, the feedback element of this design is wholly apparent in and integral to the design. Lastly, the workshop design affords the writer multiple opportunities to grow, to get it "right," as long as she participates consistently in the agenda. And, again, what makes this design so effective, according to Norman, is that each of the design principles—the conceptual model, feedback, constraints, affordances—is apparent in the design itself. The apparatus and functions of the workshop, as the primary approach to composition delivery, are contained in the object itself, much like a well-designed door with a push-bar on one side and a pull-handle on the reverse.

Or maybe not.

Delivery for the Napster Student

If we think in terms of what the physical bodies of students and instructors literally *do* while composition is delivered, we may begin to improve our understanding of the teaching of writing, and we may begin to recognize that the workshop approach to delivering composition is not as student centered as it might seem at first.

Of course, I'm not the first to attempt this kind of critique. In 1989, Kate Ronald and Jon Volkmer published an important but often overlooked essay, "Another Competing Theory of Process: The Student's." The thrust of Ronald and Volkmer's argument is that our research is perhaps hopelessly out of touch with the experience of the real, live, material students we teach. To use two clichés from the era, composition studies needed to *get real*—as, in speaking of another context, Teresa Redd suggests—and Ronald and Volmer were *trying to keep it real*. Ronald and Volkmer boldly write,

> In general, we find that students' composing processes are influenced more by contextual factors than by strictly textual ones. Most of the students we observed and interviewed say that they always do their assignments "at the last minute" and that they therefore feel they aren't doing the best job they could. . . . As we spoke with students, it became apparent that the amount of time and concentration allotted to a paper depended more on the context of the English class in the person's life than upon the rhetorical aims and attractions of the particular writing task. . . . Students' writing simply doesn't proceed as smoothly as many process theorists suggest. Here's a typical description from a student who is sitting at her kitchen table, trying to complete an assignment after work:
>
>> I finally came up with a beginning sentence that met my approval. Another interruption by my roommate. I had to leave the room or I'd never get this paper done. I moved onto the couch and rested my lap desk on my folded legs. I was not concentrating on the paper. All I could think about were irrelevant things. Another interruption, this time a phone call from a friend in Texas. I couldn't just cut her off after she called long distance. I hung up and started to panic a little and blocked everything out of my mind. . . . I started writing the introduction at 10:00 Tuesday night. At 10:30 I watched *Entertainment Tonight.* After the show, I went to the kitchen to get a snack. When I sat down at my desk with my food and my scratch paper in front of me, I noticed it was 11:07. I could not resume my writing at such an odd time. I had to begin either half past the hour or on the hour—nothing in between. So I cleaned my room a bit and thumbed through the *TV Guide* to see what else was on. At 11:30 I watched David Letterman and wrote during the commercials, composing nearly a paragraph. After the show I took a No-Doz, finished the paragraph, and went to bed.

So, it's clear that friends, family, television, and caffeine determine the way students write and the ways they receive the delivery of composition, arguably more so than sacred cows like *ethos*, *revision*, *peer feedback*, and *voice* enter into their consciousness. Note, in particular, that the student took a caffeine pill after midnight to stay awake, "finished the paragraph," and then *went to sleep*.

If you talk to students, or watch students, or watch them fall asleep in class, it's obvious that materials like caffeine and alcohol are (too) often a very large part of their college experience, not to mention illegal drugs—which further underscores this question: Why do we *not* talk about such important "centers" to many of our students' lives, since they clearly influence the way composition is received? Robert Brooke's 1987 essay "Underlife and Writing Instruction" made the point that compositionists have much to learn from unauthorized student behaviors such as passing notes and poking fun at instructors behind their backs. If contemporary composition delivery were as truly student centered as it struggles to be, we would have taken Brooke's charge more to heart, and we would now have abundant research on issues like falling asleep in class, drug and alcohol abuse, and stress. Sexual behavior presents another enormous influence on the way college students encounter the world. Of course, college courses do get at issues of sexuality through discussions of gender and representation, but they are bound to be located within the safe, insulated, intellectualized bubble of academic talk. Consider, for example, how much thought and energy our students invest in the way they dress for class and the extent to which their clothes are a projection of their sexuality—not to mention social class. Once you begin asking the questions, the threads just seem to keep unraveling: Yes, what about money and social class? What about students who act arrogantly in class and seem to base their pretentiousness on family wealth or aristocratic position? What about students on the reverse of the social ladder, namely, those who seem displaced by lack of economic privilege? All teachers have witnessed such things, and they must either consciously or unconsciously influence the ways we deliver composition instruction. But why doesn't our research delve into such prevalent, everyday issues? Joseph Harris has talked about the power of cultural homogeneity as evidenced in that way everyone in his class on a particular day wore either corduroys or jeans. But like Brooke's discussion of student note taking, our interrogation into such apparently extracurricular influences tends to stop short of the really big, though traditionally taboo, issues that determine student experience.

There are many motives and impulses that dissuade us from talking openly about students who fall asleep in our classes and who may care much more about beer consumption than peer collaboration. One prominent reason to keep quiet about these kinds of questions is that they reveal that our pedagogies are actually more institutionally centered than they are student centered. Composition is delivered so that it sustains educational institutions more than it responds to the actual, material lives of our students. Fortunately, higher education is almost certainly more responsive to lived student experience than it has ever been, as evidenced by the sway of institutions like the Carnegie Commission, widespread endorsement of active-learning methods, and the emergence of composition studies itself. But there's still a long way to go. Consider, for example, the now widely heralded (although no doubt less widely implemented) institution of active learning. Centers of teaching and learning at western colleges and universities are largely advocates for active learning. They stress how ineffective lecturing is, and they have abundant research that demonstrates extremely low rates of retention for knowledge delivered through monologue. The key component of active learning is, obviously, that students are active: they are asked to move, speak, and perform a variety of tasks that ideally shift every ten to fifteen minutes within the span of a class session. This basic template for the active-learning class maps perfectly onto the most prominent design for the delivery of contemporary composition instruction, which is the workshop model. It's how we deliver composition, and it's at least in large part an antidote for falling asleep in class, although almost no one, even at the centers for teaching and learning, describes this schema in terms of academic narcolepsy.

If we deliver composition instruction in ways to keep students awake, this fact belies an institutional rather than student center to our designs, as Donald Norman's principles help explain. Imagine, again, that we successfully lured Donald Norman and Clifford Geertz away from their think tanks. Imagine that they had no exposure to active-learning theory or research in composition studies and that they were asked to evaluate the design of instructional delivery by observing a variety of classes. I think it would be easy for them to identify the conceptual model of the workshop pedagogy: that students learn to write by active practice in writing and receiving feedback about their writing. I believe it would also be apparent that the pattern of shifting action in the workshop is a constraint that prevents students from reaching the end of their attention spans and/or falling asleep. However, note how the users' sense of feedback within the design is *actually* mediated. The instructor typically surveys the action in the workshop, often moving from student to student or peer group to peer group, able to attend to only one unit at a time. The users of the workshop design, the students, get a sense of feedback, largely from their peers, but, in truth, this feedback is only at a mediated distance from the mechanism itself. In other words, the only real feedback between the user and the pedagogical design happens when the teacher participates in a specific interaction, when she delivers. To illustrate this point, imagine that Norman was also asked to compare the pedagogical design of the writing classroom with that of the writing center. The basic template of contemporary writing centers features a single student working one-on-one with a single, trained tutor. In the case of the writing center, the feedback is not as mediated as it is in the writing workshop. Many composition theorists, perhaps most notably Peter Elbow in *Writing Without Teachers*, might argue that peer interaction in the writing classroom isn't mediated at all, because the goal is to compel students to learn from their peers without the intrusion of the teacher. To be honest, the fact that I often have my students assign grades to each other's work suggests that the real, not mediated, experience I aim to promote is between students, not between the student and the teacher. But you know what? If you ask the students, not Peter Elbow or Todd Taylor, what *they* think about peer collaboration and assessment, they will almost always tell you that they gain somewhat from peer collaboration but what they *really* want is feedback from *the* teacher. What students really want, and what I'd honestly prefer to deliver to them, is abundant one-on-one interaction like that offered at the writing center.

So, why don't we more often deliver composition instruction through the one-on-one writing-center model, not a workshop design? I'm willing to speculate that Norman would agree that the writing-center model is a better design than the workshop model for teaching writing, because the basic objects (one expert and one student with idiosyncratic needs) in the writing-center design more naturally match the conceptual model of how to improve student writing.

To use an analogy from Norman's world, classrooms of twenty or so students meeting three hours a week (typically only at the beginning of college) are like a sophisticated modern telephone with a panoply of functions but only a very limited number of buttons to press. Based upon past experiences, anyone would have a general sense of what is supposed to happen (a class is meeting), but a first glance at the new design does not reveal exactly which object will produce which function. In contrast, the writing-center design is like a well-engineered car in which each control has its own function:

> When I picked up my new car at the factory, a man from the company sat in the car with me and went over each control, explaining each function. When he had gone through the controls once, I said fine, thanked him and drove away. That was all the instruction it took. There are 112 controls inside the car. This isn't quite as bad as it sounds. . . . Why is the automobile, with all its varied functions and numerous controls, so much easier to learn and use than the telephone system . . . ? Things are visible. There are good mappings, natural relationships, between the controls and the things controlled. Single controls have single functions. There is good feedback. (Norman 22)

There's no mistaking what will happen in the writing-center design: one student will work intimately with one expert about the student's own writing. The writing center model is so simple, so Zen, so student centered, so active, why isn't all composition instruction delivered this way?

Many of us would probably argue that we, in fact, do replicate the writing-center model in classroom settings, a point made earlier in this volume by Joyce Neff. Instructors often conference individually with students. They often try to train each student in the workshop classroom to function as a tutor, like those in the writing center. But, the rub, here, is that we "often" "attempt" to "replicate" the writing-center experience, because, institutionally, professional instructors can't afford to spend so much time working individually with students. The contrast in the vocabulary used to describe the writing-center design and that used to describe the workshop model is particularly revealing. Stu dents go to the writing center to *receive* help, yet this collection emphasizes how composition instruction is *delivered*. The term *delivery* has a one-way valence to it. It connotes the packaging of content at a source that is then channeled to the user, which sounds frighteningly like the current-traditional, Freirian banking models of teaching and learning against which we have campaigned so strongly. If our pedagogical designs were, in fact, deeply student centered, this collection's title might replace *delivering* with *receiving*.

But, of course, the tension in our focus between students and institutions and between delivery and receipt is precisely why these issues need to be discussed. So, what do we do in the meantime, until educational budgets are so strong that we can achieve the utopia of one-on-one (or at least very small group) delivery of composition instruction? Well, we first have to at least keep students awake in class. To do so, we need to attend much more intimately to the material lives of students: what they think about, their priorities, what they want, who they are, how their minds and bodies operate. For instance, research has demonstrated that adolescents and young adults need more sleep than others, and this awareness has compelled some school districts to change their daily starting times. The U.S. government reports,

> According to researchers, adolescents demonstrate different biological sleep and wake patterns than adults. In fact, a recently published study by Dr. Kyla Wahlstrom at the University of Minnesota, demonstrates the impact of pushing back school start times. After the Minneapolis Public School District changed the starting times of seven high schools from 7:15 A.M. to 8:40 A.M., Dr. Wahlstrom investigated the impact of later start times on student performance and the results are encouraging. Dr. Wahlstrom found improvement in attendance and enrollment rates, increased daytime alertness, and decreased student-reported depression. The National Sleep Foundation reports that children and adolescents require 9 to 10 hours of sleep each night, however, few actually get that much sleep due to daily school routines.

Hold on a minute. Start the school day at 8:40? Any working parent is likely to see the logistical nightmare this heresy creates. With any kind of typical urban or suburban commute, how can a parent get to work by nine if his or her kids begin school so late? Teachers and air-traffic controllers are not allowed to strike, because if one of these workers stays home, they can often force dozens of others to stay home from work as well—and this kind of domino effect is very bad for the economy. Thus, it's clear that at least one purpose of educational institutions is child care; it's part of our conceptual model and the design of the everyday thing we do. Schools deliver crowd control.

Much is being currently discussed about the changing nature of the students we must control. The radically changing demographics of college students (especially their increasing cultural and economic diversity) have been discussed extensively. Spurred in part by the Americans with Disabilities Act, theorists and administrators alike have begun to understand education very differently by having to appreciate the material experiences of disabled students. This chapter has itself been leveraged upon the very serious, debilitating, widely misunderstood and misdiagnosed disease of narcolepsy. Students who fall asleep in class are, of course, typically not narcoleptic. But the fact that narcoleptics have been historically misunderstood as lazy can help us better understand what is really happening when students fall asleep in class. According to Donald Norman's view, if students fall asleep, it indicates a problem with the pedagogical design, not the user. Instructors might like to learn that the culprit may not even be their syllabus, teaching methods, or style of delivery. The problem may simply be that the school day is poorly designed, because it starts too early.

Much has also been written about the need to redeliver education as "edutainment," because our students' worlds seem increasingly fast paced and media saturated. In "The Nintendo Generation," the National Academy of Sciences writes, "The eyes of the school children glisten with anticipation. Their fingers arch lightly over their computer terminals, waiting to tap out solutions to ever more difficult problems appearing on the screens before them. Any schoolteacher would be thrilled by such concentration and receptiveness. But these children are not in school; they're playing games in a video arcade." If video games are, in fact, a defining characteristic of the next generation, our first impulse is likely to be dismay. These games are especially troubling in their representations of violence and gender. They seem dangerously hypnotic, at odds with intellectual engagement and connection with community—even encouraging moral corruption. For example, the brief but potent Napster revolution from 1999 to 2001 seems to have encouraged the current generation to participate in and shrug off media piracy. In the spring of 2003 one of my students offered, without apparent hesitation or concern, to give me a downloaded DVD copy of a major motion picture *that was to debut in theaters the following week*. How can we deliver composition instruction to the Napster generation, who seems increasingly likely to be put to sleep by instructors who will never be able to compete with the dynamism of Lara Croft, a tomb-raiding anthropologist? If we read a little further into "The Nintendo Generation," we may find some answers:

> With today's technologies, the consumers of information can engage in dialogues instead of simply absorbing monologues. They can interrupt and redirect the flow of information. They can modify the complexity of information, the speed at which it is communicated, and its manner of presentation. They can control the elements of sophisticated multisensory experiences, combining audio, video, text, and graphics into a single immersive reality.

Creating a generation of media producers from within generations of media consumers is a pretty worthwhile goal, and it's probably a lot easier than we might think. I have found, for instance, that thanks to the Napster revolution, students are shockingly adept at capturing, editing, and composing digital audio. It used to take me days to teach basic word processing to students in the early 1990s. A decade later it takes me less than an hour to teach them how to compose an NPR-style audio documentary. Likewise, if we read a little further into the material lives of our students, if we begin to discuss more openly issues like student alcohol abuse, sexuality, media saturation, and sleep deprivation, we are likely to become much more effective in the designs we create for delivering college composition. Like Clifford Geertz, we should try more often to go native. Like Donald Norman, we should deliver designs that work.

Works Cited

Brooke, Robert. "Underlife and Writing Instruction." *College Composition and Communication* 48.2 (1987): 141–53.

Elbow, Peter. *Writing Without Teachers*. New York: Oxford UP, 1973.

Geertz, Clifford. "Deep Play: Notes on a Balinese Cockfight." In *Ways of Reading: An Anthology for Writers*. Ed. David Bartholomae and Anthony Petrosky. New York: St. Martin's, 1987, 299–335.

Goin, Linda. "Principles of Design." *Graphic Design Basics*. 2000. Accessed online at www.graphicdesignbasics.com/article1043.html. May 16, 2004.

Hairston, Maxine. "The Winds of Change: Thomas Kuhn and the Revolution in the Teaching of Writing." *CCC* 33 (1982): 76–88.

Harris, Joseph. "The Idea of Community in the Study of Writing." *College Composition and Communication* 40.1 (1989): 11–22.

Mok, Clement, and Vic Zauderer. "Timeless Principles of Design: Four Steps to Designing a Killer Web Site." *New Architect* 4 (1997). Accessed online at www .webtechniques.com/archives/1997/04/mok/. May 16, 2004.

National Academy of Sciences and National Academy of Engineering. "The Nintendo Generation." *Reinventing Schools: The Technology Is Now*. Accessed online at www.nap.edu/html/techgap/nintendo.html. May 16, 2004.

Norman, Donald. *The Design of Everyday Things*. New York: Basic, 1988.

Ronald, Kate, and Jon Volkmer. "Another Competing Theory of Process: The Student's." *JAC: Journal of Advanced Composition* 9 (1989). Accessed online at http://jac. gsu.edu/jac/9/Articles/7.htm. May 16, 2004.

U.S. Government. "Sleep Research and School Starting Times." www.house.gov/ lofgren/030402.htm. June 23, 2003.

11

Toward Delivering New Definitions of Writing

Marvin Diogenes and Andrea A. Lunsford
Stanford University

As one of the world's oldest technologies, writing has been redefined down through the ages, most often in response to changes in the technology itself. Emerging in middle eastern cultures almost ten thousand years ago as a means of recording trade, western writing systems have been linked to commerce, to trade, to exchange—to making things happen in the material world. Composition studies has been slow to attend to the history of its subject, writing, preferring to study writerly processes and the effects of writing rather than writing itself.[1] More particularly, composition as a field and as a set of teaching practices has been situated primarily in schools, and this positioning has had a powerful effect on the development of the field. Writing in school has traditionally been strictly regulated—assigned by teachers and then delivered back by students in easily assessed forms. As Bartholomae explored in "Inventing the University," students come to a very specific form of writing when they come to higher education. Thus the subject of writing itself, and especially its protean and epistemic nature, has often been beside the point in educational contexts, since anything that challenges the smooth functioning of the school apparatus is potentially disruptive. In such a system, delivery on the teacher's part emphasizes clarity of instruction and instructions; delivery on the students' part requires packaging prose in the required forms: calling attention to the historical and material conditions of writing serves no practical purpose and runs the risk of exposing and calling into question the premises necessary to preserving the status quo. As a result, writing becomes a decontextualized tool of assessment, with no past and no potential for change.

Such choices are understandable, given the role of writing in schools, the extensive and complex history of writing, the need to work across at least several languages when studying this history, and—for roughly four hundred years—the relative stability of writing in western culture. With the rise of print culture in Europe, writing increasingly meant black print on white or cream-colored paper, printed left to right, top to bottom, filling the space with text. This regularization of the production and delivery of writing—through increasingly mechanized processes of standardized formats and mass production—served the growing educational apparatus well by making writing itself less and less visible as a technology and more and more a transparent means of assessment.[2] As students from diverse cultural and linguistic backgrounds gained entry into U.S. schools formerly reserved for the economically and culturally advantaged, a narrow definition of writing (as an uncomplicated transcription of thought featuring orderliness and easy-to-measure correctness) served as a gatekeeper, simultaneously guaranteeing propriety and signaling membership in an educated class (Berlin; Faigley; Miller).[3] Cutting down on the choices available to writers in content and organization and also in the look of the writing on the page—margins, font size—made it easier for large numbers of students to be measured and ranked (Williamson).

Such stability can no longer be taken for granted, as evidenced most dramatically perhaps by the emergence of a relatively new field of study referred to as the history of the book (Chartier; Feather; Kilgour; Petroski; Armory and Hall; Woodmansee and Jaszi). The outpouring of articles and monographs in this field chronicles a specific age of the traditional print book, now drawing to a close, and examines in detail the material characteristics as well as the ideologies, the epistemologies, and—to a much lesser extent—the pedagogies associated with the book. Concomitantly, scholars in rhetoric and composition have pioneered work on electronic forms of communication, studying the emergence of what Walter Ong calls secondary orality and what we think of as an accompanying secondary literacy. If we accept Ong's understanding of secondary orality as a form of communication that appears to be oral but is actually "planned and self conscious" and deeply inflected by writing and print (289), then a necessary corollary may well be secondary *literacy*, that is to say, a form of communication that still looks a lot like traditional print literacy but that is deeply inflected by other media, including spoken words and sounds, video, and images of all kinds. It is our contention that this new literacy requires us to develop and make available to our students expanded definitions of writing.

For the present generation of college-aged students, reared and schooled in a culture of cable TV, computers, poetry slams, zines, the Internet, and the World Wide Web, writing is no longer a stable, black-and-white affair: writing is Technicolor, oral, and thoroughly integrated with visual and audio displays. This explosion of media and genres, which serves to blur distinctions between academic and nonacademic forms of writing, generates a new context for the traditional tension between school uses of writing—rewarding order, clarity, and propriety—and more popular genres often associated with low or youth culture. The boom in graphic novels provides a dramatic example of this general point. In a recent undergraduate course on the language wars, students read two such novels—Lynda Barry's *One Hundred Demons!* (which she defines as an "autobifictionalography") and Eric Drooker's *Blood Song*, a visual narrative without words. As Kathi Yancey points out to us, the mix of high and low cultures featured in the summer 2003 film *The League of Extraordinary Gentlemen* and the graphic novel it grew out of marks another challenge of contemporary writing to traditional essayist literacy. Students in the language wars class debated the pros and cons of graphic novels, ending up in a bit of a language war themselves over whether such novels can or should have a place in academic writing, or even an oblique relationship to it.

If, allowing for disciplinary differences, academic writing can be said to have a distinctive style—what Walker Gibson terms "stuffy," Winston Weathers associates with the linearity of Grammar A, and Richard Lanham refers to as "CBS style" (clarity, brevity, sincerity)—the "mediated" writing of the Internet age favors immediacy, quickness, associative leaps, and ultimately a more fluid and flexible sense of correctness. Secondary literacy, then, advances a looser prose style, infiltrated by visual and aural components to mirror the agility and shiftiness of language filtered through and transformed (or, more irreverantly, goosed) by digital technologies. Such a literacy, we have learned, shifts focus from the regularized writing that could easily be assessed to writing that is increasingly performed and performative. Della Pollack describes the features of writing that is performative as evocative, metonymic, subjective, nervous, citational, and consequential, in essence, a kind of writing easier to experience than to evaluate. Scholars of performance theory have done much to articulate this sense of writing and to move it well beyond J. L. Austin's distinction between constative and performative utterances. In this milieu, is it any surprise that students are increasingly performing their writing, in digital networks, in spoken word collectives, in poetry slams, and so on? If information wants to be free, as the Free Software Foundation, the GNU Project, and other open source code movements argue, it's perhaps natural that language and writing want to share that freedom.

Many argue that these changes in the technologies of writing are as or even more momentous than those associated with the complex move from a primarily oral to a mixed oral-literate culture. Whether or not such a claim is justified, however, new definitions of writing are emerging, at least implicitly. One mark that they are doing so can be found in the definition offered by the *American Heritage Dictionary*: "Writing. Written form. Language symbols or characters written or imprinted on a surface: readable matter. Any written work" (Morris). To contemporary rhetorical eyes, such a definition seems threadbare and highly reductive. Even the *Oxford English Dictionary*'s slightly more complex "Writing. The action of one who writes, in various senses; the penning or forming of letters or words; the using of written characters for purposes of record, transmission of ideas, etc." is clearly inadequate to today's arts and practice of writing.[4] We are not alone, of course, in noting this inadequacy. In a review and critique of the relationship between words and images in composition theory and pedagogy, Mary E. Hocks makes a related call, concluding that "new technologies simply require new definitions of what we consider writing" (630). In light of these inadequate definitions, we offer a tentative rewriting of terms:

> Writing: A technology for creating conceptual frameworks and creating, sustaining, and performing lines of thought within those frameworks, drawing from and expanding on existing conventions and genres, utilizing signs and symbols and incorporating materials drawn from multiple sources, and taking advantage of the resources of a full range of media.[5]

Scholars of composition and rhetoric have done much to make such a redefinition possible, as documented in *Computers and the Teaching of Writing in American Higher Education, 1979–1994: A History* (Hawisher et al.) and especially in the journal *Computers and Composition*, founded in 1983. In its twenty-year history, *Computers and Composition* has continued to challenge scholars and teachers of writing and rhetoric to reexamine their most basic assumptions about what it means to write and to read. Jim Porter's work also points in this direction; he explores "internetworked writing," a term that invokes design, production, and publication as well as collaboration and interaction. So a revised definition of writing has been implicitly evolving for some time in our field.[6] Still, any definition presents problems, and the one we offer is no different: Does it, for example, distinguish clearly between the technologies of what we're calling writing and other technologies of communication? Does it sacrifice useful distinctions between writing and communicating in an attempt to privilege writing? Does it too easily accept that writing must incorporate all technological innovation? Is it robust enough to cover all contemporary acts of writing? Is it comprehensible to everyday readers? These are legitimate and perplexing questions, ones we hope that readers of this essay will help address.

A year ago, computer scientist and architect of Stanford's Human-Computer Interactive Collaborative Terry Winograd called up many of these problematic questions when he asked why we were so interested in writing. After all, he said, almost all the writing our students would be doing in the future would be paragraph-long "crots" or lexia for hypertexts and PowerPoint presentations. In this instance, Winograd was overstating his case on purpose, to begin a productive conversation about how current college writing relates to career writing. But his overstatement serves our purposes of definition by highlighting the need to redefine writing more clearly in the communicative context of the world Winograd sees coming to dominance. Winston Weathers' Grammar B, for example, provides a useful way to position writing in this hypertext world without dismissing what we know of the history of style. If anything, freedom from traditional print settings (the $8\frac{1}{2}$-by-11-inch page) can create a fertile ground for a new burgeoning of Grammar B. After all, crots, in Weathers' taxonomy, already function as a prefiguring of hypertext in print; crots need not have any explicit connection to what comes before or after (either on the page or on the screen), although they may certainly be linked thematically. Perhaps what's happening now is an opportunity for some digitally enhanced and reimagined form of Grammar B to become the dominant grammar of mediated writing (see, e.g., Schroeder, Fox, and Bizzell). As Weathers documents, Grammar B has long been with us, though generally suppressed or consigned to creative genres. Such a change in its status and level of use, however, could well be another source of anxiety for teachers and students, especially those invested in keeping academic writing rooted in Grammar A. And while many of us will no doubt relish an expansion of stylistic and technological adventurousness in student writing (and our own academic writing), few if any would consider it a simple matter to prepare to teach such writing effectively, or to define criteria for evaluating it.

Even this brief exploration of Winograd's question and possible ways of responding to it helps point up the growing need to expand narrow definitions of writing and to attend to the challenges entailed in doing so, particularly those related to classroom pedagogy and to teacher training practices. We may still aim to teach students to take the rhetorical situation into account when making language choices, but if the rules are in the process of changing within the rhetorical zone of electronic mediated communication, how do we begin to transform our pedagogy? Can we articulate a full rhetoric of crots or of other nontraditional units of discourse? How do we describe to students the logic of relation, of association, the ways in which a sequence of separate screens or a collage of windowed screens creates meaning—not to mention how to know in what situations these sequences are rhetorically effective? What would it mean to begin teaching students to compose or create clear and effective crots, and how would that affect the rest of their school writing? In short, if the definition of *writing* is expanded in the ways we have been suggesting, how will we deliver writing instruction and how will our students deliver their texts? From an administrative perspective, how will writing program directors position themselves and their generally required curricula in the academy, moving actively to implement new definitions of writing, or maintaining a more conservative role in relation to the traditional forms of print-based writing that will likely retain power in our institutions?

Such considerations surfaced early on in the two-year review of writing conducted at Stanford University during 1999–2001. Out of that review came a recommendation, endorsed by the Faculty Senate, to expand the writing requirement from two to three courses for all students. It's interesting to note that the discussion in the senate focused more on the appropriateness of the word *rhetoric* as part of the new program's name than on the oral and multimedia presentation skills to be developed by students in the second level of the new requirement, after they completed a print-based research-based argument in the first required course. While all accepted that students need to be more effective presenters of their research, several faculty members cited the disreputable nature of rhetoric as a concern, associating it with deceitful and dishonest language use; others amicably defended rhetoric as a worthy field of study, while still others stated that the naming of the program should be left to its administrators to decide. In the end, the faculty took to trying to outdo one another in bits of epideictic discourse in praise or blame of rhetoric—and then voted overwhelmingly to approve the new name. What was missing was any in-depth discussion of how the world had changed to make an enhanced requirement necessary and what goals this new course should pursue. What was palpable was faculty dissatisfaction with student performance: "Students can't speak" and "Students can't present their work" joined the traditional lament that "Students can't write" as shared premises, leading to approval of the new requirement. Given the tendency of those outside writing programs to oversimplify writing and writing instruction, it's likely that we'll face a similar gap between our understanding of the challenges of teaching oral, visual, and multimedia rhetoric and the perspectives of those mandating improvement in this area. In anticipation of such gaps, we have been working in all our writing courses to deliver an enlarged, enhanced definition of writing.

A longitudinal study of writing that we launched in the fall of 2001 supports the need for such enlarged definitions and for additional attention to oral, visual, and multimedia discourses. When asked whether they had opportunities for making oral presentations outside of their first-year writing class, for instance, 66 percent of students said they had such opportunities "rarely" or "never"; only 7 percent reported "often." And when asked about their use of visuals and media for writing, 50 percent reported "none." Finally, when we asked about the kinds of writing they had been assigned, students identified nineteen genres they had been asked to engage in during their first year of college, but only 12 percent of those involved Web texts. In short, while Stanford is a leading university in technologies for writing and communication, the assignments given to its first-year students call overwhelmingly for traditional print-based texts. (Since we have followed this group of 189 students through their college careers—and now into their first year beyond graduation—we will be able to report how these numbers change across the years.) We have already benefited from the study, however, in designing the curriculum for the new required course.

This new second-level course, which we began teaching in winter 2004 and implemented fully in 2004–5, bears the simple title of Program in Writing and Rhetoric 2 (PWR 2), but its mandate is anything but simple. In this new course, students build on the rhetorical analyses, arguments, and research-based writing they did in their first writing course (PWR 1) by continuing to carry out research and develop argumentative positions. But the course broadens the definition of research to invite students to consider field research, and it broadens the genres in which students work and, hence, the audiences they address. Most notably, the course shifts focus from the first three canons of rhetoric in PWR 1 (invention, arrangement, and style) to style, memory, and, especially, delivery. Thus students reflect extensively on how to present or deliver their knowledge—what genre, media, and designs are called for in particular rhetorical situations, in just the kind of mediated writing we defined earlier.

As we complete this chapter in September 2005, we are about to convene the second PWR 2 Summer Institute, a four-day gathering of our instructional team that will allow us to assess the progress of the course in 2004–5 (when seventy sections were taught) as well as prepare us to implement a revised assignment sequence in 2005–6. To help us work toward these ends, we will review the goals for the course set out with the support of the university's Writing and Rhetoric Governance Board:

- To build on the analytical and research-based argument strategies developed in PWR 1 through more intensive work with oral, visual, and multimedia rhetoric.
- To identify, evaluate, and synthesize materials across a range of media and to explore how to present these materials effectively in support of the student's own arguments.
- To analyze the rhetoric of oral, visual, and multimedia documents with attention to how purpose, audience, and context help shape decisions about format, structure, and persuasive appeals.
- To learn to design appropriate and effective oral and multimedia texts.
- To conduct research (including field or experimental research) appropriate to the specific documents being created.
- To reflect systematically on oral, visual, and multimedia rhetoric and writing.

The goals for this new course will be familiar ones for most readers of this volume. Indeed, articulating these goals seemed fairly straightforward. But how to *deliver* on them—there's the question. While composition studies began to pay renewed attention to oral discourse a decade or so ago, it is still most common for oral and written discourse to be separated in the university curriculum (indeed, in many schools, oral discourse has been conspicuously absent until very recently). And while some schools have begun working fairly extensively with multimedia writing (e.g., Michigan Tech has developed a second-year seminar in oral, written, and visual communication that aims emphatically not to separate these modes), most writing programs continue to teach writing as primarily print based. We took as our challenge, then, the blending of print-based writing, speaking, and multimedia presentation into a form of writing reflective of twenty-first-century technologies that increasingly shape students' experiences with language.

We initially pursued these goals through the following assignment sequence that would set a standard across our many differently themed sections. We began with an assignment we called "texts in translation," one that asked students to take a fairly brief text and translate it from one form of delivery to another, analyze the rhetorical strategies operative in the two versions, and then present their findings to the class. This assignment would, we hoped, set the stage for a multimedia research-based argument, one that would include substantive writing, research, collaboration, and delivery of the argument in one or more media. Spanning five to six weeks of the course, this project might include various steps such as a proposal, documentation of research, several drafts, and the final live delivery. The final assignment would ask students to create a reflective essay that essentially analyzed their work in the course, noting how various media shaped their writing, how their rhetorical choices were affected by various media, and how they used a new medium effectively in the presentation of research. This final meta-analysis would often lead to the third major class presentation.

Had we not been in such a state of euphoria, we would have noticed that this set of goals and assignments was, at the very least, daunting. And certainly our experience in trying to carry out one of our own assignments during our first one-week institute in 2004 should have alerted us to the difficulty of what we were planning to do. We plunged into teaching PWR 2 with abandon, however: in retrospect it's easy to see that we were to some extent dazzled by the possibilities presented to us, especially in the technology-enhanced classrooms specially designed for the PWR 2 classes. We and our students can do it all, we thought.

And indeed, we managed to do a lot: teachers and students alike plunged into multimedia writing, producing films and videos, extensive audio essays (which are being aired every week on our campus radio station), and Web texts of all kinds. But our students helped rein us in. In their evaluations and in the extensive focus-group discussions we held with students following their experience in PWR 2, they told us in no uncertain terms that while they loved the opportunity to explore new media in writing and to push their writing in new directions, they weren't sure their *writing* was actually improving. (In other words, they knew they were learning something, but many of them wouldn't call it writing.) So caught up were they in the fine points of Audacity or the pleasures of iMovies or the production of a zine that the actual writing (or at least what students understood as writing) in these endeavors seemed to suffer. Moreover, they noted with irritation that the class workload differed dramatically across sections and, especially, that some classes provided for very thorough instruction in presentation and for lots of drafts of oral and multimedia presentations, while others did not. In short, they echoed our own concerns. Midyear reflection told us we had not yet reached the more effective design for the course, so we went back to the drawing board. In particular, our Curriculum Committee (Kevin DiPirro, John Peterson, Shay Brawn, Alyssa O'Brien, Nancy Buffington, and Marjorie Ford in 2004–5) worked to address three major concerns:

- how to balance academic with practical, real-world writing assignments
- how to balance critique and analysis of multimedia rhetoric (skills most of us generally felt confident teaching) with practice in developing multimedia texts (here we felt less confident)

- how to balance technical training (ranging from PowerPoint to video production) with instruction in writing, rhetoric, and presentation

We had heard early on from upper administrators about their concern that we might "just be teaching PowerPoint" on the one hand, and from our Undergraduate Advisory Board about their near-violent disagreements over what constituted an effective PowerPoint presentation, much less how to teach one. So we were particularly interested to compare reactions to this newly required second course with what we hear about PWR 1, the more traditional first-year course. While some students complain that our focus on research-based argument is too limiting, and that they want a chance to write more creatively or expressively, we don't hear complaints about how we define research-based argument in the context of a research university. It's in the context of PWR 2 that everyone—and no one—is an expert, and we feel as though we are hearing from every one of these folks.

With these points in mind, a group of us, led by our Curriculum Committee, began to reconsider our course goals, to try to focus more on the role of writing and presentation in the course. We realized, for example, that just as we did not expect students in PWR 1 to conduct research at the level of graduate students, so we should not expect students in PWR 2 to create full-length films, videos, hypertexts, or other digital work at the level of students with specialized training in those areas. (Indeed, we were reminded politely, Stanford's new major in film and media studies would be grappling with that advanced task.) Instead, we posited that PWR 2 should orient students to media production as a means of persuasion in the way that PWR 1 does this task for research at the university level. What we had to remind ourselves of (over and over again) was that the core values of PWR 2 entail rhetoric, research, argument, and *presentation* rather than advanced training in media production. This rethinking and refocusing led us to develop yet another revised PWR 2 assignment sequence, one that is intensely project driven, beginning with a research proposal to focus the work of the quarter. The project includes writing to be read as well as scripting for the presentation of research and a final reflection on the process of translating a print-based research argument into an oral presentation with appropriate media support. We look forward to implementing the new sequence in the 100 sections of PWR 2 we will teach in 2005–6.

Along with developing the curriculum, another key element of implementing the new requirement is determining the most appropriate *site for delivering the courses*. As part of the process of preparing for the pilot sections and, then, the first "real" sections of the new required course, we designed three technology-enhanced classrooms. These classrooms are meant to encourage and foster writing, research, and, above all, collaboration: they feature wireless laptops, moveable rectangular tables, plasma screens with semicircular desks to accommodate groups of three, electronic whiteboards, and two large Websters, networked screens that allow for very flexible rhetorical performances and demonstrations, and a full range of software tools for brainstorming and writing, for real-time audio and video communication, and for multimedia presentations. These rooms function ultimately less as traditional classrooms best suited to lecture and discussion and more as staging areas for writing and the performance of writing. The three classrooms have spoiled us, and our students, so much so that we find ourselves having trouble spreading them around to all of our faculty. Unfortunately, and like colleagues in institutions across the country, we have had to face a dramatic economic downturn. Thus we don't see the prospects of adding additional rooms like these in the immediate future. We do have access, however, to a number of teaching spaces with smart panels, and we plan to make good use of those. As we move forward in teaching this course and then in reviewing, revising, and refining the curriculum and our pedagogy, it seems likely that space and classroom design will in some ways shape the delivery of the course; we will continue to seek out classrooms that encourage instructors to plan their teaching as performance and students to conceptualize their writing with performance in mind.

We will thus continue to face a series of challenges in mounting our new course and evaluating its effectiveness. We have already touched on the economic issue of providing enough sufficiently equipped classroom space for this ambitious course. And we have noted that our first-year students are, at this point, not doing a great deal of what we define as mediated writing in their course-assigned writing. Both of these issues call for persuasion on our part: we must continue to convince the university that investing in highly mediated classroom space is both wise and necessary, as is our commitment to fulfill the Faculty Senate's mandate to "teach writing and speaking" while allowing students an opportunity to, as our colleague Eric Miraglia puts it, "author in the most compelling discursive modalities of their generation." In addition, we must convince our colleagues to consider the broadened definition of writing offered here and to take that redefinition into their own classroom teaching. More important, we must engage our students in systematic and rigorous analysis and production of mediated writing, a goal that may call for encouraging students to actually use all of the media available to them—even if their instructors are not often assigning such tasks directly. (As Kathi Yancey points out to us, in such a case, students would actually be delivering information and curricula to the faculty, a neat reversal of roles.)

In preparing to teach and evaluate our new course, then, we have articulated a range of issues, some intrinsic to our program (such as the tension between analysis of media and its production or the need to intensify our efforts to train and retrain ourselves as writing teachers) and some external (such as the economic downturn or the habits and practices of faculty outside the program, whose definitions and understandings of writing may well not match our own). In addition, many of our faculty are not yet entirely accustomed to teaching in such elegant, high-tech classrooms. Partially as a result of this potential problem, we have added the PWR institutes in 2004 and 2005 to our expanded fall orientation.

When we began this work, we thought of a redefinition of writing (as highly mediated) as pretty much self-evident: just look around and take note of what writing looks like today and how it functions, and the need for such a redefinition becomes apparent. Redefinition is one thing; realizing and implementing redefinition is another. Indeed, we have learned that delivering composition based on a substantive redefinition of writing affects every aspect of our work: our theories of writing, our curriculum, classroom configurations, staffing, training, evaluation principles and procedures, relationships with other programs, and methods and materials. Traditional and familiar theories of writing have not focused, for instance, on the material conditions of production or accounted for the inclusion of aural and visual elements at every stage of the writing process. And while the field of composition studies has done a great deal to articulate assessment of traditional forms of academic writing, we are now engaged in the very complex work of assessing forms of digital and multimedia writing. Likewise, we find ourselves rethinking our methods—from how we use collaboration in the classroom, to how we teach research, to how we respond to students and their writing.

When we think of the next couple of years in light of such challenging changes, it's easy to slip quietly into a panic: what could we have been thinking of when we set out on this path? At such times, we remember that for all the changes we face, our program is anchored in rhetoric and in rhetorical principles. This ancient discipline has served as a means of generating frameworks or maps for negotiating other times of enormous technological and social change, and it can do so today as well. In fact, rhetoric seems ideally suited for making connections between what is old—the complex and shifting but also enduring relationship among message, text, audience, rhetor, and context—and what is new. So while we will be looking for ways to describe new aspects of these relationships and to trace their features and functionings, we will be doing so within a familiar and time-tested means of knowledge production, now adapted to engage such new elements as design.

The seemingly simple step of working toward a redefinition of writing, then, has taken us quite a long way into exciting new territory, leading us to explore how we can deliver composition instruction in light of a definition of writing robust enough to account for the very wide range of writing students need to do—that is, writing that is quite often mediated by both the media in which students work and the technologies they can employ in producing texts. As we continue this work, we look to colleagues throughout the country to respond with their own redefinitions of writing and their own experiences, both good and bad, in teaching what we have been calling mediated writing or secondary literacy. Meeting the demands of theorizing, teaching, and evaluating mediated writing calls for the kind of collaboration composition scholars have advocated as well as pioneered, a collaboration that can perhaps best begin at home but which must also move beyond U.S. borders to consider how to deliver mediated writing and its instruction in global and transnational settings.

Notes

1. While we refer to composition studies as our field of study, we use the term *writing* rather than, say, *composing* for several reasons. Foremost is the long history encoded in the term and its traditional special association with literate practices. In addition, *writing* seems the term of wider understanding and usage. Finally, *composing* too easily shades into its nominalized form, *composition,* which has been particular to the United States.

2. On the significance of such regularization for assessment and evaluation of writing, see Robert J. Connors and Sharon Crowley.

3. In the last couple of decades this same phenomenon has been occurring in other countries from Canada to Great Britain to Japan. One result of this increased attention to writing on the university level is the creation of new professional organizations such as the European Writing Centers Association and the European Association of Teachers of Academic Writing. Depending on how these organizations evolve, they can serve either as stabilizing forces defining writing's role in school contexts or as supporters of more fluid definitions of writing.

4. Both of these definitions mention imprinting or inscribing, and it's worth noting that the Latin word for writing, *scribere*, indicates incision, cutting, and this etymology is related to the case Derrida (and others) makes for the relationship between writing and violence. Consider writing with a computer, however: while we still hit keystrokes, there is no concomitant indentation or imprinting into a surface of stone, skin, cloth, or other writing surface. We can ponder how this affects postmodern selves—indeterminate, contingent, leaving no permanent mark. The ephemeral electrical impulses of writing on a computer can add to our anxiety about identity, to the extent of making us nostalgic for print's violence. It can also cause anxiety for writing teachers who must evaluate such ephemeral, shape-shifting writing—what is there that will hold still long enough to be labeled and graded?

5. This definition is, at best, very clumsy, but it captures (or at least, we hope, begins to capture) the sense of writing we are trying to evoke—as epistemic, as performative, as multivocal, multimodal, and multimediated.

6. In her recently completed MIT dissertation, "Speaking on the Record," Tara Shankar works toward such a revised definition. Arguing that the domination of print-based writing is now at an end, she introduces a set of terms aimed at clarifying communicative relationships. To begin, she defines literacy as "the knowledge of language, domains of experience, and structure of discourse that permit one to use language as an object for learning reflection and analysis" and distinguishes this from Seymour Papert's term *letteracy*, the "mechanical and presentational skills specific to writing." This she contrasts with *prosodacy*, "oral decoding and encoding abilities that indicate awareness of ways in which situated intentions, emotion, identity, and expression can be realized in and through the repleteness of spoken language." Into this mix she adds the key term *spriting*. By *sprite*, a portmanteau combining *speaking* and *writing*, Shankar means speaking that "yields two technologically supported representations: the speech in audible form, and the speech in visual form. Spriting, therefore, equally encompasses digital speech recorders, speech editing tools, and any speech dictation recognition tools that would use speech in addition to text as an output mode." The

product of *spriting* she identifies as a spoken document, or *talkument.* As one *reads* a written text, she says, so one *audes* a talkument.

Works Cited

Armory, Hugh, and David D. Hall, eds. *A History of the Book in America.* Cambridge, MA: Cambridge UP, 1999.

Austin, J. L. *How to Do Things with Words.* Cambridge: Harvard UP, 1975.

Barry, Lynda. *One Hundred Demons!* Seattle: Sasquatch, 2002.

Bartholomae, David. "Inventing the University." In *When a Writer Can't Write.* Ed. Mike Rose. New York: Guilford, 1985.

Berlin, James. *Writing Instruction in Nineteenth Century American Colleges.* Urbana, IL: NCTE, 1984.

Chartier, Roger. *The Order of Books.* Trans. Lydia G. Cochrane. Stanford, CT: Stanford, UP, 1994.

Computers and Composition. Twentieth Anniversary Double Issue 20.4 (2003); 21.1, (2004).

Connors, Robert J. "The Abolition Debate in Composition: A Short History." In *Composition in the Twenty-first Century: Crisis and Change.* Ed. Lynn Z. Bloom, Donald A. Daiker, and Edward M. White. Carbondale: Southern Illinois UP, 1996, 47–63.

Crowley, Sharon. "Around 1971: Current-Traditional Rhetoric and Process Models of Composing." In *Composition in the Twenty-first Century: Crisis and Change.* Ed. Lynn Z. Bloom, Donald A. Daiker, and Edward M. White. Carbondale: Southern Illinois UP, 1996, 64–74.

Drooker, Eric. *Blood Song: A Silent Ballad.* New York: Harcourt, 2002.

Faigley, Lester. *Fragments of Rationality.* Pittsburgh: U Pittsburgh P, 1993.

Feather, John. *A History of British Publishing.* New York: Routledge, 1988.

George, Diana. "From Analysis to Design: Visual Communication in the Teaching of Writing." *CCC* 54.1 (2002): 11–39.

Gibson, Walker. *Tough, Sweet and Stuffy.* Bloomington: Indiana UP, 1966.

Hawisher, Gail, Paul LeBlanc, Charles Moran, and Cynthia L. Selfe. *Computers and the Teaching of Writing in American Higher Education, 1979–1994: A History.* Norwood, NJ: Ablex, 1995.

Hocks, Mary E. "Understanding Visual Rhetoric in Digital Writing Environments." *CCC* 54.4 (2003): 629–56.

Kilgour, Frederick G. *The Evolution of the Book.* New York: Oxford UP, 1998.

Lanham, Richard A. *Literacy and the Survival of Humanism.* New Haven, CT: Yale UP, 1983.

Miller, Susan. *Rescuing the Subject.* Carbondale: Southern Illinois UP, 1989.

Morris, William, ed. *The American Heritage Dictionary of the English Language.* Boston: Houghton Mifflin, 1976.

Ong, Walter J. *Interfaces of the Word*. Ithaca, NY: Cornell UP, 1977.

Oxford English Dictionary. 2d ed. Oxford and New York: Oxford UP, 1998.

Petroski, Henry. *The Book on the Bookshelf*. New York: Knopf, 1999.

Porter, James. *Rhetorical Ethics and Internetworked Writing*. Greenwich, CT: Ablex, 1998.

Schroeder, Christopher, Heper Fox, and Patricia Bizzell, eds. *AltDis: Alternative Discourse and the Academy*. Portsmouth, NH: Boynton/Cook, 2002.

Shankar, Tara. "Speaking on the Record." Unpublished dissertation, Massachusetts Institute of Technology, 2005.

Weathers, Winston. *An Alternate Style: Options in Composition*. Rochelle Park, NJ: Hayden, 1980.

Williamson, Michael. "The Worship of Efficiency: Untangling Political and Theoretical Considerations in Writing Assessment." *Assessing Writing* 1 (1994): 147–74.

Woodmansee, Martha, and Peter Jaszi, eds. *The Construction of Authorship*. Durham, NC: Duke UP, 1994.

Yancey, Kathleen Blake. Personal email (2004).

12

Undisciplined Writing

Joseph Harris
Duke University

The first time I heard a chair of the Conference on College Composition and Communication address its membership was in 1985 when Maxine Hairston urged us to "break our bonds" with English and create a new discipline centering on the study of writing. A few years later, in 1988, I listened as another chair of CCCC, David Bartholomae, responded to Hairston by voicing a suspicion of such "calls for coherence," suggesting instead that "most of the problems of academic life—problems of teaching, problems of thinking—come from disciplinary boundaries and disciplinary habits" and urging us to resist the "luxury of order and tradition" (49). I admired such irreverence then and continue to do so now. Unfortunately, though, Bartholomae failed to extend his distrust of disciplines very far, instead arguing—quixotically, it now seems to me—for professors of English to take on the teaching of writing as an integral part of their work, and concluding his address by urging those of us in composition to "acknowledge our roots in English, not deny them" (49). And so an argument for resisting disciplinarity somehow became one for remaining within the discipline of English.

This is the form that most debates over the status of composition have continued to take for the past two decades—with one group arguing for establishing a new discipline and the other for reforming English to include the study of writing. Both sides of the argument locate the teaching of writing as part of a disciplinary project—as taking place under the auspices of either a new department of writing and rhetoric or a refigured department of English. But I think that Bartholomae hinted at a more compelling view of composition in describing it not as a branch of English, but as a more open (if perhaps less coherent) form of intellectual work that seeks out the margins, crosses borders, mixes methods, and disdains the status and order of the traditional academic disciplines. I believe that we need to imagine composition not as a new discipline, but as a kind of intellectual work that takes place *outside* the conventional academic disciplines, that resists the allure both of English and of becoming a separate field of its own.

In this chapter I will describe how we have tried to put such a view of composition into practice in an independent first-year writing program at Duke University. I want to be clear, though, that in doing so I am arguing not for a particular structure for writing programs, but rather for a way of thinking about the work of composition. We have shaped the Duke University Writing Program in strategic response to a set of specific institutional constraints and opportunities; simply trying to replicate this structure at a different site would almost surely be a mistake. But while I am not presenting Duke as a model for other writing programs to follow, I do want to argue for a view of composition that is centered not on graduate programs, scholarly journals, and academic conferences, but on the *labor* of teaching basic and first-year writing.

Most recent attempts to define composition as a discipline have worked from the top down; it is now possible to be a credentialed PhD in composition studies in the same way that one can be an expert in eighteenth-century literature or postcolonial theory. We have distinguished professorships, university press series, and refereed journals cataloged by the Modern Language Association (MLA). We also have the daunting task of teaching the moves and strategies of academic writing to hundreds of thousands of beginning college students each year. Whether many of those students will stay in college or not depends on the work they do with us. For me the most pressing question facing our field is thus not how to build a discipline but how to deliver, in a broad and effective manner, what we know about writing to the beginning and often underprepared undergraduates whom we are asked to teach.

Such a ground-level view of our work raises issues that are as much political as intellectual: Who actually teaches first-year writing? What are they paid and how are they trained and supported? Who evaluates their work and on what basis? In speaking of the *labor* of teaching writing, then, I refer both to the intellectual work of teaching and to the workers who do it. In rereading Hairston and Bartholomae, I am struck by how neither has much to say about the problems of staffing first-year writing courses with qualified teachers. Both were instead preoccupied, at that moment in the mid-1980s, with defining the intellectual agenda of our emerging field. Two decades later I can't imagine trying to define the work of composition in such terms alone. We now know a lot about how to teach academic writing—not everything, but a lot. And yet each year too many students pass through too many writing courses taught by indifferent, underprepared, or overworked instructors. To deliver what we know about writing to a wider range of students, we need a better qualified and better supported labor force.

Composition has long been a textbook-driven field precisely because so many of our programs are staffed by inexperienced teachers. The usual response to the problem of inexperience has been to hand the novice instructors under our charge a course—in the form of readings, assignments, exercises—that we compose for them and whose execution thereof we can monitor. I want to argue here for a shift from this focus on curriculum to one on labor—from designing preset and teacher-proof courses to be implemented by underprepared adjuncts or graduate assistants to finding ways of attracting and supporting faculty who are interested in the work of teaching writing. Let me turn to how we have tried to do so at Duke.

Creating a Multidisciplinary Writing Faculty at Duke

In 2000 Duke University put into place a new curriculum that requires all undergraduates to take a seminar in academic writing in their first year and two writing-in-the-disciplines courses afterward. Writing 20, Academic Writing, is the only course at Duke taken by every undergraduate. There are no prerequisites and no exemptions. Almost all of the sections of this first-year course are taught by a group of twenty-six postdoctoral fellows whom we have recruited across a wide range of disciplines. In the last five years our fellows have held PhDs in African American studies, architecture, biology, communications, cultural anthropology, cultural studies, economics, education, engineering, English, epidemiology, forestry, genetics, history, human environments, linguistics, philosophy, political science, psychology, queer studies, religion, rhetoric and composition, sociology, theology, and women's studies. Fellows design and teach five sections of Writing 20 per year. Sections are capped at twelve students for a total of sixty students per year. Most fellows design two different writing courses each year—one for the fall and one for the spring.

Our fellowships are not tenure-track positions, but neither are they dead-end jobs. Fellows join our program because they want to work intensely on their teaching before moving on to other academic positions. And indeed, in the past few years, several have won tenure-track jobs at other colleges or universities. The salary is reasonable ($38,200 to $41,200 per year), the support for research strong, the environment for teaching excellent, and the collegial support of the other fellows extraordinary. Fellows are offered an initial three-year contract. In the second semester of their second year at Duke, they undergo a rigorous review of their work based on a teaching portfolio that they have assembled. If this review is positive, their contract is extended to five years.

I like and admire our faculty immensely. While most have not taught first-year writing before coming to Duke, we tend to attract people who want to center their careers on teaching undergraduates and who are interested in working as part of a collective intellectual project. We tell prospective fellows that we do not want them to teach a staff course that we have composed for them, but rather we want them to draw on their interests as scholars to introduce students to the difficulties and pleasures of academic writing. And while we work closely with new fellows as they design their courses, there is no template or rubric for them to follow in doing so, no assumed pace or sequence of assignments or activities. We do, however, expect faculty to write out their course materials with a level of care and thoroughness that many at first find surprising. Before they begin their first semester of teaching at Duke, fellows participate in a three-week summer seminar on teaching writing. In this seminar we offer our new colleagues a quick sense of the history and politics surrounding the teaching of writing, model some key moves as teachers (responding toward revision, workshopping student texts), and help them draft the materials they will use in working with students in the fall. Since we represent our intellectual work as teachers in our course materials, we argue that such materials should be written with the same care we give to our scholarship. We thus spend a good deal of time talking about how fellows phrase the writing projects they set for students and how they describe the aims and concerns of their courses. As a result, we have as a program an unusually rich and varied archive of the work that goes on in our courses, and our fellows, when they look for tenure-track jobs, have strong textual evidence of their skill in teaching undergraduates.

All sections of Writing 20 are listed on the Duke Web catalog by title, brief description, and teacher. Many of these courses are centered on the ways academics and intellectuals have responded to public controversies. In 2003–4, for instance, students in Writing 20 were asked to take on such issues as the Origins of Darwinism, Church-State Conflicts in Education, Revolutionary Visions in Art, Communicating Science to the Public, Science in the Popular Media, Writing About the Web, Hippies in American History, Imagining the African Diaspora, and Academic Writing and Political Dissent, among many others. Students thus do not simply sign up for "English 101/Instructor: Staff," but rather select a section of academic writing as they would any other course—that is, by what most grabs their interest. Many fellows also post their course materials on the Web, making their work as teachers public in a sense usually reserved for scholarship. And that work has been a strong success by all measures: In their course evaluations, students report that they work harder and are more stimulated intellectually in Writing 20 than in most of their other courses at Duke. Some of their work as writers is showcased annually in *Deliberations*, a journal of first-year writing that is itself often used as a text in our courses. The teaching portfolios put together by second-year fellows form a rich archive of the range of work in our program, and we also post course materials designed by the winner of our annual Award for Excellence in Teaching Writing to our website. In the spring of 2003, with the guidance of assessment expert Richard Haswell, we conducted a programwide analysis of early and late essays in Writing 20 that offers textual evidence that students make significant progress over the course of the semester in how they draw on other texts in their own writing, moving from uses that are largely descriptive to those that are more critical and assertive.

Composition as Pedagogy

In *The End of Composition Studies*, David Smit argues that composition may have a stronger and more interesting role to play in the university than simply becoming a traditional academic discipline. What if, he suggests, rather than assuming full responsibility ourselves for teaching writing to all undergraduates, we instead defined our task as helping faculty across the disciplines take on this work? He thus proposes a curriculum in which the universal general skills course in composition is replaced by a range of discipline-specific, writing-intensive seminars. To teach such courses, Smit argues, faculty would require three kinds of expertise: (1) They'd need to be proficient writers themselves in the genre they're teaching; (2) they'd need to be able to explain the rhetorical moves and strategies that underlie such writing; and (3) they'd need to know about the ways people learn to write and how to design courses that could help them do so. The job of compositionists would be to consult with faculty on the second and third of these tasks—that is, to help them surface the rhetoric of their disciplines and to design and teach what for many of them would be a new sort of course.

And indeed that is pretty much what I now do as director of the Duke Writing Program. Working with a multidisciplinary faculty has offered me a new sense of what composition has most to offer to our colleagues in other fields—which is, in a word, *pedagogy*. The fellows in our program are ambitious and talented young scholars. They come to Duke with strong ideas about the sort of writing they'd like to see undergraduates do, but a less developed sense of how to help them learn to do so. They need help with things like figuring out how much reading to assign, how to help students use writing to come to terms with complex texts and ideas, how to compose writing projects that are well defined yet open-ended, how to comment toward revision, how to structure a course to make room for drafting and revising, how to lead a strong class discussion of student texts, how to set up useful peer response groups, and so on. And even if what I have to say to them about teaching sometimes strikes me as quotidian, as the sort of thing anyone in comp would know, that's not a complaint I've heard from our faculty. They want to learn how to do a certain kind of intellectual work, one that has a real impact on students, and they look to me to help them do so. There is a satisfaction in such work that I have seldom felt in teaching graduate seminars or in serving on dissertation committees. And so, while I understand why many of us wish to see composition solidify its status as an academic discipline, I am drawn instead, along with Smit, to a more centrifugal view of composition, to the impulse to reach out to initiatives in writing in the disciplines as well as to other reform efforts in general education, service learning, community literacy, academic ethics, and the scholarship of teaching and learning.

Before I came to Duke, I directed the composition program in a large university English department. I experienced that job as an ongoing siege: How much training do graduate teaching assistants really need just to teach comp?

Who gets to offer graduate courses and on what topics? Who directs dissertations? Why should research on teaching count toward tenure? And so on. A set of questions and anxieties about the intellectual status of work in composition seemed to define everything I did and thought. It wasn't until about two years into my new job that I realized that I simply didn't have those worries anymore. Our program is defined not by a set of disciplinary concerns but by a collective teaching project. We all teach the same course, albeit in very different ways. The focus of our talk together is thus on teaching—and, at least to me, such talk seems more useful, collegial, focused, and sane than the familiar and internecine struggles of disciplinary argument.

Negotiating Coherence

We offer about 140 sections of Academic Writing at Duke each year, and we work toward coherence among them in a number of fairly loose and informal ways. One of the first tasks we took on as a faculty in our first year of work together was to articulate a set of four teaching goals for Writing 20: (1) *reading closely and critically*; (2) *responding to and making use of the work of others*; (3) *drafting and revising texts*; and (4) *making texts public*. In crafting these goals, we tried to define both those aspects of writing that we thought were teachable (drafting and revising, making texts public) and those qualities that distinguished a certain sort of writing as *academic* (a close attention to texts, a responsiveness to the work of others). Each year since, we have returned as a faculty to these goals in order to debate what they mean and to share our various ways of working toward them. In particular, over the last few years, we have moved from an understanding of the goal of making texts public as one centering on the tasks of editing and document design to one that takes on the question of how and where student texts *circulate*—within a seminar itself, on the Web, in class or program publications, and perhaps beyond. What seems crucial to me in this process is not that each of us interprets these four goals in the same way, or even that the goals always remain the same, but that all of us position our work as teachers in conscious relation to a vision of Writing 20 that we have collectively defined.

In addition to the summer seminar for new fellows, we also hold an annual retreat for all of the teachers of Writing 20, along with a series of symposia throughout the year, designed and led by the fellows themselves, at which we talk about various issues in teaching. We visit one another's classes frequently, and there is a remarkable amount of hallway conversation about students and courses. We try to form a sense of identity as a program, that is, not through imposing a fixed syllabus or a set of mandated classroom practices (small groups, portfolios, grading rubrics, etc.), but through sponsoring a set of ongoing conversations about the course we are all teaching.

But in fact our versions of Writing 20 are far from the same. On the contrary, the success of our approach rests in large part, I think, on the sense of our faculty that they and not the program own their courses. Why should one expect a writing course taught by an epidemiologist or an architect to follow the same template as one designed by a historian or a political scientist? And so students in the various sections of Writing 20 often end up reading and writing very different sorts of texts, considering very different kinds of problems, and talking about their work in very different ways. Some teachers have students look closely at intricacies of phrasing; others tend to work more at the level of paragraph and essay. Some make extensive use of the Web in circulating and responding to texts; others continue to handwrite comments in the margins of essays. Some ask students to imitate the forms of writing in their disciplines, others ask for something more like critical essays or literary journalism. Some ask students to do substantive research; others work with assigned texts alone. Some divide students into groups all the time, others never do. And so on. There are, however, some practices that we do insist on: Since our charge is to teach *academic* writing, we expect that students will be asked to write on complex issues and texts, that they will have the chance to revise their work in response to the comments of readers, and that they will discuss the work they are doing as writers with their peers—in the form of workshops, discussion lists, seminar discussions, or the like. In short, we expect the work of the course to center on the writing of the students in it, and that the writing that students do will engage the work of other thinkers. But beyond that, we want faculty to own their courses, to shape the work that goes on in them according to their own sense of what is involved in learning to write as an academic and intellectual.

Encouraging Faculty Ownership

What I want to argue for, then, is a willingness to tolerate a good bit of programmatic diversity and even incoherence. Of course you can do so only if you trust both the abilities of your faculty and their commitment to the goals of your program. And so we've worked hard to offer fellows a sense of ownership of our collective project. A subcommittee of fellows drafted formal bylaws for the Duke University Writing Program, which the fellows as a group then approved. We meet as a faculty each month both to share information and to discuss and vote on questions of policy concerning issues like student evaluations and course archives. Fellows hold four of the seven seats on the program steering committee that implements such policies. Fellows serve as members of our Executive Steering Group and on the Editorial Advisory Board of *Deliberations*, the annual journal featuring the work of students in Writing 20. Three fellows also serve each year as associate directors of the University Writing Program, with no one holding such a position for more than two consecutive years. More experienced fellows are often paired as mentors with newcomers to the program—visiting classes, reading materials, and talking informally about teaching. And perhaps most importantly, fellows hold five out of the seven positions on the search committee charged with recruiting new members of our program, giving them a very strong voice in deciding who will actually join them in teaching writing at Duke. Fellows who serve on this committee often seem, perhaps through finding themselves talking to candidates about what "we" do, to form a stronger attachment to the program. They also report that the experience of reviewing some 350 applications, and of interviewing about twenty-five candidates for the six or so fellowships that we have to offer each year, gives them an invaluable set of insights into how people gain (and lose) academic jobs.

Near the end of their second year at Duke, fellows are required to put together a teaching portfolio for review by the directors of the program. If this review is positive, their contract is extended from three years to five. We have structured this review to offer fellows a chance to represent their teaching as complex intellectual work. This involves both *documenting* that work—through selecting examples of course materials, student writings, letters of observation, and standard course evaluations—and also *interpreting* it in an essay that discusses how their aims and practices in teaching writing have evolved over the past two years. In writing such an essay, fellows somehow have to situate their own work in relation to the goals of our program, to define for themselves the ways in which they both do and do not identify with our project. We also hope, on a practical level, that composing such a portfolio will prove of use to fellows when they look for jobs in their home disciplines.

But while I think this process of review is both fair and appropriate, it also points out the considerable gap in status between the directors of the program, who are regular-rank faculty, and its fellows, who are on limited-term contracts. Fellows know that they can only teach in our program for at most five years. These are positions that one takes on in order to prepare to move somewhere else. Even still, I have been struck by the energy that fellows bring to the program and their commitment to it. These are, for the most part, people who are interested in learning both how to become better teachers and also how programs and departments get run. And while there are, to be sure, the occasional complaints about meetings and programmatic chores eating into time needed for teaching or research, these are no more frequent than those voiced by tenure-stream faculty in other departments I've worked in. In any case, not being eligible for tenure, it seems to me, is not a reason for being denied a voice in the academic workplace. We want fellows to be involved as much as they want to be in shaping and governing our program.

Creating Alternatives to Tenure

Since I agree with many of the concerns voiced about the growing use of non-regular-rank faculty in the academy, let me say a little more about the thinking behind these limited-term positions. Would it be better if these were not post-doctoral fellowships but tenure-track professorships? Well, yes, of course. But I also need then to note that such a proposal—which would turn the writing program into one of the largest departments in the university—has never been a remote possibility at Duke or at most other American universities and colleges. So the real question is: Do postdocs offer a stronger labor force for teaching first-year writing than the usual mix of graduate teaching assistants and adjunct instructors? At Duke the answer has been an obvious yes. But then more questions follow: Why limit the term of these positions? If you have good teachers of writing, why not just keep them?

This is the case made by Michael Murphy in "New Faculty for a New University," and I can well imagine that at many schools it would be desirable. However, since promotion at Duke hinges almost entirely on scholarly publication, I would worry about creating a permanent underclass of teachers who, when asked to work year after year with only minimal raises and recognition, might become increasingly prone to burnout and resentment. On a more positive note, I also think that a program like ours, charged with training a young multidisciplinary faculty in teaching writing, can hope to influence higher education in ways that extend both beyond our local campus and beyond first-year composition. In the last few years, we have had fellows leave Duke for assistant professorships at other schools in cultural anthropology, education, English, history, linguistics, psychology, public health, science communications, women's studies, and writing. Still others have taken jobs in university programs or centers focusing on service learning, multiculturalism and diversity, and teaching and learning. Most past fellows report that their experiences in our program have profoundly shaped the work they are now doing at other sites in the academy.

As someone who holds tenure, I don't want to slight the problems—both practical and psychological—that fellows face in being required to find and move to new positions. Indeed, managing a faculty composed entirely of inexperienced and anxious young teacher-scholars can pose challenges faced by few department chairs. But if the pattern of the last few years holds, and fellows continue to land good jobs in a tight academic market, then I think we will be able to say that we have not only established a strong first-year writing course for Duke students, but also influenced undergraduate teaching at other universities.

Duke is an affluent and prestigious university. We can offer material and intellectual incentives for young PhDs to come work with us that many other institutions cannot, and we have resources to help our fellows develop as teachers and scholars that few universities can rival. In addition our program has also been supported by a generous grant from the Mellon Foundation. So I don't want to suggest here that other composition programs should also be staffed by postdoctoral fellows. But I do want to argue for an approach to our work that begins with the needs and the interests of first-year writing students. I realize that this may seem a truism, but in fact most university writing programs serve several competing interests and constituencies. And so, for instance, I'm not asking what serves the best interests of the tenure-stream composition faculty, or the graduate program, or the English department, or even the current cadre of writing instructors. Nor am I asking what is best for rhetoric and composition as an academic field. (If such a starting point seems far-fetched, remember how the "new abolitionism" of the 1990s was fueled in strong part by worries that the intellectual credibility of composition would be tainted by its association with the service role of first-year writing.) I'm asking what is best for students in basic and first-year writing courses.

This is not an argument, I need to insist, against the value of scholarship in composition or against its establishment as an academic discipline. All of my own writing as a scholar has been in composition, and I think that the best recent work in our field—of Marilyn Sternglass, Deborah Brandt, Jackie Royster, Richard Miller, Linda Flower, Tom Fox, Bruce Horner, Mary Soliday, Suresh Canagarajah, and others—is clearly as rigorous as most of what I now read in literary or cultural studies while at the same time far more lucid and useful. And I'm glad that graduate programs in rhetoric and composition like those at Syracuse, Southern Florida, Purdue, Texas, and Rensselaer now exist to promote such scholarship. But I don't believe that first-year writing programs should belong to the discipline of composition studies any more than they should be owned by English. The teaching of writing should be a university-wide and multidisciplinary project, not a departmental fiefdom.

Good Teaching for Fair Pay

This returns me to the question about who teaches in our programs, to questions of labor. But I do so, I think, with a difference. For me, the argument for better working conditions is better teaching. I can't imagine how a writing program can exploit its teachers and still hope to serve its students well. But I don't think we will improve how writing gets taught simply by raising salaries. We also need to change how we select and train the teachers in our programs, and how we support and evaluate their work. We need, that is, to connect our demands for better working conditions to clear plans for improving the quality of instruction, to link good teaching directly to fair pay.

I am thus worried by how the 2003 CCCC resolution "Standards to Support High-Quality Professional Instruction" insists that "all full-time writing positions will be tenurable or covered by continuous employment certificates" (384) but says nothing about the sorts of expertise teachers of writing should be expected to bring to their work and little about the sorts of support they should be given. This resolution almost exactly mirrors the position taken by the 1989 CCCC "Statement of Principles and Standards for Postsecondary Writing Instruction," that much-debated attempt to implement the Wyoming Resolution. The 1989 statement argued that the teaching of writing should be made the responsibility of tenure-stream faculty; the 2003 resolution simply asserts that all writing teachers should be made tenure-stream. Like Hairston and Bartholomae before them, both of these documents respond to the problem of who should teach writing by trying to normalize that work within the familiar structures of departments, disciplines, and tenure. While I have long argued for involving tenure-stream faculty in teaching writing whenever possible—and continue to do so—I think we also need to admit that the odds are overwhelmingly against a widespread return of such faculty to the basic or first-year course.

If that is the case, then I suspect it will prove counterproductive to insist on a principle of tenure that, on the one hand, few programs can ever hope to implement and, on the other, seems to put us in the position of censuring other, more immediate ways of improving the working conditions of writing teachers. I'd note, for instance, that our program at Duke is in clear violation of both the 1989 statement and the 2003 motion. Our fellows don't accrue tenure, and they aren't paid as much as regular-rank faculty at Duke. And yet, I think, we do an excellent job of teaching first-year students and an ethical one of supporting our faculty. My sense is that, as a field, we have to learn how to think less in terms of ideal structures, of disciplines and tenure lines, and more in terms of possible reforms. We *should* argue for tenure for good writing teachers whenever that is a realistic option. But we also need flexible and strong ways of delivering composition, that is, of supporting the teaching of writing in situations where tenure is not possible.

The principle I'd insist on is not tenure but this: *To teach academic writing, you should have to be good at it—or at least show a strong promise of becoming good at it.* This means that decisions about who teaches in a writing program need to be made by someone whose main concern is with the quality of instruction in that program—and not with supporting graduate students, or with balancing faculty workloads, or with finding work for the protégés or spouses or friends of powerful professors. It also means that we need to put into practice ways of assessing the work of faculty that account for the complexities of teaching writing and that are as open and transparent to the people involved as possible. It means, in short, that we need to structure our programs so it is clear that the only way to advance in them is through teaching writing well.

I can imagine such programs existing within the framework of university English departments—although their directors would need to be given much more control over staffing than they are usually allowed. I can also see them as part of departments of writing and rhetoric, or in other sorts of interdisciplinary units, but with the same caveat that first-year writing needs to be staffed by the best teachers available. Jane Hindman has recently shown, for instance, how simply creating a separate writing department does not in itself solve the problem of finding and supporting strong teachers for the first-year course. On the other hand, Daniel Royer and Roger Gilles offer their experiences at Grand Valley State as an example of how one can structure such a department to make sure that both first-year and advanced courses in writing are taught by the same faculty. Or such programs could be freestanding, unaffiliated with any particular department or discipline, like ours at Duke. My sense is that, in the end, the disciplinary location of first-year writing programs doesn't matter that much—that what really counts is our ability to recruit good teachers of writing and to support their work. And that problem is less disciplinary than political.

Making Our Own Mistakes

Near the end of *The Remains of the Day*, Kazuo Ishiguro's protagonist, the consummate butler Mr. Stevens, finds himself sitting by the sea, reflecting on a life that he has focused on the careful observance of the forms and rituals of dignified behavior. The irony is that the fastidious Stevens has spent his life working for a philistine aristocrat with few interests beyond sport, drink, and conservative politics. And yet, Stevens comes to realize, it was not his employer whose life lacked dignity but his own. "At least he had the privilege of being able to say at the end of his life that he made his own mistakes," Stevens admits of the man he served.

> He chose a certain path in life, it proved to be a misguided one, but there he chose it, he can say that at least. As for myself I cannot even claim that. . . . I can't even say I made my own mistakes. Really—one has to ask oneself—what dignity is there in that? (243)

Teachers of writing also need to be allowed the dignity of making their own mistakes. Those of us charged with directing writing programs have too long accepted a view of our task as one of delivering a *curriculum*. I am arguing that we should instead see our job as recruiting and supporting a *faculty* who can design and teach their own, strong courses in writing. The status of disciplinarity means little for first-year teachers if it doesn't come with a practical authority over their work. I'd rather have an undisciplined writing that supports good first-year teachers than a discipline that doesn't.

In interviewing candidates for fellowships at Duke, I've been struck by how many of them tell some version of what I once thought of as the "comp story"—the one that begins, "Well, I was the one who actually *liked* teaching this course that everybody else said they hated." I've also had the chance to work at Duke with faculty members from departments like biology, mathematics, physics, music, and German who share my political commitments to teaching beginning undergraduates and my intellectual interests in the complexities of doing so, far more than do most of the English professors whom I've met. As a faculty consultant to our Preparing Future Faculty Program, I've seen how graduate students and postdocs in fields as diverse as biomechanical engineering, marine biology, and art history urgently want to structure their careers around teaching undergraduate students. Composition has many friends in the academy (and the public) beyond English. My experiences suggest that many faculty across the disciplines are interested in and good at teaching first-year writing. We should ask them to join us in that work.

Works Cited

Bartholomae, David. "Freshman English, Composition, and CCCC." *CCC* 40 (1989): 38–50.

Hairston, Maxine. "Breaking Our Bonds and Reaffirming Our Connections." *CCC* 36 (1985): 275–82.

Hindman, Jane. "Learning as We G(r)o(w): Strategizing the Lessons of a Fledgling Rhetoric and Writing Department." In *A Field of Dreams: Independent Writing Programs and the Future of Composition Studies*. Ed. Peggy O'Neill, Angela Crow, and Larry W. Burton. Logan: Utah State UP, 2002, 107–29.

Ishiguro, Kazuo. *The Remains of the Day*. New York: Knopf, 1989.

Murphy, Michael. "New Faculty for a New University: Towards a Full-Time Teaching-Intensive Faculty Track in Composition." *CCC* 52 (2000): 14–42.

O'Neill, Peggy, Angela Crow, and Larry W. Burton, eds. *A Field of Dreams: Independent Writing Programs and the Future of Composition Studies*. Logan: Utah State UP, 2002.

"Resolution 5: Standards to Support High-Quality Professional Instruction." *CCC* 55 (2003): 383–85.

Royer, Daniel J., and Roger Gilles. "The Origins of a Department of Academic, Creative, and Professional Writing." In *A Field of Dreams: Independent Writing Programs and the Future of Composition Studies*. Ed. Peggy O'Neill, Angela Crow, and Larry W. Burton. Logan: Utah State UP, 2002, 21–37.

Smit, David. *The End of Composition Studies*. Carbondale: Southern Illinois UP, 2005.

"Statement of Principles and Standards for the Postsecondary Teaching of Writing." *CCC* 40 (1989): 329–36.

13

Asynchronicity
Delivering Composition and Literature in the Cyberclassroom

Richard Courage
Westchester Community College, State University of New York

My first opportunity to teach online came with tempting perks: a stipend for course development, a more flexible teaching schedule, a lower enrollment cap, and of course the allure of the new. I'd had a love affair with computers since using an Apple 2e to complete a dissertation begun on a typewriter, and teaching online seemed the next step after word processing, email, discussion lists, and Web-based research. It offered, as well, a potential antidote to the burnout that comes of teaching the same courses the same way once too often.

Teaching English at a community college inevitably means teaching writing, given that composition sections far outnumber literature. In a typical semester at Westchester Community College, we offer approximately ten sections of freshman English and remedial writing for each elective. Even the literature electives are designed to be writing intensive, as students explore texts by writing extensively about them. Years ago, the English department made a successful case for a contractually lower course load than other departments based on the number of papers we read each term. In my Short Story elective, for example, each student produces at least seven thousand words of formal and informal writing. With typical rosters of thirty students, these classes offer a formidable paper load. Teaching online, I hoped, would provide some relief from what one colleague dubbed the "sigh factor," that moment of despair many composition teachers experience as they lift the first paper from a tall stack of student essays.

When my proposal to teach a distance-learning (DL) version of Short Story in fall 2001 was accepted, I undertook the attendant tasks with enthusiasm:

visiting model course sites, learning WebCT software, uploading course files, choosing layouts and icons, and developing online substitutes for the intensely discussion-based format I use in face-to-face classes. Besides teaching Short Story online, I would be teaching Composition and Literature 2 in person. I think of Short Story as Comp Lit 2½ since I employ the same interactive pedagogical approach in both courses. In Comp Lit 2, students read and write about texts in different genres. Short Story focuses on a single genre, but students continue to use writing heuristically and to deepen compositional and reading skills. I begin both courses the same way, by exploring the personal and autobiographical lenses that students bring to literature. Genre knowledge, historical and intertextual considerations, different methods of working (and playing) with texts are gradually folded in, but finding something to say is the first threshold every student must cross. They accomplish this by writing informal responses, raising questions, examining specific passages, describing what happened as they read a text, and making connections with other texts or with their own experiences; nearly anything is welcome except plot summary. Every assigned work—whether short or long, play, story, poem, or essay—requires a written response.

Typically, I begin a class session by describing my own experiences reading and teaching a particular text, sometimes providing background information on author or context. This opening move is largely ceremonial. The real work starts with students' initial reactions shared in small groups. A recorder notes questions and disagreements that arise during subsequent discussion, and eventually these fill the blackboards. Some questions are essentially requests for information, which I address quickly. Others open broader interpretive possibilities and serve as springboards to move from the text of their responses back to the literary text. Discussions often spark controversy, puzzlement, and laughter and require ongoing textual detective work. Some of the more provocative questions become the basis for essay assignments. Variations of this approach have served me well for a long time. Instead of wrapping a text into a deceptively neat interpretive bundle (as some students expect), I invite them to unwrap it at leisure and make it messy. The extended interplay of reading, writing, talking, rereading, more talking, more writing seems to spur students' level of engagement with texts and their skills in writing analytically about what they read.

Adapting this pedagogy to the cyberclassroom was the key challenge posed in designing an online version of Short Story. If the course consisted only of my giving reading and writing assignments, students sending them back, and my evaluating their work, it would be little more than an old-fashioned correspondence course in electronic format. I decided that an asynchronous discussion board would be the centerpiece, that neither email nor chat rooms would serve as well. Email would not foster the group interaction that injects vitality into face-to-face classes. Chat rooms seemed too chaotic; twenty-four people typing at once is not much different from twenty-four people talking at once. The discussion board, on the other hand, allowed me to divide the class into small groups with a separate forum for each story, and the visual organization of messages into discrete discussion threads would lend a degree of order and coherence impossible in chat rooms. I could post introductory comments to each forum, and students could post responses. I liked the prospect of having responses publicly and permanently recorded, an improvement over the sometimes hasty, mumbled, or partial "read-around" that takes place in face-to-face classrooms. Far more difficult was to create a substitute for spontaneous discussions. The nearest equivalent was a second posting after students had read each other's responses and reread the story. I hoped that this process would foster dialogue through threaded postings and email exchanges, that it would lead students to reconsider their initial views in light of others' insights and questions. I added an "Essay Topics" page to post a set of extended writing assignments drawn from issues arising on the boards.

In the opening days of the course, I realized how the DL format constantly immersed students in writing. *Everything* they did in the course—completing required assignments, participating in public discussions, conferring with me, even just establishing their presence in class—was accomplished or at least mediated through writing. This central, instrumental role of writing was transforming Short Story into a virtual composition course. With Short Story online and a face-to-face section of Comp Lit 2, that semester offered rich possibilities for comparing different modes of delivering composition.

First Days

The first meeting of Comp Lit 2, my face-to-face course, was familiar terrain. The majority of students worked full-time during the day and attended classes part-time at night. Most appeared several years older than typical day students. By evening's end, I had reviewed the syllabus, learned several names, collected a piece of writing, and led a discussion about the reading students do on their own. I had begun getting acquainted with this class, laying the basis for an increasingly detailed mental picture of each individual. Every subsequent class meeting adds something new to the files—one per student—that I carry in my head throughout the semester. I learn their faces and names. I observe where they sit and whom they interact with. I notice who wears business attire, who wears denims or khakis, who wears tie-dye, who has tattoos or piercings—how many and how extreme. I notice who speaks without prompting and the sorts of comments they make. I listen for the soft voices and the strong. I look for potential peer leaders. I also scan the room for potential problems: students who doze, who seem distracted, whose comments seem incoherent or hostile, who huddle down into desks with coats and hats on, who chat audibly as if waiting at a bus stop. Although I like my students and enjoy working with most of them, two decades in the classroom have created a certain self-preserving alertness to all that students communicate about themselves before I even see a piece of writing.

The cyberclassroom was eerily different. There were no students behind desks, no blackboard, no windows opening onto the campus—only a date to begin the semester's work and a course site to be logged on to with posted information including an initial assignment due the following day. This virtual ghost town was populated instantly the moment I downloaded student files from the global database. Here I was no longer a professor, or even an instructor. According to WebCT, I was now a "course designer." For the first time in two decades, I had to compose a teaching persona solely through the written word. My physical appearance, body language, tone of voice, gestures, use of classroom space, spontaneous reactions to students' comments and questions—all were irrelevant in (or, more precisely, absent from) this asynchronous, nonspatial site. Yet these are the essential physical details with which we present ourselves in public spaces. Like ancient rhetoricians, contemporary sociologists such as Erving Goffman and Richard Sennett delineate the manner in which we are accustomed to establishing our status and credibility. As Sennett notes:

> In a milieu of strangers, the people who witness one's actions, declarations, and professions usually have no knowledge of one's history, and no experience of similar actions, declarations, and professions in one's past; thus it becomes difficult for this audience to judge, by an external standard of experience with a particular person, whether he is to be believed or not in a given situation. The knowledge on which belief can be based is confined to the frame of an immediate situation. The arousal of belief therefore depends on how one behaves—talks, gestures, moves, dresses, listens—within the situation itself. (39)

Or: what the authors in this volume call delivery. Although the presence of my name in a course schedule confers a certain ascribed status, my ability to really establish myself as *Professor* Courage—as someone worthy of belief, who knows something about writing and literature, who can successfully manage a class and teach and assist students, who has the right to lay claims on students' time and energies—depends on the words I speak *and* on the manner in which I deliver them. My task is to "arouse belief in a part" (Sennett 39), which requires a ritualized litany of first-day behaviors that I became acutely aware of when the medium of course delivery changed. These include the tastefully casual sports jacket I wear; the confident manner with which I walk to the front of the room and begin to speak in a loud voice to everyone present; the worn, overstuffed leather briefcase I carry; and the well-organized folders of materials I extract and array across the oversized teacher's desk.

Just as I could not establish myself in the classroom in my accustomed manner of delivery, students too were limited to a single channel of communication. I didn't meet them, see them, or hear their voices. The only initial data to file in my head came from their biographical statements, which were often brief and perfunctory. Jay's is typical: "hi everyone, my name is Jason but you can all call me jay. I am 19 years old and this is my 3rd semester here. I am a full time student and i have a part time job at a gas station. I am taking this class because any class that i dont have to leave my house for is ok in my book. Well thats about it."[1]

By default, I found myself *inventing* Jay and his classmates, overlaying a template of experience onto such terse descriptions. In my mind's eye, Jay wore a carefully shaped baseball cap, Tommy Hilfiger polo, baggy khakis, and scuffed but expensive running shoes. He was majoring in marketing or computer science with little concrete idea of his next step. He read sports magazines, was passionate about cars and basketball. He presented himself with a certain brash irreverence (even in his cavalier approach to mechanics) and could be fun to engage as long as he put sufficient time and attention into the coursework. A semester's worth of responses and essays would reveal a lot about his actual academic profile and replace idle speculation with information; composition teachers are, after all, accustomed to reading our students between the lines of their writing. Yet I was already sensing the cental role of imagination in compensating for the one-dimensionality of student-teacher interaction online.

Some students took up my invitation to write at length about themselves. Elaine, for example, included these comments:

> I am a hundred years old on some days because somewhere back in the 80's I thought it would be so cute to have 3 teenagers at the same time. Wasn't I clever! I'm with you because my daughter has grown tired of my correcting her English homework, so it's time to do my own. For me, reading is the avenue to feeling. "Feeling" as in empathy. "Feel" as in changing the way I feel about things. Writing is the path from the soul to the paper. I challenge the writer to bring me to another level of growth.
>
> I've been a Registered Nurse for about twenty-five years, and I am now on a long journey toward opening a nursing practice. The credits from this course are another step.
>
> I'm also here because I want to play! I plan to play hard in this course and have fun with our chosen short story writers.

Elaine seemed to consciously shape a persona, using language to claim a certain role in relation to her readers: older and consequently wiser, academically engaged for the pleasures of learning, not just for grades, but also witty and playful. The new medium demanded the successful substitution of words alone for all the accustomed methods of establishing one's status and credibility.

Several introductions, among them Tina's, were posted after the deadline. They raised an issue of technical competence to which I had given little thought:

> My name is Tina, and I live in Rockland County with my mother. I'm sorry this is late, but I had a difficult time with the computer in the last few days. I am currently in my fourth semester at WCC, and this is my first time taking

an online course. My major is liberal arts/teaching. I like to read novels and write poetry, go to the movies and spend time with friends. I work full-time as a secretary for a construction company and am a part-time WCC student.

I was accustomed, in face-to-face classes, to a certain number of students who appear on my roster but miss the first meeting. They come a day or more late, sometimes alluding to a family emergency, conflicting work schedule, financial or other problems. In fact, every semester some students register and never show up. I call them ghost students and am continually perplexed by the phenomenon. The online course presented an additional set of challenges, however—browsers, Javascript, caches, URLs, user names and passwords—and I received phone calls from several students for whom these proved daunting. I duly noted how they had reverted to a more familiar, comfortable mode of communication. I referred them to the DL office for technical support and hoped for the best. Eventually, nineteen of the twenty-two students made their way to the course site and posted bios. Three ghosts remained on my roster without ever logging on—apparent casualties of the medium itself.

The Unexpected

"Expect the unexpected" is wise counsel. That semester began on September 4, 2001. A week later, while getting dressed, I learned of the monstrous attack on the World Trade Center. I spent that morning alone in front of the television, watching the towers fall over and over. When I could no longer bear the nightmarish images, I went online to visit my course, yearning for the distraction of work. Instead, I found a message that the Website was unavailable. I learned later that the server's connection to the Internet ran through the World Trade Center; nearly a week passed before I could reestablish contact with my online students.

Meeting my face-to-face class on September 12, I was sick at heart, overcome by grief, fear, anger, and confusion over the horror that had transpired in lower Manhattan. I hated the terrorists but had no confidence in the venal coterie in Washington that would determine how the nation would respond. I had no idea how to act or what to say. I feared that I might burst into tears or launch into an incoherent diatribe that would lead students to conclude that they were being taught by a madman or a terrorist sympathizer. I was keenly aware that we had spent a scant three hours together and were still building rapport and trust. I was reluctant to expose the churning current of conflicting thoughts and feelings that engulfed me and determined to offer only calm reassurance in this charged atmosphere. Already I had received a phone call from one student whose husband and uncle, both firemen, were missing. I had no idea who else had been personally affected. I began class with perfunctory comments about "our common grief and outrage" and added: "Many people have asked you to pray, to hug your loved ones, to maintain a minute of silence. This is a writing course, so I will ask that you write." We wrote in silence and then went on with the class. I spoke about a graduate school professor who continually reminded his students that "literature is one of the healing arts." I hoped that the readings contained something that might actually bring an ounce of comfort. For the remainder of the semester, I struggled to maintain my composure in that classroom. Normally, I draw energy from the give-and-take of discussion and openly share my personal history and views on any subjects that arise. That term, I tried to rein in my feelings, control vagrant thoughts, and keep everyone on a steady course.

By contrast, the asynchronous, distant cyberclassroom provided a space to compose myself and my thoughts. I was never so grateful for the cool detachment of the written word. I wasn't afraid of falling apart in front of my students or of alienating them by airing—unedited—my many reservations about the mindless rush to retaliate. Although the reality of the September 11 attack hovered above us like a dark cloud, we were at least given an opportunity, in the quiet company of our keyboards, to hold the pain at arm's length and shape a response. I welcomed students with a revised schedule and these words: "We are back online with an ISP that does not run through the World Trade Center, but not back to normal by any stretch of the imagination. I do not know how directly you were affected by this tragedy, but I know how difficult it is to concentrate in such a situation. We are all in need of healing, and I hope that reading and writing about culturally rich literature may help."

Students reported back in, one by one over the course of a week, like scattered soldiers in some tale of the Lost Patrol. Many of their postings alluded to our common nightmare. Jay wrote, "Im a little late getting started with the responses in this class but who could blame me with all that is going on so close to us. It seems like i watched more tv in the last few days then in my whole life." Tina informed her group: "I was having a difficult time dealing with the tragedy because one of my friends was missing but, thank God, she turned up safe." As weeks passed and something like normalcy began to return to my life and my work, I continued to notice how different online teaching is and how I made adaptations to accommodate it.

The insights gleaned under those extreme circumstances have been deepened by subsequent semesters of teaching both online and face-to-face and might be sorted under the categories of classroom management, channel(s) of communication, and issues of evaluation.

Classroom Management

Classroom management problems can weigh heavily in the lives of composition teachers, who typically encounter students early in their college careers. Face-to-face teaching makes intense emotional demands on us. Students sometimes take a long time to adjust to the expectations of higher education; some never do, but remain for a period in our classrooms, playing out their confusion and unhappiness. In that first difficult semester, and subsequently, I came to view the cyberclassroom as a refuge where discipline problems in the conventional sense do not occur: no dozing, no rude chatter, no hostile glares, no one sauntering in half an hour late—just responses and essays submitted on time or not and a surround of informal email exchanges. No doubt Jay, Elaine, Tina, and their classmates had their share of personal difficulties and emotional baggage, but they weren't acted out in front of me. Instead, they were on occasion communicated in writing, but without affecting the classroom experience of other students.

Accountability issues do not, of course, disappear in the cyberclassroom, but they are significantly reshaped. In face-to-face composition teaching, missed deadlines, for example, can create problems for students and professors alike. When essays come in late, the slow, recursive process by which students deepen their abilities is short-circuited. Late essays also subvert my strategies for managing the paper load, often making the last days of the semester a hellish affair of nonstop grading. Students who come to class without their writing also affect the dynamics of small-group work. While their peers read responses or essay drafts aloud, they sit smiling sheepishly behind empty desks as if their physical presence were sufficient evidence of good intentions. That semester my evening, face-to-face students were a relatively serious and hardworking group, yet in the middle weeks of the term, while they were taking midterms in other courses, a distressingly large number showed up empty-handed. To communicate how seriously I took deadlines and the group processes they enabled, I roamed the classroom noting the names of those without their assignments and threatening dire consequences. I recalled the high school teacher I had once been, neither very happy with this particular strategy nor with the felt need to strategize at all.

Online, enforcing deadlines was much easier. When I announced in the "Course Information" page that "I will not read and you will not receive credit for any response posted after the deadline," students saw only this stark warning. They took my words literally, and indeed the WebCT software provided an impressive set of tools for turning this warning into reality. Dates and times were permanently recorded; there was no disputing the electronic record. I could even lock a discussion board, making it impossible to post assignments late.

The first time I locked a board, I recalled the wonderful scene near the end of *The Wizard of Oz* where Dorothy and her companions are ushered into the inner sanctum of the Emerald Kingdom for an audience with the Wizard himself. A thunderous voice resonates from a giant, disembodied head: "I am the great and glorious Oz!" The effect is terrifying until Toto pulls back the curtain and reveals the rather ordinary man at the controls. I pulled off a similar stunt for the entire semester. If someone missed the occasional deadline, he or she simply suffered the consequence of a lower grade without imposing a future claim on my time. Four of nineteen active students dropped the course, but mostly, overwhelmingly, the students got the work in on time. Three ghost students who never logged on, four who withdrew, fifteen who completed and passed—this was comparable to my experience over many semesters of face-to-face teaching. Toward the end of the term, when the pattern of steady, disciplined reading and writing was well established, I did agree to several requests for extensions, in the process encountering the one student who would lift the curtain, the one who demanded to "meet the man behind the words."

The Man Behind the Words

Elaine's strengths as reader and writer were apparent from her first response, to Chekhov's "Lady with the Pet Dog." Here is an excerpt:

> Suppose I told you that I had written a story about the color gray? Would you want to read it? Well, maybe if I said I'll include a clandestine love affair. Would that interest you a little more? I might add in the battle between what is pure and impure. Piqued your interest yet? One more thing. The guy is a self-centered womanizer and the woman is a naïve little adulteress. I'll put them in a frigid climate and watch the temperature rise. Have I got you now?

It was great stuff—smart, confident, conversational—and continued to meet her own high standard week after week. If the cyberclassroom was my refuge, it was Elaine's playground, and she could roam freely among the discussion boards, posting comments in response to anyone in the class. She embodied Roger Akers' observation about how the same student can play different roles in different kinds of classrooms: "In many classrooms, one or two students often respond to nearly all questions and tend to monopolize the discussion. These same students may be prolific writers on discussion forums as well, but their actions do not impede upon others because the time and place constraints are no longer in place." Elaine might "monopolize the discussion" in a face-to-face class, but online, her decision "to play hard . . . and have fun" was not a problem for other students. In fact, her emails to me indicated that she had become a mentor to several classmates: "I didn't send you a copy of my discussion with Tina. I'm not sure that I wish to give full disclosure of my critique lunacy. Tina asks me a two-line question about how I can get so much out of a brief story. I reply with two or three pages of my analyzing methodology."

Elaine wrote often to me: "I smile when I read the boards. Tina is almost always the first one to post. Her enthusiasm is infectious." It was as if we were colleagues chatting about students in our classes, developing what Linda Boynton calls a "partnership": "Online courses allow more of a 'partnership' to develop" with students (303); Boynton adds that "'Partnership' is really a synonym for 'power shift.' . . . [P]erhaps . . . their 'faceless' identity breaks down some of the artificial authority our now invisible bigger desks traditionally project" (306). Despite the positive spirit of Boynton's claims, I reacted to several of Elaine's emails with vague unease. "Did Jay drop out?" she asked one day. "I got a big kick out of reading his raw responses." I knew that Jay's responses were quite "raw," that he was submitting work only sporadically, and that I had warned him that he might fail, but professional boundaries obviously prevented my sharing such information.

For the most part, however, I continued to savor Elaine's lively writing until I was jolted by another turn of events. About eleven weeks into the term, Elaine requested a deadline extension for a major essay, citing unnamed "major family challenges." I readily agreed. When her paper eventually arrived, it read like an extended response, intelligent but rambling, not at all what I was expecting. Concerned that her course grade was in jeopardy, I sent a gentle warning. Her response stunned me: "There's a first time for everything. A first time to tell a professor that my life is filled with 'challenges.' . . . A first time to leave out what the word 'challenges' meant." She then provided a catalog of calamities: medical treatments that left her "sick as a dog"; a husband threatening to leave; a violent, alcoholic son; a daughter healing from a recent injury. Her tone was sharp and accusatory: "I believed you. You told me to be kind to myself. I took you for your word. That paper was written under duress. You knew that I was going through something. . . . Did you stop and wonder why you would receive a paper so out of character?"

Over the years, I have encountered students suffering the full spectrum of disasters: physical illness, mental or emotional disorders, financial woes, academic failure, family discord, problems on the job. But here was nearly every possible ill heaped on one student's head—Elaine's—and I'd had no warning. Until that disappointing essay, Elaine had done a remarkable job maintaining her composure and keeping her problems to herself. Perhaps I might have missed visual clues available in the conventional classroom, but at least they are available. By contrast, the online medium forces us into a single channel of communication in which we present ourselves solely through the written word, not unlike the writer of a letter. Near the end of Walter Ong's classic essay "The Writer's Audience Is Always a Fiction," he examines that rhetorical situation:

> The dimensions of fiction in a letter are many. First, you have no way of adjusting to the friend's real mood as you would be able to adjust in oral conversation. You have to conjecture or confect a mood that he [*sic*] is likely to be in or can assume when the letter comes. And, when it does come, he has to put on the mood that you have fictionalized for him. . . . Letters do not have this normal give-and-take: they are one-way movements. (19)

Even letters transmitted electronically and instantaneously exhibit this fictionalizing quality, I realized. I had written to my "best student," the clever, committed one who always came through. Moreover, Elaine and I both had a stake in her ability to enact this narrative, but only she knew the forces that threatened it. Unable to play the role any longer, recognizing herself and her writing as "so out of character," she erupted in anger at me for assigning her the role.

I sorted through my shock at discovering Elaine's crisis, anger at being attacked for what I considered a helpful gesture, and dismay at facing this difficulty near the end of an already challenging semester. I composed the most diplomatic note I could and, within hours, received a request to meet in person. It appeared the storm had broken, yet I seriously considered asking for a security guard near my office in case I had misread the situation again. I was suddenly aware of how limited was my sense of Elaine—and of other students—whose contact had been limited to cyberspace. Our long meeting was, in fact, friendly and constructive. She left with a plan for completing the course and, I hoped, a sense that she had been heard and the complexity of her situation recognized. I left with renewed appreciation of the value of in-person conferences for understanding students' writing within the context of their lives and literacy histories.

Online Writing, "Good" Writing, and Teaching Writing

Somewhere behind that vexed interaction lay another set of issues: the relation of different types of writing to each other and to the electronic medium and appropriate standards for evaluation. Informing Elaine that her paper had received a C, I noted, "It read more like a very long response than a formally constructed essay. . . . The clever asides, rhetorical questions, stray thoughts that mark your responses are just fine—for responses—but I'm looking for focus, organization, strategic use of evidence, and carefully crafted sentences when I read an essay." Although she acknowledged that the grading criteria were reasonably clear and that her paper was inadequate, the experience shifted certain questions from the margins of my thinking toward the center. Does a new medium of writing and course delivery create new conventions—both rhetorical and typographical—that may trouble composition teachers and others concerned about "good writing"? Is writing online fundamentally different from writing on paper? Is an essay or response transmitted electronically different from an essay or response submitted on paper? How do the answers to such questions affect our thinking about this mode of delivering composition?

I confess that I paid minimal attention to such questions while initially designing the course. Many of the materials were existing Word files copied into html format and uploaded to the site. While they indicated significant differences between essays and responses, they made no distinction between online essays and essays on paper or between online responses and responses on paper, and they said nothing about email. (One exception was a brief set of "Netiquette" injunctions against "flames" and overuse of capital letters.) However, I soon found myself making unanticipated changes in the ways I handled writing assignments and thinking about the implications of such changes. After some difficulties opening essays sent as email attachments and concerned about downloading a virus, I asked students to write in a word processor, then copy, paste, and send their essays as email messages. This shift required immediate adaptations in grading. When a Word file is pasted into an email window, it changes significantly. The window is narrower and the essay becomes a visually longer document. Highlighting features are erased. Indentations and white space between paragraphs are lost and must be manually reentered. Fonts and type size revert to the default Times New Roman at 12 CPI. Such changes made it impossible for students to follow every aspect of MLA format, such as italicized or underlined book titles or hanging indentations in the works cited list, and my grading had to take account of such technical limitations.

The question of standards also arose regarding responses. While I did not expect precise editing or the reshaping of content that produces a finished essay, I did expect students to demonstrate a minimal level of competence associated with college-level writing. Responses were shared publicly in a writing class (and posting to the discussion board made them even more public), and therefore I believed that they required some elementary attention to sentence craft. Yet early in the semester, I noticed responses full of errors. I winced when I encountered such haphazard approaches to grammar and mechanics as Jay exhibited. Here, for example, is his response to "The Lady with the Pet Dog":

> I did not like this story very much. I mean it could of been worse but it also could of been alot better. I usually have trouble reading stories that are translated or are from another country. I do not know what it is, maybe its the difference in the vocabulary or the grammar but it gives me trouble.
>
> This story was very indepth. While there was a lot of action going on in the real world, a big part of the story took place in Gurovs mind. Gurov is a good character, I like him. He thinks of himself as a ladies man and i guess he is. He has a wife and 2 kids but he just goes on these trips to meet up with women.
>
> Now what takes place between anna and gurov is strange and hard to follow. Gurov meets with her and just sees her as another potential target but after a while falls in love. Then when anna leaves he tells himself it will all be OK but its not. After she is gone the ladies man finds out he isnt as tough as he thought he was. Gurov becomes almost infatuated with her and travels to Anna's home and basically stalks her. Then they realize they both love each other but what they do after that is not clearly explained in the story so who knows what happened.

However superficial, the content of Jay's response covered the ground: acknowledgment of what he brought to his reading of the text, some exploration of a main character and his motivations, and a brief reaction to the open question at the story's end. But I was distracted by the errors, like static in a radio broadcast. I wondered whether he didn't know how to edit his work or whether he might be carrying over habitual practices from other online contexts (email, instant messaging, chat rooms) where speed can count far more than form.

Comparing Jay's early responses with his emails and essays, I thought I could discern a pattern. The essays showed evidence of basic competence in grammar and mechanics, but the emails seemed like breathless utterances through the keyboard:

> hi prof., couple of requests if you dont mind. i was wondering if maybe i could get some sort of insight into how im doing in the class so far, that would be nice. and also i was wondering when you were gonna do the calendar for october, because that calendar is my guiding light (no i dont watch saop operas haha) its a big helper. Ok thats about it!

I regard such email as spontaneous functional communication. I would no more correct its flawed mechanics than point out the nonstandard usages I hear in a phone call or a quick chat after class with a student. But responses are different, falling somewhere between essays and emails. Perhaps Jay and some of his classmates interpreted my description of responses as "informal" or "less polished" than essays to mean that they could follow whatever practices they normally followed in email and other online contexts. After I alerted Jay that this was a problem, his responses showed more careful editing, indicating that he had the language skills to correct his work when he thought it worth his time and attention. He may, for all I know, have shifted from composing in the message window of the discussion board to composing in Word, taking advantage of its autocorrect features and then copying the text into a discussion message.

The question of standards for evaluating online writing is, unsurprisingly, a source of controversy. Nearly a decade ago, Gail Hawisher and Charles Moran offered "the beginnings of a rhetoric and a pedagogy" for electronic communication, approvingly citing a Rand Corporation report that characterized email as "a fundamentally new medium with significantly new characteristics that cannot be treated with the old rules alone" (629). A recent book takes the opposite tack, offering guidelines for writing in an environment compared to the "Wild West . . . with everybody shooting from the hip and no sheriff in sight" (O'Conner and Kellerman 6). While acknowledging that "e-mail has single-handedly revived the epistolary tradition" (9), the authors complain that "the spelling in e-mail is rotten, the grammar is atrocious, the punctuation—don't ask" (3). Undergirding the argument that "the old rules" apply equally to magazines, college essays, and chat rooms is an explicit discounting of the significance of medium: "People who still ask whether online writing has to be good writing just don't get it. Words, whether etched in stone, written in sand, sent by Morse code, inked on parchment, or transmitted in bytes, serve only one purpose: to connect us with other people" (5). One reviewer chides O'Conner and Kellerman for not "examining why online writing is so undisciplined and attempting to appreciate the virtue of such impertinence. . . . The Internet, so long as it remains in . . . its 'Wild West stage,' offers an opportunity for the unwashed masses to rethink accepted rules of grammar, to reclaim them and to reinvent them to suit new meanings" (Keats). Engaging the debate from the perspective of composition theory, Joe Wilferth argues that "the dichotomy between public and private or academic and nonacademic-based literacies need not be so prevalent in the electronic medium. Students might benefit from a hybrid form of writing which blends their private reading (e.g. comic books, popular magazines, and favorite websites) with a school related assignment."

Implicit in Wilferth's analysis is the need to shape new standards of evaluation for this new medium for inscribing texts and delivering composition.

Delivery and the Future

Such clashing views evoke familiar battle lines: basic skills versus higher-order thinking, phonics versus whole language, prescriptive versus descriptive linguistics, tradition versus reform. I suspect both sides miss the point. The medium of communication *must* have an effect. Writing with a pen (not to mention a chisel or a stylus) is quite different from writing with a typewriter, from writing with a computer, and from writing online. The medium in which students shape their texts changes how they write and develop as writers. It changes the dynamics of the composition classroom. I rediscover this every time I teach a lab-based remedial course to a group composed of some students who have used computers at home and in school all their lives and others who have never touched a keyboard. But to have an effect is different from (*pace* McLuhan) determining everything. The continuities between writing online and offline in a word-processing program are at least as pertinent as the differences, so too the continuities between writing in Word and writing by hand in a bluebook. In an earlier period, composition teachers gradually embraced computers and word processing as an instructional tool, indeed as a ubiquitous facet of our professional lives, and we made conscious and unconscious changes in our classrooms and pedagogies as a result. As online teaching continues to grow, we will adapt again, continuing to slouch toward the goal of bringing students into the modes of language use and intellectual activity valued by the academic community. Even as we discover unanticipated difficulties and demands for adaptation, we may also conclude that—by cutting through classroom management problems, by replacing ephemeral classroom talk with a permanent record, and by immersing students deeply and continually in writing—online courses do a better job of inculcating the extended exploration and analysis of texts and the elaboration of a point of view and the marshaling of supporting evidence that mark real scholarly work.

We may, in short, learn to love the cyberclassroom as a site for delivering composition.

Note

1. Excerpts from students' communications are used with permission. All names have been changed.

Works Cited

Akers, Roger. "Web Discussion Forums in Teaching and Learning." University of North Carolina at Chapel Hill. http://horizon.unc.edu/TS/cases/1997-08a.asp. Aug. 6, 2002.

Boynton, Linda. "When the Class Bell Stops Ringing: The Achievements and Challenges of Teaching Online First-Year Composition." *Teaching English in the Two-Year College* 29.3 (2002): 298–311.

Goffman, Erving. *The Presentation of Self in Everyday Life*. Garden City, NY: Doubleday, 1959.

Hawisher, Gail E., and Charles Moran. "Electronic Mail and the Writing Instructor." *College English* 55.6 (1993): 627–43.

Keats, Jonathon. Review of *You Send Me: Getting It Right When You Write Online*, by Patricia T. O'Conner and Stewart Kellerman. *Salon*. Accessed online at www.salon.com/books/ review/2002/08/26/o_conner/index.html. Aug. 7, 2003.

O'Conner, Patricia T., and Stewart Kellerman. *You Send Me: Getting It Right When You Write Online*. New York: Harcourt, 2002.

Ong, Walter. "The Writer's Audience Is Always a Fiction." *PMLA* 90 (1975): 9–21.

Sennett, Richard. *The Fall of Public Man*. London: Faber, 1974.

Wilferth, Joe. "Private Literacies, Popular Culture, and Going Public: Teachers and Students as Authors of the Electronic Portfolio." *Kairos* 2 (2002). Accessed online at http://english.ttu.edu/kairos/7.2/sectionone/wilferth/1.htm. Aug. 7, 2003.

14

Distributed Teaching, Distributed Learning

Integrating Technology and Criteria-Driven Assessment into the Delivery of First-Year Composition

Rebecca Rickly
Texas Tech University

In our program at Texas Tech, three writing program administrators collaboratively run first-year composition (FYC). We offer—in fact, we require—multiple means of professionalization before teaching assistants can teach FYC. PhD and MA students must take a course in the history and theory of teaching composition (or have had the equivalent in transfer credit), and both must attend at least two professional development workshops each semester, attend a two- to four-day orientation before fall and spring semesters, and be observed by a WPA during their first semester. MA students who have never taught serve as "apprentices" their first semester. Before teaching, they complete a practicum of teaching methods and spend three hours a week observing and holding reflective conversations with a mentor teacher. During their apprenticeship, they practice grading, teaching, and curriculum development as well as read and discuss pedagogical articles.

Before we began our new program, all PhD-level TAs taught two courses a semester (capped at twenty-five students each), and the new MA apprentices would teach one course of twenty-five their first semester (after the semester of preparation) and then two courses each subsequent semester. Contractually, full-time TAs were responsible for a twenty-hour week. All graduate students were required to take three classes a semester to maintain funding. The same textbooks (a rhetoric and a handbook) were to be used in each class, and all TAs were strongly encouraged to use the "default" syllabus. Because the senior WPA, Fred Kemp, was one of the developers of the LAN-based Daedalus Integrated Writing Environment in the 1980s, TTU has been a leader in integrating technology into the FYC curriculum. Though access to technology had increased and we now had four computer classrooms, we simply did not have enough computer lab space for every class. To address this situation, Fred created a Web-based writing application, TOPIC (Texas Tech Online Print-Integrated Curriculum). This homegrown Web application, programmed in Interdev using an SQL database structure, allows students to see the syllabi online at any time, turn in work outside of class, and conduct peer critiques online. In effect, it serves as a course management system similar to commercial systems like WebCT and Blackboard. Teachers are able to post syllabi, keep attendance, comment on drafts, and submit grades (which the program compiles, weights, and makes available to students in real time). Initially, all FYC students submitted all work on TOPIC, and teachers recorded grades and attendance on TOPIC. Teachers were strongly encouraged to make comments on TOPIC as well, though many chose to ask students to print out papers so they could make comments on hard copies; that way, students would have immediate access to commentary, grades, and attendance, something they often complained they had not received in a timely fashion. This, then, was our "new" version of FYC.

However, the following problems quickly arose:

- We received notification from our departmental chair that the university was expecting a huge increase in freshman enrollment in the next two semesters. The FYC budget would not receive an increase; thus our only recourse would be to increase class size (currently capped at twenty-five students)—something we had fought successfully for the last three years. Our dream of cutting down the required teaching load to a 2/1 seemed out of reach.
- After the first class day, more than thirty students lined up and officially complained that they could not understand their English teacher. We had at least four nonnative speakers teaching in the program, and we found that two of them in particular were getting strong, frequent complaints. The number of students in our offices doubled by the next class day.
- In the first week alone, we saw at least six students with grade complaints from the previous semester, most of them based on "I didn't get any feedback, so I have no idea why I got the grade I got" and "My teacher hated me."
- Upon analyzing the last semester's statistics, we found that while most teachers (twenty out of fifty-five) received good to moderate evaluations for this required class, we still had four teachers who had a horrendous add-drop rate (they ended the semester with fewer than six students in

their classes), three whose student evaluations were well below both departmental and university averages, and eighteen whose grades were ultra-inflated (mostly As and a few Bs, or more than 50 percent As).

- A seemingly never-ending parade of TAs tramped through our offices, asking how to download the default syllabus, although we had already covered this topic extensively. We spent a good part of our first few days showing them how to download the syllabus and customize their classes on the Web, since it was a requirement for all FYC classes to have a syllabus online, keep grades and attendance online, and have students turn in papers online.

These problems are typical, and not at all earth-shattering, but it was just this sort of semester start that led us to our reenvisioning of the FYC program. In particular, I would like to concentrate on the second item—students not being able to understand their instructor—because that is where our breakthrough occurred. I will also come back to the other items later in the chapter.

A Quick Fix?

All three of the WPAs at TTU coadministered the writing program, with the help of a full-time secretary and a graduate student assistant. All of us (including the graduate student) received a course release for our administrative duties, part of which included holding office hours and handling student complaints. During this semester, we continued receiving a steady stream of student complaints about two new graduate instructors, both nonnative speakers. As the senior (and, at the time, the only tenured) WPA, Fred Kemp offered to observe these two teachers on a regular basis. Because our TAs teach two courses (and take three) each semester, this meant that Fred spent four hours observing class three times a week. In short, he ended up coteaching one TA's class and taking over the second TA's class. Teaching four extra courses was one thing, but grading them was something else—after all, he was teaching his own FYC course, as well as a graduate course in technical communication and rhetoric, and he was one of the coadministrators of a large FYC program. But these students needed feedback on their writing, perhaps more so since their awkward shift in teachers midway through the semester.

Fred had proposed a writing-across-the-curriculum-based initiative several years prior that would utilize his own Web-based writing application, TOPIC. He argued that students could turn in papers online that would be graded collaboratively by English graduate students and graduate students and professors in a particular discipline. He decided to tweak the system so that we could use the same principle, and *we* could be the "expert readers." Students in both of his new FYC classes were required to turn in their papers online, which would then place the papers in a queue. The five of us—the three WPAs and two graduate student assistants—would log onto TOPIC and anonymously grade all papers that appeared in the grading queue. Because the grading was distributed, we would be able to do little bits at a time, and because Fred wanted to make sure the students felt they were getting a fair deal, he decided that each paper would have at least two readings: one with a grade and a comment, one a grade only (the second grader could see the first grader's comment, but not the numeric score). If the two scores were more than eight points apart, it would go to a third reader. In addition, each draft was commented upon by two student peer critiques, so students were receiving a copious amount of focused feedback.

All of us, including the graduate students, had ample experience teaching and grading FYC, so the extra work was familiar. And, in fact, the anonymity of the papers made the grading quicker: each paper went through two drafts before a final draft was turned in. The first drafts of the paper took about five to ten minutes each to grade and comment on (and only a few minutes to assign a grade only), and final drafts averaged about fifteen to twenty minutes each, with extensive commenting and a grade (and assigning a grade only took about five minutes each). However, in spite of the "ease" with which we were able to grade, we would soon find that our collective experience did not necessarily lead to the same conclusions. Our first stab at grading blindly online was draft 1.2, for example, the second draft of a three-draft sequence of the initial exploratory essay, and it resulted not only in a dismal interrater reliability rate (we had more than 30 percent third reads) but also in a heated discussion of what makes writing good, in our weekly composition meetings. Disappointedly, while between us we had more than one hundred years of combined experience, we found ourselves grading according to our personal preferences and arguing those preferences in terms of the assignment description and the generic final draft grading rubric ("An A paper will . . ."). Ultimately, we graded the drafts according to our own idiosyncratic likes and dislikes and then defended our grading vehemently to one another.

Fred immediately revised the syllabus so that each draft had specific criteria that would apply to it alone but that related to the larger completed text. He did the same for the peer critiques and self-evaluations that we would be grading (we all agreed that, for students to take these reflective assignments seriously, they needed grades—but these documents had only one reader each). During the weekly composition meetings, we went over these criteria, negotiating what they meant, determining how they should be applied, and adding, subtracting, or clarifying when we felt the need. Similarly, Fred shared the criteria in process with his class, and they underwent a similar reflection and negotiation process. The next time we graded papers, it was to grade assignment 1.3, the final draft of the exploratory essay, and using the new, focused, negotiated criteria to guide us, we were able to grade and comment on final papers in about eighteen minutes each (with substantial comments both intertextual and comprehensive, an error log based on the *St. Martin's* twenty common errors that TOPIC would calculate an "error weight" for, and a numerical grade). Second and third reads, where we had to enter a grade only, took about three to five minutes each. What was really exciting, though, was that with these negotiated criteria, our interrater reliability was much improved—we now had a 4 percent third-read rate.

What was amazing about this process (and the consistency continued, with a final average of third reads around 14 percent) was that even though we were experienced teachers and administrators, we found that we learned more about grading—and, subsequently, about teaching—this semester than we had in a very long time. The five of us had lengthy email and face-to-face discussions about what we had learned (concerning the importance of criteria that were public, defensible, and understood by all, what seemed to make a "helpful" comment versus a nonhelpful one online, and so forth). All of us were invigorated by the experience; we felt like we were learning to be teachers all over again, engaging in the reflection-in-action that Donald Schon has described as we participated in, revised, and further examined the system we were using. What's more, the students in Fred's classes were engaging in a similar discussion, clarifying the criteria, and learning to apply the criteria in their own peer critiques, mirroring the reflection-in-action we were experiencing.

It is not unusual for a WPA to have to cover a class or two in emergency or extenuating situations. In this case, Fred had to take over two classes in addition to the two he was already teaching. We thought we had hit upon a good solution to distribute the preparation, teaching, and evaluating that was part of taking over a class so that one person would not be overwhelmed yet the students in the classes would still have a good, consistent experience. Fred became the classroom instructor for two classes of twenty-five, focusing on modeling good writing, good peer editing, and helping students understand the criteria by which each of the documents would be evaluated; the five of us became the collaborative curriculum planning, negotiating, and evaluating team—what we would later call document instructors.

Problems on the Horizon

I would like to return to the scenario at the beginning of this chapter to discuss other problems that arose this semester and point to how they contributed to the growth and expansion of this experimental program. We had been told in no uncertain terms that we would be getting 25 percent more freshmen in the subsequent fall but that we would not be receiving any more money to hire graduate or adjunct instructors. We knew already that our teaching load for TAs—teaching two classes while taking three classes—was difficult to manage and do well. We were concerned, then, when our only option for meeting the increased demand seemed to be an institutionally ordained increase in class size, from twenty-five to possibly thirty. We had to find a way to meet the needs of the FYC program and the FYC students while still providing the TAs with experience and a professionalization opportunity. Perhaps, we thought, our experiment could be expanded.

Two of the most common student complaints we get as WPAs revolve around grades. The first is that students feel the teacher was biased, subjective, or unfair, usually because he or she didn't like the student (according to the student). The second complaint is that the students do not understand why they got the grade they got, because they did not pay attention, the teacher was not clear, or some combination of the two. During the semester in question, the latter situation arose when we had a student come to one of us saying, "I don't understand how I can get better." When we looked at the comments he had received, we were as perplexed as the student. The only comments were "85—Very Good." Because we had required that students turn in papers on TOPIC and had encouraged teachers to grade online (and required teachers to record grades and attendance online), we were able to log on to this section as the teacher to see if there was any information the student had missed. What we found was that while this teacher did grade online (online comments were this student's only source of feedback), most papers had just a short sentence or two and a numerical grade as the only source of evaluation. We knew that our TAs were under a lot of pressure, taking three courses while teaching two, and yet students needed better feedback if the goals of FYC were to be met, so we decided that we would have a workshop on responding to student writing, and we went to TOPIC to find good examples of commenting. While our intentions were good, what we found on TOPIC was discouraging.

Many of the TAs were behind in their grading. In fact, during the eighth week of class, after students had turned in almost half of the writing required for the course, some students had yet to receive *any* feedback. Others got short comments and a grade. Still others received a grade only. To be fair, many TAs had spent a goodly amount of time grading, and students had plenty of good, evaluative feedback from these teachers and from their peers (since frequent peer editing sessions were built into the default syllabus), but there were nonetheless a frightening number of TAs who had not graded anything or who had graded only cursorily, who did not encourage revision or application of new ideas. Perhaps only five teachers were in question (though I recall the number being higher)—but those five teachers were exclusively responsible for two classes of twenty-five students each semester. That means that five hundred students each academic year may have been in a writing class where no feedback by the teacher was received in a timely fashion, or else in a class where the only feedback received from a teacher was a numerical grade and a sentence or two of vague, generic commentary ("Very Good").

As good, traditionally trained WPAs, our initial reaction was to respond with increased training in the form of workshops or with what we had come to call "intensive mentoring" (meeting one-on-one with a TA who had received multiple student complaints or consistently poor student evaluations to reflect on specific practices and target specific areas of improvement).[1] However, this process was time-consuming—as is all teacher development—and we had no real proof that it yielded long-term improvement; most TAs who had participated in multiple workshops and/or intensive mentoring had left the FYC program to teach in literature, creative writing, or technical communication. Like many other schools of our size, we have a 25 to 35 percent turnover rate each year. Providing increased training and support aimed at teaching FYC, therefore, often falls flat since the participants know that they soon will be teaching a different course, one in their area of expertise. We do have some excellent teachers in our program, but they soon leave to teach elsewhere; we also have a few substandard teachers who, in spite of various training and remediation, still do not provide students with the feedback or instruction they need to become better writers. Our own experience taught us that even good teachers tended to rely on their own individual preferences, their own idiosyncratic notions of what good college-level writing is, personalizing even a default syllabus to the point that the more than twenty-five hundred students who took FYC each year were given very different messages on how to write and what makes for good writing.

Meeting Needs in Context

How could we better meet the goals of FYC? How could we prepare students to be successful in college writing while still giving the TAs a valuable experience learning to teach? As we went back to these core questions, we tried shifting our view from the individualistic to the programmatic. We began to sort the facts surrounding our situation and think about what we might do to better meet the administrative needs of the program, the scholarly needs of the FYC students, and the pedagogical and professional needs of the TAs. Instead of being tied to a "this is how it's always been done" mentality in the teaching of writing, we found our experience in distributing the various aspects of the writing classroom among ourselves gave us the courage to see beyond the brick-and-mortar classrooms and helped us envision some exciting—and frightening—new systems-level possibilities in terms of teaching writing.

Before we began, however, we brainstormed what our constraints were. *Constraints* is a broad term we used to include the organizational, institutional, bureaucratic, regulatory, financial, and material realities that dictated the program's scope and mission. Next, we listed the principles that we all agreed led to good writing and good writing instruction. While the representation in Table 14–1 is not intended to be parallel, it does compare the various constraints

Table 14–1
Constraints and Principles of Good Writing Instruction

Constraints for the Writing Program	Principles of Good Writing Instruction
• Number of rooms available • Seating in the rooms available • Equipment available to students • Equipment available to instructors • Number of entering freshmen needing to take FYC sequence • Number of TAs, adjuncts, and faculty able to teach FYC • Money available to pay FYC instructors • Institutional requirement for FYC sequence • Departmental contractual requirement for TAs	• Students should have frequent and varied opportunities to write • Students should engage in frequent peer and self-critique • Students should receive timely feedback • Students should receive helpful feedback • Students should engage in a drafting sequence for assignments • Assessment should be public, understood, and defensible; students should know and understand what criteria are being used to evaluate their work • Students should be taught to integrate technology into their researching, writing, editing, and revising processes • Students should have access to models of good writing

with the theoretical, pedagogical goals we had. We needed to think outside the box—in fact, outside the building—if we were going to be able to achieve our goals in terms of delivering good writing instruction on a programmatic level.

As we analyzed the information we had brainstormed, we tried to think critically about our situation. How could we meet the needs of the graduate teaching assistants in terms of support, training, and professional development? How could we get TAs to fulfill their contractual obligation (twenty hours a week) without increasing (indeed, trying to decrease) the time they already spent teaching and preparing to teach? How could we assure the FYC students of a consistent, positive experience that would lead to more successful writing in the future? And, given the proposed increase of students, how could we reenvision our FYC program despite our constraints? As we examined our situation in light of our beliefs and our constraints, we started to posit solutions as to how we might be able to apply the principles of good writing instruction within the specific confines of our particular program. Table 14–2 outlines some of this thinking, along with some proposed benefits and drawbacks of our solutions.

Table 14–2
Programmatic Pedagogical Applications and Our Solutions Assessed

Pedagogical Concepts to Be Applied	Our Solution, Benefits, and Drawbacks
More and varied writing experiences	*Solution*: Require less time in the classroom, and compensate for less seat time with more writing outside of class *Benefits*: Students often perceive class time as "a waste"; gives them more practice writing *Drawbacks*: To make this program work, we need to put more students in each class, increasing the normal load if we remain with the cohort teaching model; the subjective relationship that is often positive between teacher and student is minimized; getting to a computer may be difficult for some students
Classroom time spent on learning and understanding criteria by which writing will be evaluated	*Solution*: Separation of teaching and assessing activities; with more students and less class time, teacher must focus on making sure the assignment, the criteria, and the sequence of assignments are understood *Benefits*: Students can focus on skills that will translate to other academic writing tasks; students will be assessed anonymously, thus more fairly, according to criteria they have learned and understood *Drawbacks*: Either teaching or assessing might be perceived as more desirable; TAs will not immediately be given ownership of a classroom
Timely, helpful feedback	*Solution*: Employ a grading pool of trained assessors; each paper gets at least two anonymous evaluations according to specific criteria *Benefits*: Students will receive feedback that they can use as they draft their assignments; they will become critical consumers of information, deciding what to pay attention to and what to leave alone *Drawbacks*: Grading must be done on a regular basis, which means that waiting until the weekend to grade is not an option
Frequent peer and self-critique	*Solution*: Engage in these activities outside of class on TOPIC; use assessors to evaluate *Benefits*: Students not only engage in peer critique, modeling what the assessors do with their own drafts, but these critiques are assessed, too, according to criteria they learn and understand, so the critiques have both inherent and programmatic value *Drawbacks*: Could begin to seem like busywork if students do not take it seriously; so much writing might seem overwhelming

Our Systems-Based Solution

Based on the success of our needs-based model of distributed teaching and evaluating during the fall of 2001, we opted to test the program on a larger scale in spring of 2002. We asked three experienced TAs to serve as classroom instructors, meeting once a week with eight classes, capped at thirty-five.[2] We also asked six TAs, some new and some experienced (each one had at least been through the required course and several workshops, but three had not taught before), to become document instructors. Based on their contractual obligation in terms of hours they were supposed to spend teaching for us, we allotted a quota of assignments to be graded (drafts and critiques) each week. The classroom instructors were also given a small quota of grading, based on their contractual obligation, too, minus the time spent preparing for and teaching class—but we allowed them some "free" time too, since they would be the negotiators, holding office hours, handling student questions, and interfacing with the document instructors.

Here, then, are the logistics of the new pilot program:

- Class time was cut in half, and writing assignments were increased. Classes that used to meet twice a week now met only once a week, but students turned in more writing outside of class on TOPIC than they did before (approximately one-third more).
- The major activities of the FYC class—teaching and responding—were physically split. Classroom instructors met with students once a week face-to-face, and document instructors read, responded to, and evaluated student writing, all online. The WPAs also participated in this project by grading occasionally.
- Criteria, specific to each draft or critique, were presented, discussed, and modeled in class by classroom instructors. Students used this information as they wrote, critiqued, and reflected on their drafts online outside of class.
- Document instructors used these same criteria to assess each draft and critique.
- Each major writing task was assessed twice; if the scores differed by more than eight points, the document went to a third reader.
- Classroom instructors also assessed papers blindly according to specific criteria, and since the papers submitted on TOPIC were distributed randomly, it was unlikely that a classroom instructor would have to evaluate his or her own students, at least not on a regular basis.
- Classroom instructors handled complaints, questions, and other classroom management issues. Because classroom instructors had access to all papers, comments, and grades for students in their sections, they also had the option of overriding a grade if they believed that the agreed upon grade

was inappropriate or if there were extenuating circumstances that those in the grading pool were not aware of.

- The classroom instructors, document instructors, and WPAs met once a week for about an hour to negotiate definitions, discuss issues, model feedback, assess feedback, and ask questions. These individuals also used email for the same activities during the week.

The pilot program showed us much about our practices and program—first, that our hypothesis was true: TOPIC kept track of time spent grading, and the participants spent only 30 to 60 percent of their contractually obligated time actually grading (we included for professional development time to attend weekly meetings and to talk with us in that number). These numbers, while not completely accurate, gave us a concrete sense of what we already knew: some TAs lingered over grading papers; some sped through. Feedback, a vital component of teaching writing, was disparate. Our response—a systems-based delivery—did provide a more uniform, distributed model of feedback, one where grading was a bit more consistent both in terms of what was graded (drafts according to assignment-specific criteria) and how grading was done (in this case, online and blind). Second, it was heartening for us to find that our overworked graduate students were actually able to work fewer hours than they had been working.[3] Third but not least, it was exciting to see the timeliness and consistency with which all of the participants responded to student papers; and because they received multiple sources of feedback before the next draft was due, students were (theoretically, anyway) actually able to use the feedback they received (from both document instructors and peer critiques) to write subsequent drafts or to write better peer or self-critiques.

Programmatic Benefits and Drawbacks

The program carried many benefits for us as administrators. TOPIC allowed us to capture an enormous amount of data, from word counts to turn-in rates, and these data allowed us to speak about this program with enhanced ethos to parents, students, TAs, and other administrators. By raising class size and cutting down seat time, we had done the impossible in the eyes of the institution: made FYC fiscally responsible. And by pointing to the criteria-driven multilayered assessment students were receiving, we were able to show how our program prepared students for the kind of writing experiences they would have in the future, both in and after college, in which their work would often be judged by a variety of people out of context. Students who are used to writing to specific criteria are more likely, we hope, to ask about specific criteria they will be assessed according to in the future. In other words, we hope that this experience will make them more aware of the rhetorical situation surrounding the delivery of their own writing.

In terms of training and professionalizing new TAs, the program gave us insights we had not had access to before. First, because each major draft had two readers, the second reader always saw the first reader's comments (but not the numerical grade). Good comments tended to be imitated; bad comments usually ended up as a discussion point in email or in our weekly meetings. Through the process of second reads, new TAs were receiving solid, incremental training on how to respond to student documents. By reading what others had written, by asking questions about and negotiating the meaning of the criteria, and by simply practicing, they were getting better at responding to student papers. In addition, the WPAs created a rubric for evaluating document instructors' comments, and we began evaluating comments on a regular basis, not as a punitive measure, but simply as a means for TAs in this new program to get a sense of where their strengths and weaknesses might be. If a document instructor had consistently high rankings, we asked him or her to help out with the weekly session or to work with other TAs; if a document instructor had consistently low commentary ratings, we would have an intensive mentoring session before the end of the semester to try to remediate the TA's commenting.[4] Early on, we asked the pilot participants to assess anonymous commentary, to generate criteria that commentary should be assessed according to, or to model good commentary. We hoped that this type of reflective activity would translate into more criteria-driven, helpful commentary to students.

Students benefited, too, from a speedy turnaround time. Most documents were graded and back to the student in three to six days. Students were then able to critically read the responses and decide which they should respond to, given their understanding of the criteria and the assignment. The criteria-based feedback they received clarified what was wrong and right with their writing and gave them focused, specific direction to improve. When at least two trained, intelligent people agreed, they were more likely to believe that the assessment was not biased or subjective.

However, the program had its drawbacks. Students did not all uniformly embrace the program. Many disagreed with the assessment they were given and came to the classroom instructor to "translate." Most of the time, though, if the evaluation was made according to the stated criteria, such negotiations were fairly quick, mandating that the student fully understood the criteria and how his or her paper responded (or failed to respond) to it. Other students missed having "their" teacher respond to their work; the students who normally benefited from the more subjective cohort model were, they thought, disadvantaged by the lack of relationship with the teacher. Showing eagerness, being prepared, speaking out in class, and simply "working hard" did not influence their grades, and many who had relied on these strategies in the past felt frustrated.

Teachers, too, particularly those who had taught under the cohort model, were loath to give up ownership of their classrooms, suffering from what Fred Kemp calls the "psychology of loss." The teachers in our program had been trained in immediacy: they were the ones who had to look at the faces of their students, and they initially wanted to immerse themselves in this immediacy. However, as they graded papers on TOPIC, many soon came to feel a different sense of ownership: programmatic ownership. They were now stewards of a pilot program in FYC at Texas Tech. No longer were they responsible for twenty-five or fifty students; they were responsible for the entire FYC population. As they came to believe in the criteria-driven curriculum, they became better able to handle student questions and complaints, moving from "cop" to "coach" as they pointed students to the benefits of learning to assess, identify, and write to specific criteria.

The Role of Digital Technology in Delivery

In his 1986 study, Hillocks argued that, aside from a one-to-one mentor model, the "environmental mode"—a task-based combination of process and product models of teaching—was the most effective means of teaching. Our new program takes the concept of the environmental teaching model and applies it systematically, allowing for incremental instruction for both students and TAs, while keeping the big picture (assignment sequence, how criteria influence a document, the most effective ways to teach, etc.) in place. As a teacher and an administrator, I find this system-based delivery of solid pedagogy exciting, but I recognize that, for it to indeed include both process and product, the teachers participating in the program need to interact with it, learning about it and constructing new aspects as it is implemented so that it might best address the various classroom (and out-of-class) contexts.

Much has been written in the past few years about technology as a delivery mechanism for education, but we must exercise caution when reading and then reflecting on and enacting what we have read, lest we mistakenly equate technology with delivery. In his theory of technology, Andrew Feenberg argues for "deep democratization" of systems as a way of reclaiming technology from technocrats, of injecting users and their situations into complex tools. For him, technology is colored by the perceptions of its users. If we perceive systems and techniques as mere tools (what Feenberg terms an instrumental view), then we retain human agency but miss opportunities of design and redesign of these tools, since they stand finished in relation to society. If we perceive technology as having a life of its own (technological determinism), then we lose all possibility of participation in the design and maintenance of systems, as these systems are seen as predestined to move in a certain direction. By looking at technology as a mere tool of delivery that we can utilize as is (say, for instance, by integrating a commercial course management system without modification so that it addresses local constraints), or as a means in and of itself (focusing the course so much on technology that writing skills as identified by the WPA Outcomes Statement [Council of Writing Program Administrators] aren't addressed), then WPAs will not be delivering courses effectively in the twenty-first century. The balance between these two approaches—the neutral instrumentalist and the agency-filled determinist—is the realistic and rational approach of the postmodern human, and of the WPA in the age of the corporate university.

Technology is not nearly as simple as mere tools, nor does it have agency of its own. It is not the technology that is vital to us as people or as a culture; it is how we use or implement it, not in a passive way, but in a participatory stance. In this light, actual use surpasses design (as Taylor notes in this volume), and when assessing value in terms of education and delivery, we must look at use rather than at design, and we must look at that use within local contexts. In these terms, educational technology is neither inherently bad nor inherently good; how we choose to use it—and what influences our use—is what determines success or failure. Too often, words like *technology, systematic,* and *efficient* are seen as suspect by those of us in the humanities; I would encourage us to see beyond our knee-jerk reactions and critically examine how technology is *used* before reacting, either positively or negatively. Our model of delivering technologically distributed teaching, learning, and assessment may not be easily replicable, especially in schools that rely heavily on faculty or adjunct labor. Nor will it be appropriate for other local situations wrought with individual, particular constraints. But for those large programs like ours, underfunded and understaffed, that rely primarily on graduate students to teach, we feel it offers the best—the most pedagogically enlightened, the most economically responsible, and the most efficient for both students and teachers—model of delivering FYC to date.

Lingering questions remain, and I would like to conclude by offering some questions WPAs need to consider critically and often in light of the changing circumstances under which FYC is (and will be) delivered.

If FYC serves a socializing and normalizing process in college, perhaps the inclusion of online, database-driven delivery mechanisms forecasts a new normalization focus: away from the aesthetic and toward the pragmatic. Perhaps our programs should concentrate less on preparing students to be successful in humanities-type classes (devaluing the read-and-respond pedagogy often associated with small-group discussion in FYC) and instead emphasize real-world communication skills as does Iowa State in its new program: business letters, reports, argumentation, analysis. Does such a program benefit students by preparing them to function successfully in a capitalist society? Does it undermine the original purpose of a liberal arts, humanistic education?

As Yancey notes in the first chapter, programs that are not fiscally responsible do not survive—or their survival is on a temporary, semester-to-semester basis (see, for example, practically any writing center). How, then, can we be both pedagogically *and* fiscally responsible in our delivery of FYC? Is it better to cling to old goals and practices, only to have programs disappear?

WPAs are notorious for embracing idealist, leftist notions and rejecting corporate, Taylorist ideas. Yet by rejecting such ideas without reflection, aren't we dooming ourselves to failure? Krista Ratcliff suggests that we learn to "listen rhetorically" to those ideas unfamiliar (or unpalatable) to us; should we listen rhetorically to ideas about delivering college composition surrounding corporate culture before dismissing them outright? What do we have to lose? To gain?

If we do not try new means of delivery, approaching them theoretically and pragmatically, but not understanding them completely, knowing that we will stumble, fall, and perhaps even fail, aren't we in danger of having new means of delivery thrust upon us? In other words, if we don't do it, won't someone do it to us?

Not least, if composition as a general education requirement is "amorphous," as Yancey notes in Chapter 1, it is likely to have little or no value to those taking it. How can we assign greater value to this generic requirement? As Martin Jacobi asked in Chapter 2, how can delivery be a mechanism to help us prepare students to be responsible citizens in a democratic society?

Acknowledgments

The author wishes to acknowledge the others involved in the collaborative WPA structure at TTU who allowed this program to evolve and—we hope—thrive: Fred Kemp, Susan Lang, and Rich Rice. Thanks also to Locke Carter for his valuable feedback on this chapter.

Notes

1. For a fuller description of our intensive mentoring program, see Rickly and Harrington's "Feminist Approaches to Mentoring Teaching Assistants: Conflict, Power, and Collaboration."

2. While we capped the pilot sections at thirty-five, students were informed that they would be part of a pilot class, and many chose to drop the course; thus our pilot classrooms had an average of twenty-three students each.

3. When we say that TAs spent less time than they were contractually obligated, we're assuming that everyone teaching under the cohort model was, in fact, working twenty hours a week. Many TAs, I know, put in more hours than they contracted for; a few put in fewer.

4. We found that ranking a comment even with a rubric proved problematic in that TAs were concerned about having their work as teachers graded. During our second year of implementation, we added a rubric so that second readers could rank a response, and students could rank a response on the basis of how helpful the commentary was. While our purpose in providing these rankings was to encourage reflection, and *not* to punish, some TAs still felt troubled by the continual assessment of their work.

Works Cited

Council of Writing Program Administrators. "WPA Outcomes Statement for First-Year Composition." Adopted April 2000. Accessed online at www.ilstu.edu/~ddhesse/wpa/positions/outcomes.htm.

Feenberg, Andrew. *Questioning Technology*. New York: Routledge, 1999.

Hillocks, George. *Research on Written Composition: New Directions for Teaching.* Urbana, IL: National Conference on Research in English and ERIC Clearinghouse on Reading and Communication Skills, 1986.

Kemp, Fred. "Computers Innovation, and Resistance in First-Year Composition Programs." In *Discord and Director: The Post-Modern Writing Program Administration.* Eds. Carolyn Handa and Sharon Mcqee. Logan, UT: Utah State UP 105–22.

Ratcliff, Krista. "Rhetorical Listening: A Trope for Interpretive Invention and a 'Code of Cross-Cultural Conduct.'" *CCC* 51.2 (1999): 195–224.

Rickly, Rebecca and Susan Marie Harrington. "Feminist Approaches to Mentoring Teaching Assistants: Conflict, Power, and Collaboration." In *Preparing College Teachers of Writing: History, Theories, Programs, Practices.* Eds. Betty Pytlik and Sarah Liggett. New York: Oxford UP, 2001, 108–120.

Schon, Donald. *The Reflective Practitioner: How Professionals Think in Action.* New York: Basic Books, 1991.

15

Delivering College Composition into the Future

Kathleen Blake Yancey
Florida State University

My initial interest in the question of the delivery of college composition was motivated by four factors.

One is that I was aware that my teaching of composition had changed: in the terms of medium, today I *deliver* something that is quite different than the course in composition I delivered when I first began teaching. What I teach now is not my mother's composition, nor is it even my own composition of another time and place. Thirty years ago, as a first-year TA, I taught freshman composition, which in terms of *medium* was delivered similarly at *every* institution in the country: in print. It's also fair to point out, however, that print could mean more than one material. It might mean typed copy; it might mean a handwritten submission—and in fact, although it probably sounds quaint now, when we gathered at the ditto master to run copies, we debated passionately about the ethics of *requiring* students to type their final copies, and this, by the way, was the language we used to describe the final text. Today, by way of contrast, composition-as-delivery, for me as for many faculty, is multimedia at least in that it includes pen-and-paper writing as well as word-processor composing.[1] Moreover, today's composition for me is explicitly materially laden, informed and invented by way of print of various kinds (markers, pens, and pencils); by way of word processors and printers and plotter printers; by way of other software (e.g., Excel, Adobe Photoshop); by way of digital cameras; by way of Web searches; by way of sticky notes and whiteboards and Smart Boards and tackboards and classroom walls and hallways. Delivery of both products and practices of *this* first-year composition, then, is multiply and materially textured.

Two is that as I reflected upon my own teaching of composition, I was aware that even as an early teacher, I—like so many of us—pushed against *the physical dimensions of delivery*, against the bare cinder-block classroom walls and the plastic seats designed (it seems) for very small students (not adults) and chipped linoleum floors. I had to work within the assigned space, of course—in the winter you will write outside only so often—but I took it as part of my job to find ways to *rearrange* the given space so that I could invent and deliver something that space was not designed for: learning rather than teaching. (As I have argued elsewhere, as in the case of electronic portfolios, what you arrange is indeed what you invent.) Sometimes I simply abandoned the assigned space for the outside, but more typically I asked students to work with me, rearranging the seats so that we could talk to each other, rearranging them again for peer review and workshop. In other words, first intuitively and later intentionally, I understood given space as something I might shape, and I also intuited something about the relationship between and among space and curriculum and pedagogy. Still, as Joyce Neff so clearly articulates in this volume, the size of the classroom is (surprisingly) deterministic in terms of the number of students it permits. While for those of us committed to small classes, that may be a good thing, for programs it reduces not only flexibility but also, as Neff argues, the ability of programs even to consider alternatives that may enhance learning.

Three is that I was aware that my delivery of composition had changed radically in terms of content. In that first year of TA teaching, I found that the three terms of freshman composition in fact comprised something else, a program in *freshman English*, with—as the catalog copy proclaimed—the first quarter devoted to nonfiction discourse; the second to novels and short stories; and the third to poetry and drama. Composition, in other words (ironically, anticipating Joe Harris' argument in Chapter 12), seemed to be located in pedagogy only—workshopping, journals, peer review—rather than in pedagogy *and* content. Not least, what I taught that year was very similar to what I had taught the previous summer when I student-taught high school English in that while both curricula employed writing practices—writing to learn and writing to perform—both were finally *about* literature. These writing courses are of course quite different from the composition course I currently teach, a course where composition is pedagogy and content both.

Four is that I was aware that many kinds of institutions lay claim to delivering college composition and that we could categorize them into three types. Postsecondary institutions, of course, provide the principal site of delivery, but college composition is also delivered in high schools through dual-enrollment programs and, as Jolliffe and Phelan argue against in Chapter 7, through what tends to function basically as an exemption program, the College Board's Advanced Placement testing program. Do the *non*postsecondary forms, I wondered, really deliver the same composition that I do? Moreover, I thought that if we took a look at representatives of some of the more common forms of college composition, we might find patterns, and in inquiring into those—as well as into places where patterns do not obtain—we would understand composition and its teaching in ways we previously have not.

And that, I thought, might make for a fuller understanding of what college composition is and, perhaps, for a better composition.

We in composition studies are in the midst of a Kuhnian moment unlike any previous such moment. A new SAT writing test—with one impromptu writing delivered in paper and pencil worth 30 percent of the total score paired with a test of grammar and usage accounting for 70 percent of the score—seeks, in the College Board's words, to help prepare students for college, while to many compositionists, it seems to call us back to the past when composition was in search of process, vocabulary, and content. In fact, as the "Portraits of Composition" study (Yancey et al.) demonstrates, what *college writing faculty* say is that one of the four biggest writing challenges new college students face is elaborating the truncated writing process they bring to college with them, which process of course is exactly what twenty-five-minute tests of writing evoke. Moreover, if the process of writing is truncated, so too will be the conception of writing.

At the same moment that the SAT is harkening us to the past, however, compositionists are fast-forwarding us to a very different kind of composition, although even in this curricular and campus site, it's difficult at first glance to see patterns. In Richard Courage's chapter, for example, we see a composition digitally mediated and delivered exclusively online. In Carol Rutz's description of Carleton's program and Joe Harris' of Duke's, we see a composition delivered by faculty whose areas of expertise lie not only outside the field of composition but also outside of English. In other, technologically rich environments, like that at Texas Tech, the teaching function is being radically reconceived; tasks traditionally assigned to a single person are being divided and reassigned to different people. Composition's curriculum, as at Howard, is often specific to the culture of both institution and student population. And in terms of classroom space, the Purdue model shows us a curriculum that, instead of being delivered in a classroom space without regard to the role that space plays in learning, is specifically *designed* (as Todd Taylor advocates in Chapter 10) for *three* learning spaces—the classroom; the computer classroom; and the conference setting. As important in contrast to the world of high school paper-and-pencil tests, in all these postsecondary models of composition, digital technology plays a role—in some cases, as technology light, with word processing assumed; in other cases, as the Stanford model suggests, with technology changing both genres and circulation of composition.

Moreover, the chapters in this volume have provided answers to the questions that initiated them. To take up the first: Is there a difference in composition curriculum between high school and college? Yes. The chapters authored by Chris Farris, Paul Bodmer, and David Jolliffe and Bernard Phelan speak to serious, worthy efforts to bring college composition to the high school classroom, with the underlying assumption that yes, without these efforts, there is a *very* clear difference between the two compositions. So that's one answer. With these efforts, which import writing and reading activities located in rhetorical analysis into the high school classroom, the composition curriculum is enhanced, but as David Jolliffe and Bernard Phelan argue, these practices do not *replace* college composition. Their intent, in fact, isn't replacement at all, but rather better preparation of students *for* college composition. Significantly, that argument—that AP provides preparation rather than replacement—is documented by Kristen Hansen and her colleagues, showing that students who attempt to replace college composition with high school AP scores, particularly those with scores in the 3 range, find themselves at a distinct disadvantage.

> Our results show that students who score a 3 on the AP exam and do not take a first year writing course are likely to suffer real consequences in sophomore courses that require writing assignments . . . . At BYU, as is likely true of most institutions, FYC provides an introduction to the discourse of the university, to a university library, and to genres of writing students have likely not encountered before. (41)

Moreover, Hansen's research, like that of Jolliffe and Phelan, shows that the students who perform *best* are those who combine first-year composition and AP: "The students in our sample who performed best overall were those who combined a quality AP experience (as indicated by a 4 or 5 on the exam) with a first year writing course" (Hansen et al. 40). In these terms, college composition *takes place at college*.

A comparable program, that of dual enrollment, seems through its emphasis on the *dual* to show more promise of providing college composition off the college campus. Chris Farris describes the best of such a program, located (as she says) in a bridging of cultures: the Indiana program brings instructors from the high school to the college so that the faculty members of the cultures can work *together*. Still, given what Paul Bodmer shows us about the differences in high school and college cultures—especially in terms of the students and their developmental needs, their parents, and the state-mandated high school curriculum—such bringing together is likely to work better for faculty than for students. Put differently, from a cultural perspective such bringing together would be necessary, but would it be sufficient? Some data suggest not. According to Tom Miller, research conducted at the University of Arizona shows that dual-enrollment programs do not provide whatever it is that *college* composition does. As he explains,

> we are continuing our research on dual enrollment programs. As noted in a previous posting, Thomas Kinney, a PhD student here, did a study of several thousand students' performance on our former mid-career writing assessment (a timed writing task). Dual enrollment students failed the assessment at a third higher rate. Some administrators did some additional research that they thought would mitigate this striking finding, but which actually compounded

> it. Their research found that the dual enrollment students also had lower verbal SATs and lower high school GPAs. When these factors were controlled, dual enrollment students still failed the writing assessment at a significantly higher rate, but the factors themselves are interesting because one of the most justifiable reasons for selling college credits to high school students is that it serves to motivate highly qualified students who might otherwise not be challenged by their high school courses. If these students are actually less qualified on key measures, there is little justification other than economics to shortchange students by allowing them to fulfill their high school and college requirements by taking a single course, which is by and large what concurrent enrollment programs do. (np)

This research, then, like that of Hansen's, documents the claim that college composition provides a kind of learning that requires *college*.

Other evidence supports this claim. High school composition, as researched by Applebee and Hillocks, is largely an exercise in literature, with writing-to-learn playing something of the same role it played in my classroom thirty years ago, although often even *less* of a role. In other words, process—prewriting, drafting, peer review, and revising—can be in place, but often only in abbreviated form, as documented in a recent *RTE* study by Scherff and Piazza. Interestingly, this study, which used a survey to inquire into the school writing practices of two thousand Florida high school students, found that of all high school students reporting on their school writing activities, the *only* students engaged in peer revision and editing were the dual-enrollment students (288–89). Moreover, the primary form of high school writing is "literary" (Scherff and Piazza 292), and the exigence, echoing Britton's study some thirty years ago, is test preparation. The high school composition curriculum thus differs from its college cousin in part because of the influence of tests—some thirty-eight states assess students' writing with an essay (Ketter and Pool)—and in part because the focus of the writing in both classroom and test is literature.[2]

Another way of making the same point—and that allows us to attend more specifically to college composition—is to think in terms of the discourse communities that host the different composition programs. In the 1960s and 1970s, as my own experience attests, both high school and college composition curricula were situated within a *literary* discourse community. Increasingly, that's not so. In high school, the discourse community is still and appropriately that of literature, and certainly that of English studies, the intent to foster writing practices and understandings that will help students successfully write the texts on literature required in the high school curriculum. By way of contrast, as the "Portraits" study shows and as chapters (Rutz, Harris, and Redd) in this volume illustrate, the discourse communities contextualizing *college* writers are diverse by design. Put in the terms of activity theory or circulation, the general intent is for college students to write texts that carry them forward from high school into the first year of college and that prepare them for the multiple discourse communities that *college* requires. In other words, the composing of high school and that of college are located in two different discourse communities. The high school discourse community is quite focused, immersed in the world of literature; the college discourse community quite plural and even if informed by English studies, not composed of it, but rather of something loosely called academic writing. Likewise, the tasks in the two sites are fundamentally different, which may well explain the recent research on how non-college-delivered writing courses *prepare* students for college but fail to substitute for it.

A continuing concern about college composition, of course, is that the agents delivering college composition—the faculty who in terms of rank range from part timers and teaching assistants to tenured faculty—don't receive the support required, however defined (e.g., salary, working conditions). As important, and a related factor, is the preparation many faculty bring to the teaching of college composition. Such preparation is especially important for college composition, given that the focus is composition, and yet too often the preparation is not in composition or rhetoric. As explained by Bill Thelin, it's a preparation keyed to literature rather than to composition.

> I do not believe there are a lot of people wandering around who are qualified to teach composition. There are, however, a lot of people wandering around who [the] administration is willing to use to teach composition. These people pick up on the current-traditional, quasi-process precepts of textbooks and outdated program guidelines, teach a few years, and declare themselves compositionists, writing experts, or whatever. The lack of undergraduate programs in composition makes the MA in comp the introduction to the field for most students. Many if not most MA students still take the majority of their classes in literature, so they might have 2 or 3 courses in the discipline of comp before becoming employed as adjuncts. Perhaps I am wrong, but in no other discipline would someone who had taken only 0–3 courses in a subject be permitted to teach it. It would be nice if people teaching writing actually were published, free lance authors, so they could at least cite practical experience in writing, but that is rarely the case, as adjunct work sucks the life out of far too many. So what passes for expertise in teaching is not making waves and hanging on as a teacher with what would barely be the equivalent of a BA or BS in any other field. (np)

The result of this kind of staffing practice—that is, staffing courses with faculty who are underpaid and also underprepared for the teaching task—is that composition itself is too often not defined as the concepts, materials, and methods of a discipline. Instead, it is loosely defined as a set of writing processes geared to composing argument (Yancey et al.); expertise is pragmatic and generalized, or almost a contradiction in terms. The impact of this is seen in Joe Harris' argument for staffing composition classes with PhDs not necessarily even in English, his argument that even if the discipline cannot be delivered, good pedagogy can. It's also so, as he says, that he incorporates the *materials* of composition into the curriculum writ large, which is another way to influence delivery. Another response is articulated by Becky Rickly, who narrates Texas Tech's shift to a division-of-labor model of teaching based on a perception, shared by Joyce Neff, that TA preparation is insufficient to guarantee an intellectually defensible delivery of composition. In other words, how composition can be delivered in terms of faculty agent is very much part of curricular design.

At the same time, there is also some evidence that composition is increasingly defined as a discipline, which shift could have the potential to change all composition courses precisely because the faculty agent is *expert*. According to the January 2005 issue of *Rhetoric Review*, we are redefining the MA degree, such that there are now at least fifty-five MA programs in rhetoric and composition, which means that we will have more graduates specializing in this discipline—and presumably, more faculty conversant with the field. Many compositionists are also in the process of creating a major in composition and rhetoric; the Conference on College Composition and Communication has established a committee that will compile a list of such programs as well as a typology of them. With more undergraduate and graduate programs, we have the hope that we'll create more faculty who *elect* to teach composition and who do so from a position of expertise.

Moreover, the larger curricular site of first-year composition and its historical antecedent, general education, is likewise changing. For evidence of this, we can revisit Bloom's taxonomy, a common intellectual framework for student development in college and university settings. As is well known, the original Bloom model includes knowledge as recall and comprehension; understanding; application; analysis; synthesis; and evaluation. A newer model (and there are several variants of a new Bloom) elaborates this schema and adds to it in at least two ways germane to composition. First, in addition to including the other items (e.g, synthesis), the framework adds one culminating item: creation. In the first model, then, students were positioned ultimately as consumers whose cumulative and most complex act was judgment making. In the new model, through "create," students are positioned as agents themselves. Second, the new framework appears not as a pyramid, but rather as a matrix, and running along the side is another set of factors related to knowledge: factual, conceptual, procedural, and metacognitive. Historically, disciplines have been defined through the first three: facts, concepts, and procedures. What's new is metacognition. Viewed through this lens, and given composition's history and the accounts presented here, "our" composition is dominated by procedural knowledge, and as Carol Rutz shows in her discussion of portfolio assessment, we know a good deal about metacognition.

What of the other two, factual and conceptual? One possibility is that facts and concepts are becoming more the stuff of composition, that is, what has (already) been delivered at the PhD level for more than three decades, and what now, according to *Rhetoric Review*, is increasingly delivered at the MA level. Included in such expertise, as Greg Columb argues, is a vocabulary that is critical for our work both inside and outside the classroom. He begins by noting that

> the terms students bring to our classes are not up to the job. They are a hodge podge of folk theory, terms invented locally by various K–12 teachers, handbook terms based on antique and false theories of language, and a little MTV and Reading Rainbow thrown in. Because terms like "attention grabber" or "the clincher" are too vague and too easily misunderstood. As Jay points out, not only is the language students bring or teachers invent seldom helpful, it is most often detrimental to a writer's performance.

He also notes that the problem isn't that students can't grasp the terms:

> Besides, are we seriously going to say that any of the following terms are too difficult for students who are contemporaneously learning organic chemistry and calculus: claim, reason, evidence, acknowledgment and response, warrant, noun, verb, character, action, topic, stress, old information, new information, topic string, main character, point of view, problem statement, common ground, destabilizing condition, cost, response, solution, etc. What do we say about ourselves when we say that we want to work in a field with NO special terminology?

What's interesting about this articulation when you read Columb in the context of the revised Bloom, of course, is that even Bloom's taxonomy, which is frequently employed for general education, calls for concepts and facts. As important, given that it has a separate category for procedures, our language for process would be necessary for a composition curriculum, but *by itself* insufficient. Identifying that vocabulary, particularly the vocabulary appropriate for first-year composition—terms like *process* and *revision*, but including newer terms like *discourse community* and *rhetorical situation* and *visual rhetoric*—would (and I hope, will) take us to a composition characterized for intellectual rigor as much as for our current innovations in process and metacognition.

Not least, Columb makes another valuable point about what happens when we *don't* employ vocabulary of the discipline. Briefly, needing some kind of vocabulary, our past students and our colleagues revert to the only language they have been given, that of grammar and rules.

> Few writers in or outside the academy have an adequate vocabulary for talking about writing because WE FAILED to teach them such a vocabulary back when they were our students. Past failures are hardly a good reason not to do what's best now.

In other words, in our classes we not only teach students to write but, by omission or design, also deliver a vocabulary that writers, parents, and citizens will take with them and use during *the rest of their lives*. This identification of vocabulary is important on the first level because providing an appropriate category helps students learn; it is important on a second level because it shapes how we and our teaching and our discipline are seen; and it is important on a third level because it forecasts how the public will see writing and its delivery. As Columb notes, identifying and defining this vocabulary and making it a centerpiece of composition is a new task, but one that, as this volume makes clear, is increasingly urgent.

What the key terms of this vocabulary will be is in process; I have argued elsewhere (Key) that they include three principal expressions: (1) the circulation of composition; (2) the canons of rhetoric; and (3) the deicity of technology. We see circulation in Columb's description of how the vocabulary of writing takes on a life of its own and shapes our own practices and in Harris' account of the shift from document design to the activity cycles of texts; we see the canons of rhetoric in the topic of this volume, delivery, using it as a lens to examine composition; and we see the deicity of technology—put simply, the ability to use multiple softwares and technologies for our own purposes—in the Stanford program. At the 2004 Council of Writing Program Administrators conference in Delaware, I added *space* as another term, and we see this in Purdue's composition curriculum, which intentionally uses spaces and the ability to work across them as a way of designing curriculum and assisting students to become composers of the twenty-first century. In this thinking, I'm influenced as well by the ways my colleagues at Clemson (Teddi Fishman, Summer Smith, Morgan Gresham, and Michael Neal); we made material space a part of the cocurricular composition curriculum. In designing the Class of 1941 Studio for Student Communication, we planned for multiple physical spaces that would accommodate a dynamic, evolving cocurriculum putting individual consultations in dialogue with team drafting and formal group presentations. The walls support and represent that curriculum intentionally in presenting many media—tackboards and whiteboards and Smart Boards and computer screens—on which to write, to peer review, and to display. Interestingly, one way to think about this set of spaces is as a twenty-first-century iteration of Robert Zoellner's talk-write pedagogy. Vilified at the time for seeming to advocate a Skinnerian approach, Zoellner conceptualized a composing curriculum intentionally located in public drafting—on flip boards—and in simultaneous talking about and returning back to the drafting process. Materially located in circulation, composing in these spaces is social; is grounded in talk and in multiplicity and in iteration.

At the heart of this volume is the claim, of course, that there *is* such a person as a compositionist; that this person has a discipline; and that as a participant of a discourse community, she or he theorizes, practices, and conducts research, in the process defining the field and assuring that our students—who historically have remained at the center of our thinking—become the best composers possible. In terms of Martin Jacobi's definition of delivery, the compositionist brings experience that can be delivered to students, that can be used to support and guide them in their composings, and that can research the effects of this kind of practice, one located in expertise.

* *

Is there such a thing as college composition? Yes.

Is this composition specific to the postsecondary context? Yes.

Does it make a difference to students? Yes.

And not least, does the way it is delivered matter to composition? Yes.

What being delivered today is radically different than the composition of twenty years ago—as we see in the faculty construct at Texas Tech, as we see in the student outcomes at Stanford, as we see in the curricular design at Purdue, as we see in the single teacher's reflection on student-teacher interaction in an online class. Increasingly, delivery is occurring in multiple sites, which themselves can function as a design principle for curriculum. And even as you read this passage, digital technologies are remediating the very concept of delivery.

As important as process has been and (still) is to composition, composition is today more and other than processes; it's a set of practices located in a vocabulary living at the center of a discipline. Where there are insufficient resources or political will to provide tenure lines, compositionists deliver twice—once to their faculty colleagues, once to their own students. In part, that is what makes compositionists unique in the academy, that their delivery is dual. And in delivering to both, they also eventually deliver to a third audience, to the world at large in Columb's sense, and to democracy in Jacobi's sense (Chapter 2).

As we continue to move into the twenty-first century, the delivery of college composition will remain at the center of the field, helping us surface hidden assumptions; challenging us to design a composition to be delivered into the future; shaping subject, practices, and person.

Notes

1. And as the recent "Portraits of Composition" study shows, this model of composition is commonplace (see Yancey et al.).

2. For instance, in North Carolina, the tenth-grade statewide end-of-course test, called a writing test, asks students to write about non-Western literature, an appropriate topic for a high school English test, of course, but not a topic focus for college composition.

Works Cited

Applebee, Arthur N. *Contexts for Learning to Write: Studies of Secondary School Instruction*. Norwood, NJ: Ablex, 1984.

———. "Stability and Change in the High-School Canon." *English Journal*, 82 (1992): 27–32.

Britton, James, et al. *The Development of Writing Abilities*. London: Macmillan, 1975.

Brown, Stuart C., Monica Torres, Theresa Enos, and Erik Juergensmeyer. "Master's Programs in Rhetoric and Composition Studies." *Rhetoric Review* 24.1 (2005): 13–127.

Columb, Greg. Re: Toulmin Method—Terms in Writing Education. WPA-L. March 1, 2005. Accessed at http://lists.asu.edu/cgi-bin/wa?A2=ind0503&L=wpa-l&D=1&O=A&P=451.

Hansen, Kristen, Suzanne Reeve, Richard Sedweeks, Gary L. Hatch, Jennifer Gonzalez, Patricia Esplin, William Bradshaw. "An Arguement for Changing Institutional Policy and Granting AP Credit in English: An Empirical Study of College Sophomores' Writing." *WPA: Writing Program Administration* 28 (2004): 29–54.

Ketter, J., and J. Pool. "Exploring the Impact of a High-Stakes Direct Writing Assessment in Two High School Classrooms." *Research in the Teaching of English* 35 (2001): 344–93.

Scherff, Lisa, and Carolyn Piazza. "The More Things Change, the More They Stay the Same: A Survey of High School Students' Writing Experiences." *Research in the Teaching of English* 39.3 (2005): 271–99.

Yancey, Kathleen Blake, "Made Not Only in Words: Composition in a New Key." *CCC* 56 (2004): 297–328.

Yancey, Kathleen Blake, Teddi Fishman, Morgan Gresham, Michael Neal, and Summer Smith Taylor. "Portraits of Composition: How Writing Gets Taught in the Early 21st Century." CCCC San Francisco, 2005.

Zoellner, Robert. "Talk-Write: A Behavioral Pedagogy for Composition." *College English* 30 (1969): 267–320.

Contributors

Paul Bodmer taught first-year college composition, survey of American literature, and western American fiction at Bismarck State College, a comprehensive community college in Bismarck, North Dakota, for thirty years before joining the staff at the National Council of Teachers of English. While on the faculty at Bismarck State College, he chaired the English Department and the Communications Arts Division during the introduction of interactive telecommunications courses in first-year college composition and introduction to communications courses. He also served as interim chair and past chair of the Two-Year College English Association of the National Council of Teachers of English during its formative years. He is currently the Senior Program Officer for Higher Education in the Washington, DC, NCTE office.

Richard Courage is Professor of English at Westchester Community College, State University of New York, where he continues to teach composition and literature online and in person. He serves on the editorial board of the *Journal of Basic Writing* and has written about composition pedagogy, basic writing, African American literature, and public education for *College Composition and Communication (CCC)*, the *Journal of Teaching Writing*, *CLA Journal*, and the *New York Times*. He is currently (2005–6) codirector of an NEH (National Endowment for the Humanities) "We the People" project called "The Shaping Role of Place in African American Biography." The project is based in Berkshire County, Massachusetts, where he lives.

Marvin Diogenes is Associate Director of the Program in Writing and Rhetoric and Assistant Vice Provost for Undergraduate Education at Stanford University. Prior to joining the program at Stanford in 2000, he taught at the University of Arizona and San Diego State. At Arizona he directed the University Composition Board, responsible assessment, outreach, and writing-across-the-curriculum programs. He is the coeditor of two books, *Living Languages: Contexts for Reading and Writing* (Prentice Hall, 1997) and *Crafting Fiction: In Theory, in Practice* (McGrall Hill, 2000). He is an original member of and lead archivist for the Composition Blues Band.

Christine Farris is Professor and Director of Composition in the Department of English at Indiana University, where she teaches courses in writing, rhetoric and composition theory, and literature. She also coordinates the dual-credit college composition course for high school teachers as part of IU's Advance College Project. She is the author of *Subject to Change: New Composition Instructors' Theory and Practice* (Hampton, 1996), coeditor with Chris Anson of *Under Construction: Working at the Intersections of Composition Theory, Research, and Practice* (Utah State UP, 1998), and coeditor with Judith H. Anderson of *Integrating Literature and Writing Instruction: First Year English, Humanities Core Courses, Seminars*, forthcoming from MLA.

Joseph Harris directs the Duke University Writing Program (http://uwp.aas.duke.edu). He is the author of *A Teaching Subject: Composition Since 1966* (Prentice, 1997) and several essays on teaching academic writing. From 1994 to 1999, Harris served as editor of *CCC*. His latest book, *Rewriting: How to Do Things with Texts*, will be out soon from Utah State University Press.

Martin Jacobi is Professor of English at Clemson University, where he teaches classical and modern rhetorical theory and American literature. He has published articles in rhetorical theory, professional communication, and the rhetorical analysis of literature, and he is coeditor of *Research in Basic Writing* (Greenwood Press, 1990) and coauthor of *The Politics of Rhetoric: Richard M. Weaver and the Conservative Tradition* (Greenwood Press, 1993). He is currently working on an attempt to define the nature and use of lying in rhetorical practice.

David Jolliffe holds the Brown Chair in English Literacy at the University of Arkansas. Most recently, he was the coauthor, with Hephzibah Roskelly, of *Everyday Use: Rhetoric at Work in Reading and Writing* (Longman, 2004). **Bernard Phelan** has taught English and coordinated Advanced Placement examinations at high schools in the suburbs of Chicago. Jolliffe and Phelan regularly conduct workshops for high school teachers interested in preparing their students for the Advanced Placement English Language and Composition Examination.

Andrea Lunsford is the Louise Hewlett Nixon Professor of English and Director of the Program in Writing and Rhetoric at Stanford University. She has designed and taught undergraduate and graduate courses in writing history and theory, rhetoric, literacy studies, and intellectual property and is the author or coauthor of fourteen books, including *The Everyday Writer* (Bedford St. Martin's, 2003); *Essays on Classical Rhetoric and Modern Discourse* (Southern Illinois UP, 1984); *Singular Texts/Plural Authors: Perspectives on Collaborative Writing* (Southern Illinois UP, 1992); and *Reclaiming Rhetorica: Women in the History of Rhetoric* (University of Pittsburgh, 1995), as well as numerous chapters and articles. Her most recent books include *Everything's an Argument*, 4th ed. (with John Ruszkiewicz; Bedford St. Martin's, 2004) and, with Lahoucine Ouzgane, *Exploring Borderlands: Composition and Postcolonial Studies* (University of Pittsburgh Press, 2004).

Joyce Magnotto Neff is Interim Chair and Associate Professor of English at Old Dominion University, where she teaches courses in professional writing, composition pedagogy, and research methods. She is coauthor of *Professional Writing in Context* and has published numerous articles and book chapters on writing across the curriculum, writing centers, grounded theory, and workplace writing. Her current projects include a collaborative study of writing in counselor education and a longitudinal study of distributed learning (*Writing Across Disciplines and Distances*, forthcoming from Erlbaum).

Teresa Redd is an Associate Professor of English and Director of the Center for Excellence in Teaching, Learning, and Assessment at Howard University. She has published numerous articles and chapters about teaching composition to African American students. In addition, she has edited *Revelations: An Anthology of Expository Essays by and About Blacks* (Pearson, 2002) and recently coauthored *A Teacher's Introduction to African American English: What a Writing Teacher Should Know* (NCTE, 2005).

An Associate Professor at Texas Tech University, **Rebecca Rickly** serves as Codirector of the ICON program (Interactive Composition Online). At the center of her work is what she calls "applied rhetoric," which includes such diverse applications as technology, feminisms, methods and methodologies, literacy study, and administration. She has served on the CCCC Committee on Computers and Composition and NCTE's assembly on computers in English, and she has chaired NCTE's Instructional Technology Committee. Her publications include *The Online Writing Classroom* (with Susanmarie Harrington and Michael Day; Hampton, 2000), and her work has appeared in numerous edited collections, as well as *Computers and Composition*, *CMC Magazine*, *The ACE Journal*, and *Kairos*. Currently, she is working on an edited collection (with Krista Ratcliffe) titled *Feminism and Administration in Rhetoric and Composition Studies*, as well as articles and chapters on the required research methods course and seeing research rhetorically.

Carol Rutz has directed the writing program at Carleton College in Northfield, Minnesota, since 1998. Her research interests include response to student writing, assessment, and faculty development. Recent publications include a collection co-edited with Ed Nagelhout called *Classroom Spaces and Writing Instruction* (Hampton, 2004), a volume that theorizes the writing classroom in terms of space and time. With Susan Singer, she coedited *Reflections on Learning as Teachers* (College City Press, 2004), a collection written by Carleton faculty and staff. A companion volume of essays on collaboration among Carleton faculty, students, and staff is under way.

Todd Taylor is Director of the Writing Program and Associate Professor of English at the University of North Carolina at Chapel Hill. Much of his later work has taken the form of scholarly film, presented at conferences and on DVD. Consult his website (www.unc.edu/~twtaylor) to learn more.

Irwin Weiser is Head of the Department of English at Purdue University, where he has been a member of the faculty since 1981. Prior to becoming department head, he served as the director of composition. His teaching and scholarship are in composition and composition pedagogy, the preparation of teachers of writing, and writing program administration. He is a former member of the Executive Committee of CCCC and is active in the Council of Writing Program Administrators, having just completed a term on the executive board and previously serving on the editorial board of *WPA*. His most recent published work includes the companion collections *The Writing Program Administrator as Researcher* (1999) and *The Writing Program Administrator as Theorist* (2002), both edited with Shirley K Rose of the Department of English and published by Heinemann.

Kathleen Blake Yancey is Kellogg W. Hunt Professor of English at Florida State University, where she teaches undergraduate and graduate students and directs the graduate program in rhetoric and composition. A recent past president of WPA and past chair of CCCC, she is Vice President of NCTE. She has edited, coedited, or authored eight books, among them *Voices on Voice* (NCTE, 1994); *Reflection in the Writing Classroom* (Utah State UP, 1998); and *Teaching Literature as Reflective Practice* (NCTE, 2004) as well as many articles and book chapters. Her current projects include completing a book exploring the uses of digital portfolios in college and high school English classrooms.